Collins Advanced Modular Sciences

Chemistry Core

Lyn Nicholls and Mary Ratcliffe

Series Editor: Mike Coles

Collins Educational

An Imprint of HarperCollinsPublishers

Northern
Modular Science Scheme

Published by Collins Educational
An imprint of HarperCollins*Publishers*
77–85 Fulham Palace Road
Hammersmith
London
W6 8JB

© HarperCollinsPublishers 1995

First published 1995

ISBN 0 00 322382 5

Typographic design by Ewing Paddock at PearTree Design
Design by Moondisks Ltd, Cambridge

Edited by Jean Macqueen, Donna Evans, and Gina Walker

Picture research by Dee Robinson
Cover photo researched by Caroline Thompson

Illustrations by Tom Cross, Jerry Fowler, Fraser Williams,
Hardlines, Mainline Design

Printed and bound by Rotolito Lombarda, Italy

Acknowledgements

Text and diagrams reproduced by kind permission of:
Ford Motor Company; *New Scientist*; *The Times*;
COMA Report, *The Road Traffic Act* and MAFF Food
Surveillance reports, HMSO; Readers Digest
Association; *Nature* Magazine, Macmillan; Open
University; Pergamon; J Wiley and Sons Publishing;
Ann Arbour Science Publishers Inc; Tioxide Europe;
Professor Kroto, School of Molecular Sciences,
University of Sussex; The Federation of Bakers;
Oxford University Press; Harcourt, Brace &
Jovanovich Ltd; *The Observer*; *The School Science
Review*; *The Chemist and Druggist's Book*.

Every effort has been made to contact the holders
of copyright material, but if any have been
inadvertently overlooked the publishers will be
pleased to make the necessary arrangements at the
first opportunity.

Contents

To the student

This book aims to make your study of advanced science successful and interesting. The authors have made sure that the ideas you need to understand are covered in a clear and straightforward way. The book is designed to be a study of scientific ideas as well as a reference text when needed. Science is constantly evolving and, wherever possible, modern issues and problems have been used to make your study interesting and to encourage you to continue studying science after your current course is complete.

Working on your own

Studying on your own is often difficult and sometimes textbooks give you the impression that you have to be an expert in the subject before you can read the book. I hope you find that this book is not like that. The authors have carefully built up ideas, so that when you are working on your own there is less chance of you becoming lost in the text and frustrated with the subject.

Don't try to achieve too much in one reading session. Science is complex and some demanding ideas need to be supported with a lot of facts. Trying to take in too much at one time can make you lose sight of the most important ideas – all you see is a mass of information. Use the learning objectives to select one idea to study in a particular session.

Chapter design

Each chapter starts by showing how the science you will learn is applied somewhere in the world. Next come learning objectives which tell you exactly what you should learn as you read the chapter. These are written in a way which spells out what you will be able to do with your new knowledge, rather like a checklist – they could be very helpful when you revise your work. At certain points in the chapters you will find key ideas listed. These are checks for you to use, to make sure that you have grasped these ideas. Words written in **bold type** appear in the glossary at the end of the book. If you don't know the meaning of one of these words check it out immediately – don't persevere, hoping all will become clear.

The questions in the text are there for you to check you have understood what is being explained. These are all short – longer questions are included in a support pack which goes with this book. The questions are straightforward in style – there are no trick questions. Don't be tempted to pass over these questions, they will give you new insights into the work which you may not have seen. Answers to questions are given in the back of the book.

Good luck with your studies. I hope you find the book an interesting read.

Mike Coles, Series Editor
University of London Institute of Education, June 1995

Radiocarbon detective

In 1908, a workman digging in a gravel bed near Piltdown Common, Sussex, uncovered part of a human skull. Some geologists thought that the skull was from a creature which was the 'missing link' between present-day humans and our ape-like ancestors. This rare discovery led to much debate about the origin of humans.

In 1953, a newly developed scientific test, called radiocarbon dating, revealed the truth about 'Piltdown man': he was only a few decades old. Reports about him being the missing link were dismissed.

Reconstruction of Piltdown man's skull: the bones found (brown) came from two individuals

The frozen corpse of Ötze, discovered in an Austrian glacier

In 1991, two German hikers were climbing through a remote mountain pass in the Tyrolean Alps, in Austria, when they discovered the remains of a frozen corpse in a glacier. Forensic scientists from Innsbruck University were called in to investigate. Within a week it was announced that the body was the oldest ever discovered frozen in ice.

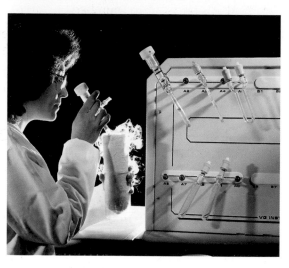

'Scientific tests on the body, nicknamed Ötze, revealed that the corpse was between 5100 and 5300 years old. This dated Ötze back to the late Stone Age. Samples of Ötze were prepared for more detailed analyses which are still throwing new insight into human genetic history.'

Radiocarbon dating, developed after World War II, revealed the Piltdown man a hoax and determined Ötze's true age. This technique – which can reliably date samples up to 70 000 years old – has had a major impact on the way we practise archaeology today. It is a reliable, scientific method of determining the age of living things. How does the technique work?

1.1 Learning objectives

After working through this chapter, you should be able to:

- **recall** that atoms are made of protons, neutrons and electrons and that these particles have different masses and charges;

- **describe** the structure of the atom;

- **explain** the terms atomic number and mass number;

- **explain** the terms relative atomic mass and relative molecular mass;

- **explain** the term isotope;

- **explain** how a mass spectrometer can detect different isotopes;

- **describe** the principles of the mass spectrometer in terms of ionisation, acceleration, deflection and detection;

- **explain** simple mass spectra of elements and compounds, and use them to calculate the relative atomic mass or relative molecular mass.

1.2 Inside the atom

All matter, including Ötze, is composed of atoms. Atoms are very small, usually around 2×10^{-10} m or 0.2 nanometres (nm) in diameter. They, in turn, are composed of even smaller particles called **protons**, **neutrons** and **electrons**.

The nucleus, at the centre of the atom, contains most of the atom's mass. The nucleus is made of protons and neutrons (Fig. 1). The protons are positively charged and the neutrons are neutral, giving an overall positive charge to the nucleus. You would think that the positive charges on the protons would repel each other, and tear the nucleus apart. However, this repulsion is overcome by a **strong nuclear force** that holds them together. This force only acts within the nucleus.

 1 **What does this tell you about the range of the strong nuclear force?**

A 'cloud' of negatively charged electrons surrounds the nucleus. In an atom, the number of electrons is equal to the number of protons, so that the overall charge on the atom is neutral. An electron has a very small mass and a negative charge (Table 1). The number of electrons and the way they are arranged determines how an atom behaves in a chemical reaction. The attraction of the positive nucleus holds the electrons in the atom.

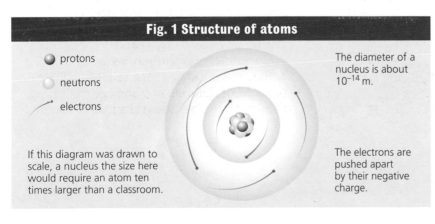

Fig. 1 Structure of atoms

- protons
- neutrons
- electrons

The diameter of a nucleus is about 10^{-14} m.

If this diagram was drawn to scale, a nucleus the size here would require an atom ten times larger than a classroom.

The electrons are pushed apart by their negative charge.

Table 1 Mass and charge of atomic particles

Particle	Charge	Mass/u
proton	+1	1.0073
neutron	0	1.0087
electron	−1	5.4858×10^{-4}

The masses of atoms and their particles are measured in atomic mass units (u); 1 u = 1.661×10^{-27} kg.

 2 **Where in the atom do you find most of its mass?**

1.3 Same element, different atom

Atomic number and mass number

Scientists describe atoms in terms of *two* numbers: **atomic number** and **mass number**. These are based on the numbers of protons and neutrons in the nucleus of atoms (Fig. 2).

 3 **What is the atomic number and the mass number of:**
  a sodium?
  b aluminium?
  c iron?

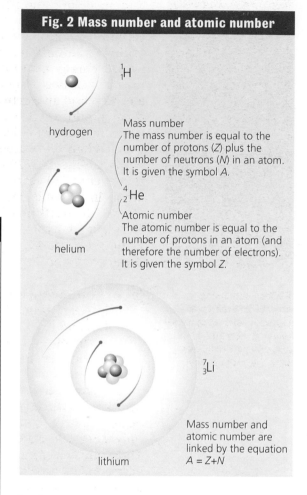

Fig. 2 Mass number and atomic number

$^{1}_{1}$H

hydrogen

Mass number
The mass number is equal to the number of protons (Z) plus the number of neutrons (N) in an atom. It is given the symbol A.

$^{4}_{2}$He

Atomic number
The atomic number is equal to the number of protons in an atom (and therefore the number of electrons). It is given the symbol Z.

helium

$^{7}_{3}$Li

Mass number and atomic number are linked by the equation $A = Z+N$

lithium

Table 2 Isotopes of carbon

Name	No: of protons	No: of neutrons	No: of electrons	Abundance/%
carbon-12	6	6	6	98.9
carbon-13	6	7	6	1.1
carbon-14	6	8	6	10^{-10}

Isotopes

Radiocarbon dating concerns *two* types of carbon atoms. Both atoms have the same atomic number, but they have different mass numbers. Atoms with the same atomic number but different mass numbers are called **isotopes**.

All **biological materials**, including the corpse of Ötze, contain carbon. The most common form of carbon is carbon-12, but other less abundant forms exist (Table 2). Most of the carbon present in Ötze's body was carbon-12. However, a small amount of the carbon in Ötze's corpse was the carbon-14 isotope.

 4 **Different isotopes of carbon behave identically in chemical reactions. Explain why.**

Half-life

The nuclei of carbon-12 and carbon-13 are stable. This means that carbon-12 and carbon-13 atoms do not change over time. Carbon-14 atoms, however, are unstable and do change over time. Neutrons in the nuclei of carbon-14 atoms can split to form a proton and an electron. This radioactive decay produces nitrogen-14 atoms. We can measure the rate of decay of an isotope from its half-life. Carbon-14, for example, has a half-life of 5730 years. This means that every 5730 years half of the carbon-14 atoms in a sample decay into nitrogen-14 atoms. The **half-life** of an isotope is the time taken for half its atoms to decay. Radiocarbon dating depends on this slow decay of carbon-14 atoms.

Radiocarbon dating showed that the Turin shroud – believed by many to be Christ's burial shroud – actually dates from the 14th century

 5 When a carbon-14 nucleus decays into a nitrogen-14 atom, what happens to
  a the atomic number?
  b the mass number?

The rate of decay of carbon-14 (Fig. 3) decreases as the amount of carbon-14 decreases. In a 1 g sample of carbon-14, only 0.5 g will remain after 5730 years. There will be 0.25 g left after another 5730 years, and so on. Radioactive decay is called a **first-order reaction**.

Carbon cycle

The radioactivity of atoms such as carbon-14 contributes to the normal background radiation around us. However, the amount of carbon-14 on Earth remains fairly uniform, because it is constantly replenished in the upper atmosphere. Cosmic ray protons, showering the Earth from outer space, transform nitrogen-14 atoms into carbon-14 atoms. Later this carbon-14 reacts with oxygen atoms to form carbon dioxide gas. During photosynthesis plants take in carbon dioxide, some of which contains carbon-14. When animals feed on plants, they consume the carbon-14. Ötze's diet of plants and animals contained carbon-14 which became part of his body cells (Fig. 4).

While Ötze was alive – eating, breathing and excreting – he was constantly exchanging carbon with the world around him. So even though carbon-14 decays, the proportion of carbon-12 and carbon-14 in Ötze's body remained constant, i.e. the same as that of his environment.

 6 What do you think happened to the ratio of carbon isotopes in Ötze's body when he died?

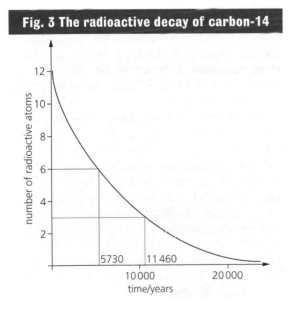

Fig. 3 The radioactive decay of carbon-14

number of radioactive atoms / time/years

5730   11 460

10 000   20 000

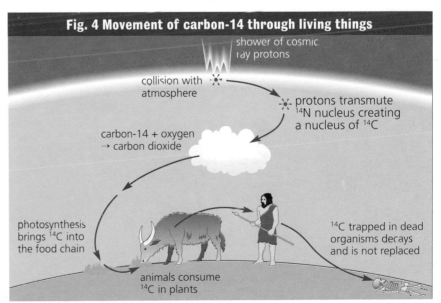

Fig. 4 Movement of carbon-14 through living things

shower of cosmic ray protons

collision with atmosphere

protons transmute ^{14}N nucleus creating a nucleus of ^{14}C

carbon-14 + oxygen → carbon dioxide

photosynthesis brings ^{14}C into the food chain

animals consume ^{14}C in plants

^{14}C trapped in dead organisms decays and is not replaced

When Ötze died, the carbon-exchanging processes stopped but the carbon-14 trapped in his body continued to decay. After 5730 years Ötze's remains would contain only half the original amount of carbon-14. The amount of carbon-12 in the body would not have changed, giving a clue as to how much carbon-12 it contained. By measuring the amount of carbon-14 left in a sample from Ötze's body and comparing it with how much he would have had when he died, scientists could calculate how long ago he died. This is called **radiocarbon dating**.

1.4 Detecting isotopes

Mass spectroscopy

To determine Ötze's age, scientists needed to measure accurately the amount of carbon-14 present in a sample from his body. This is done using a machine called a mass spectrometer, by a process known as **mass spectroscopy** (Fig. 5).

The recorder in a mass spectrometer produces the mass spectrum of the sample being analysed (Fig. 6). The x-axis in Fig. 6 shows the mass numbers of the isotopes present (i.e. 35 and 37). The heights of the lines are proportional to the amounts of the isotopes present in the sample. The spectrum shows that this element is composed of two isotopes of mass numbers 35 and 37, in a 3:1 ratio. This information can be used to calculate the average mass number (Fig. 7). We call this figure the **relative atomic mass**.

Q7 What element is shown in Fig. 6?

Fig. 6 Mass spectrum of an element

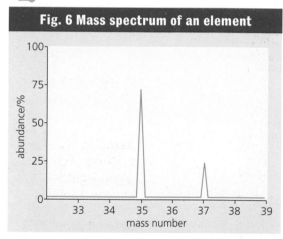

Carbon-14 dating can be used to date some cave paintings – the paint often contains materials like blood. (This painting from Australia has been repainted over the years.)

Fig. 5 Basic principles of a mass spectrometer

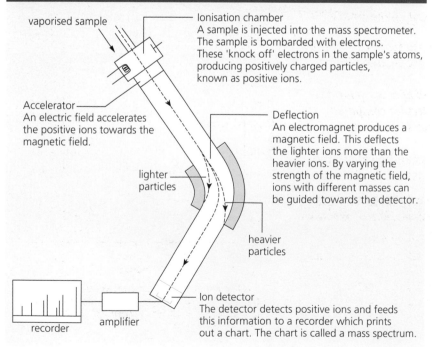

vaporised sample

Ionisation chamber
A sample is injected into the mass spectrometer. The sample is bombarded with electrons. These 'knock off' electrons in the sample's atoms, producing positively charged particles, known as positive ions.

Accelerator
An electric field accelerates the positive ions towards the magnetic field.

Deflection
An electromagnet produces a magnetic field. This deflects the lighter ions more than the heavier ions. By varying the strength of the magnetic field, ions with different masses can be guided towards the detector.

lighter particles

heavier particles

recorder

amplifier

Ion detector
The detector detects positive ions and feeds this information to a recorder which prints out a chart. The chart is called a mass spectrum.

Relative atomic mass

Relative atomic mass is given the symbol A_r. It is formally defined as follows:

relative atomic mass of an element is the mass of one atom compared with one-twelfth the mass of one atom of carbon-12.

The values of relative atomic mass given in data books are the average for all naturally occurring isotopes, taking relative abundance into consideration (Fig. 7). Remember that the numbers are just an average – there may be no atoms with the actual values given. However, relative atomic masses are still very useful for the purpose of chemical calculations.

Fig. 7 Calculating relative atomic mass

In a sample of 100 atoms of chlorine:
75% will be chlorine-35
25% will be chlorine-37.
So, the total mass for 100 atoms
$$= (75 \times 35) + (25 \times 37)$$
$$= 2625 + 925$$
$$= 3550$$
Therefore, the relative atomic mass for chlorine is 35.5.

Relative molecular mass

A similar system is used to calculate masses of molecules. Instead of relative atomic masses, molecules have **relative molecular mass** (M_r). Relative molecular mass is defined as follows:

relative molecular mass of a compound is the mass of one of its molecules compared with one-twelfth of the mass of one atom of carbon-12.

Relative molecular mass can be calculated using relative atomic masses (Fig. 8).

Fig. 8 Calculating relative molecular mass

To calculate the relative molecular mass of a molecule, add together the relative atomic masses of its atoms.
Thus for magnesium carbonate ($MgCO_3$):
relative molecular mass $= 24 + 12 + (3 \times 16)$
$$= 84$$

 8 Calculate the relative molecular mass of
  a ethanol, C_2H_5OH;
  b calcium hydroxide, $Ca(OH)_2$;
  c ammonium sulphate, $(NH_4)_2SO_4$.

Mass spectroscopy can also be used to find relative molecular mass. The molecular substance is bombarded with electrons, in a similar way to the element in Fig. 6. Some of the molecules lose electrons to form positive ions. This makes little difference to the mass of the original molecule, because electrons have a tiny mass. These ions are therefore representative of the original molecules in the sample. However, some of the molecules can split into fragments when bombarded with electrons, again forming ions. All the ions and fragments can be detected as separate lines on the mass spectrum. This means that the mass spectrum can give useful clues about the structure of the molecule, as well as its relative molecular mass (Fig. 9).

 9 Explain the lines at mass numbers 1, 2, 12, 13, 14 and 15 in Fig. 9.

Fig. 9 Mass spectrum of methane

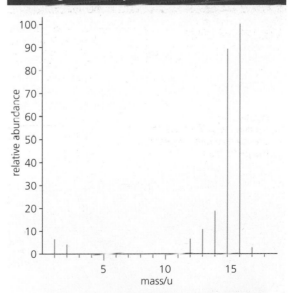

The line representing the highest molecular mass is the CH_4^+ ion. This gives the relative molecular mass of methane. The other lines represent fragments of methane molecules.

1.5 Ötze's age

Most mass spectrometers require several grams of sample substance to produce a spectrum. Fortunately, a new breed of mass spectrometer has been developed (called an accelerated mass spectrometer) which only requires a 1 mg sample.

Accelerated mass spectroscopy differs from ordinary mass spectroscopy in that it actually counts the atoms present. To determine Ötze's age, a 1 mg sample of bone was used. The first stage in the analysis was to extract protein molecules. Pure carbon was then isolated from the protein molecules. Burning the carbon in oxygen produced carbon dioxide. Most of the carbon dioxide contained carbon-12 atoms, a small amount contained carbon-13, and very small amount carbon-14. The accelerated mass spectrometer was used to measure the ratio of carbon-12 atoms to carbon-14 atoms. The results were compared with standard values. This showed that the carbon-14 content of Ötze's protein was approximately half the carbon-14 content of the 1990s level.

10 What does this suggest about Ötze's age?

Ötze's tools and other artefacts (found near him) are providing a valuable insight into his way of life. He wore leather and fur clothes with a grass cloak. He carried an axe, dagger, bow and arrows, and various tools. He also carried mushrooms with antibiotic properties in a birch-bark container. Dr Konrad Spindler – who has been in charge of the overall investigation – concluded that Ötze was a shepherd who, on returning to the village at harvest time, became caught in a fight and broke two ribs. He fled up the mountainside but paused to rest. There he fainted, or fell asleep, and froze to death.

Key ideas

- An atom consists of a nucleus containing protons and neutrons, surrounded by a 'cloud' of electrons. The mass is concentrated in the nucleus. The positive charge of the protons is balanced by the negative charge of the electrons.

- The atomic number of an atom is equal to the number of protons it contains.

- The mass number of an element is equal to the number of protons plus neutrons it contains.

- Isotopes have the same atomic numbers but different mass numbers.

- Isotopes can be detected in a mass spectrometer.

- Mass spectra can be used to calculate the relative atomic mass of an element, or the relative molecular mass of a compound.

- The relative atomic mass of an element is the mass of one atom of the element compared to the mass of one twelfth of an atom of carbon-12.

- The relative molecular mass of a compound is the mass of one molecule of the compound compared to the mass of one twelfth of an atom of carbon-12.

Reacting quantities

The Tioxide logo: the left half represents water birds, whose health is a measure of the pollution in estuaries and inshore waters; the right half represents the people employed by Tioxide and Tioxide's customers

'I've worked at the Tioxide Europe factory at Grimsby for a number of years. Tioxide have been making titanium(IV) oxide here ever since 1949. Everyone round here knows the factory – you can see it from all over the Grimsby area. The locals call it "Titans".'

In 1984, the Anglian Water Authority found raised levels of pollutants around Tioxide's waste outlet into the Humber estuary. The Water Authority recommended longer outlet pipes to carry the waste into deeper, faster-flowing waters to disperse it. When these were installed the pollution fell dramatically, but the waste did not disappear. It just passed more quickly into the North Sea.

In 1989, a directive from the EEC required that discharges from the factory should be reduced by about 75% by 1992. Tioxide has done a lot of work to meet that requirement.

2.1 Learning objectives

After working through this chapter, you should be able to:

- **explain** the idea of a mole of particles;

- **calculate** empirical formulae of compounds given the composition by mass;

- **derive** balanced chemical equations;

- **calculate** amounts of reactants/amounts of products from balanced chemical equations;

- **calculate** reacting volumes of gases;

- **calculate** unknown molarities from acid/base titrations.

2.2 Why make titanium(IV) oxide?

Titanium(IV) oxide is one of the whitest substances known. The starting material for manufacturing titanium(IV) oxide is ilmenite, a black sand

Paints containing titanium(IV) oxide pigment have exceptionally good covering power

Titanium(IV) oxide is brilliantly white; it reflects almost all the light that falls on it. It is thermally stable, insoluble in water, non-toxic and very unreactive. These properties make it a first-class white pigment: its whiteness and covering power are far better than any of its competitors.

Most of the titanium(IV) oxide produced in the UK is used in paints. Some is used as a white pigment in plastics, and some is sold to paper manufacturers. Titanium(IV) oxide is used to whiten all types of paper, from bank notes and postage stamps to books and journals. It has many other uses too – in cosmetics, toothpaste, printing inks and food, for example.

The demand for titanium(IV) oxide is growing steadily. Every year, about 250 000 tonnes of titanium(IV) oxide are produced at three British factories, two of which are owned by Tioxide Europe.

2.3 The raw materials

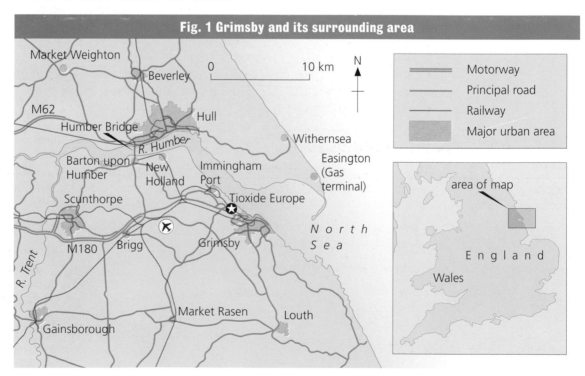

Fig. 1 Grimsby and its surrounding area

Market Weighton
Beverley
M62
Humber Bridge
Hull
R. Humber
Barton upon Humber
New Holland
Immingham Port
Withernsea
Easington (Gas terminal)
Scunthorpe
Tioxide Europe
M180
Brigg
Grimsby
R. Trent
North Sea
Market Rasen
Louth
Gainsborough

0   10 km   N

Motorway
Principal road
Railway
Major urban area

area of map

England
Wales

Titanium(IV) oxide is usually made from ilmenite, which is mined in Western Australia. Ilmenite consists mostly of iron(II) titanate, $FeTiO_3$, with some iron(III) titanate, $Fe_2(TiO_3)_3$, and impurities of silicon compounds. Tioxide import ilmenite through the nearby deep water port of Immingham (Fig. 1).

At Grimsby, Tioxide Europe make titanium(IV) oxide by the sulphate process (Fig. 2). This process essentially removes the iron from ilmenite to produce titanium(IV) oxide. The product is then treated to form crystals of the correct size and shape – the excellent covering power of the pigment depends on having the right crystal form.

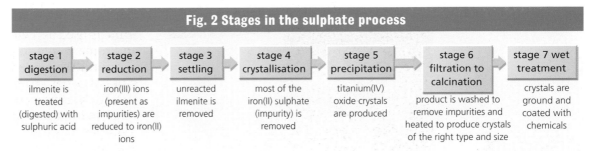

Fig. 2 Stages in the sulphate process

stage 1 digestion	stage 2 reduction	stage 3 settling	stage 4 crystallisation	stage 5 precipitation	stage 6 filtration to calcination	stage 7 wet treatment
ilmenite is treated (digested) with sulphuric acid	iron(III) ions (present as impurities) are reduced to iron(II) ions	unreacted ilmenite is removed	most of the iron(II) sulphate (impurity) is removed	titanium(IV) oxide crystals are produced	product is washed to remove impurities and heated to produce crystals of the right type and size	crystals are ground and coated with chemicals

2.4 Empirical and molecular formulae

Chemists at Tioxide are able to identify which titanium compound a sample consists of, if they know its relative molecular mass and the amount (mass or percentage) of each element present. This helps Tioxide to decide whether samples are worth processing or not. For example, if a compound contains 2.8 g iron, 3.6 g titanium and 3.6 g oxygen and has a relative molecular mass of 352, its formula can be found using the method in Figure 3.

The formula obtained by this method is called the **empirical formula**. It shows the ratio of the elements present. It does not necessarily show the numbers of atoms present in a molecule. The actual numbers are given in the **molecular formula**. To find the molecular formula of the compound:

Mass of empirical formula, $Fe_2(TiO_3)_3$:

$$2 \times Fe = 112$$
$$3 \times Ti = 96$$
$$9 \times O = \underline{144}$$
$$= \underline{352}$$

Since this is the molecular mass given in the example, the empirical formula is also the molecular formula; i.e. molecular formula is $Fe_2(TiO_3)_3$.

Fig. 3 Calculating empirical formulae

Element	Iron	Titanium	Oxygen
Mass/g	2.8	3.6	3.6
Relative atomic mass (A_r)	56	48	16
$\dfrac{Mass}{(A_r)}$	$\dfrac{2.8}{56}$	$\dfrac{3.6}{48}$	$\dfrac{3.6}{16}$
No. of moles	= 0.05	= 0.075	= 0.225
Ratio (divide by lowest)	1	1.5	4.5
Ratio of atoms (whole number)	= 2	= 3	= 9

So the formula is $Fe_2Ti_3O_9$, or $Fe_2(TiO_3)_3$.

 1 a Calculate the empirical and molecular formula of a compound containing: 3.6 g carbon, 0.6 g hydrogen and 4.9 g oxygen.
 b Its relative molecular mass is 60. Calculate its molecular formula.

2.5 Making sulphuric acid

In the first stage of the sulphate process, the ilmenite ore is treated with sulphuric acid. This means that Tioxide needs large amounts of sulphuric acid. They find it cheapest to make the acid themselves on site. Sulphuric acid is made by the contact process. There are four sulphuric acid plants on the Grimsby site.

The Tioxide factory, close to the Humber estuary at Grimsby

In the contact process, liquid sulphur is reacted in a furnace with dry air to produce sulphur dioxide. We can represent the reaction of the sulphur with the oxygen in the air using a word equation:

sulphur + oxygen $\rightarrow$ sulphur dioxide

or, better, with a chemical equation using symbols and formulae:

$$S(s) + O_2(g) \rightarrow SO_2(g)$$

In a balanced chemical equation, the number of atoms of each type on the left-hand side of the equation must equal that on the right-hand side. This equation is already balanced.

The sulphur dioxide gas is then made to react with oxygen at 450 °C and a pressure of 2 atm to produce sulphur trioxide. A catalyst of vanadium(V) oxide is used to speed up the rate of the reaction.

$$SO_2(g) + O_2(g) \xrightarrow[\text{450 °C, 2 atm}]{\text{vanadium(V) oxide}} SO_3(g)$$

This equation is not balanced. There are four atoms of oxygen on the left-hand side and only three on the right-hand side. In one molecule of oxygen there are enough oxygen atoms to react with two molecules of sulphur dioxide, producing two molecules of sulphur trioxide.

$$2SO_2(g) + O_2(g) \xrightarrow[\text{450 °C, 2 atm}]{\text{vanadium(V) oxide}} 2SO_3(g)$$

There are now six atoms of oxygen and two atoms of sulphur on each side of the equation. The equation is now balanced. The sulphur trioxide produced will react with concentrated sulphuric acid to produce oleum or fuming sulphuric acid:

$$SO_3(g) + H_2SO_4(l) \rightarrow H_2S_2O_7(l)$$

Water is then added to the oleum to produce sulphuric acid:

$$H_2S_2O_7(l) + H_2O(l) \rightarrow 2H_2SO_4(l)$$

Sulphuric acid is not made by adding sulphur trioxide directly to water. This reaction is **exothermic** (gives out a lot of heat) and any sulphuric acid produced may be vaporised. Tioxide Europe save on energy costs by using the heat produced in the contact process to provide hot water and steam for use in other parts of the plant.

2.6 Calculating reacting quantities

When chemists manufacture a substance, they need to be able to calculate the amounts of reactant and product involved. At the contact process plant in Grimsby, chemical engineers need to know how much sulphur needs to be reacted to produce a set amount of sulphuric acid.

In any chemical reaction, a certain number of particles react together. For example, two molecules of sulphur dioxide react with one molecule of oxygen (see equation). When we measure reacting quantities of chemicals, we need to think in terms of the actual numbers of reacting particles.

Chemists measure the amount of a substance in **moles** (symbol mol). A mole contains 6.022×10^{23} particles. One mole of an element contains 6.022×10^{23} atoms, but we may refer to a mole of molecules, electrons or ions. The quantity 6.022×10^{23} mol^{-1} is called the **Avogadro constant**, after the Italian chemist Amadeo Avogadro who first discovered its importance.

Atoms have different masses, so moles of different elements have different masses too. The following masses of elements all contain 6.022×10^{23} atoms:

12 g	24 g	59 g
carbon-12	magnesium-24	cobalt-59

197 g	207 g
gold-197	lead-207

These masses are the relative atomic masses of the elements in grams. So 12 g of carbon-12 is one mole of carbon-12, and 24 g of carbon-12 is two moles of carbon-12.

2 How many moles are there in:
a 414 g lead?
b 6 g magnesium?
c 60 g calcium?

3 What is the mass (in grams) of:
a 2 mol gold?
b 0.5 mol oxygen?
c 1.5 mol iron?

The mass of one mole of a substance is called its **molar mass**, M. Its units are g mol^{-1} (grams per mole). The molar mass of carbon-12 is 12 g mol^{-1}.

In the Contact process, chemists can calculate how much sulphuric acid can be produced from a given amount of sulphur. Since balanced equations tell us the ratio in which the particles react and since moles of different substances all contain the same number of particles, equations also tell us the ratios in which moles react.

S(s)	+	O_2(g)	$\rightarrow$	SO_2(g)
one	reacts	one	$\rightarrow$	one
molecule	with	molecule		molecule
sulphur		oxygen		sulphur
				dioxide

It follows that:

one	reacts	one	$\rightarrow$	one
mole	with	mole		mole
sulphur		oxygen		sulphur
				dioxide

Or,

32 g	reacts	32 g	$\rightarrow$	64 g
sulphur	with	oxygen		sulphur
				dioxide

4 How many tonnes of sulphur dioxide are produced from 1.4 tonnes of sulphur?

5 How many tonnes of sulphur trioxide are produced from 2.8 tonnes of sulphur dioxide?

Key ideas

- Chemists measure amounts of particles in moles.

- A mole contains 6.022×10^{23} particles.

- A balanced chemical equation can tell us the amounts of reactants and products involved in a reaction.

- An empirical formula gives the ratio of atoms present in a molecule.

- The molecular formula of a compound can be found from its empirical formula and the relative molecular mass.

2.7 Other calculation methods

The amount of a gas

It is not always convenient for chemical engineers and research chemists to measure an amount of substance by finding its mass. When we are dealing with gases, volumes are much easier to measure than masses. Since differences in the sizes of gas molecules are far smaller than the distances between them, equal volumes of gases contain equal numbers of particles (provided that they are at the same temperature and pressure).

Research has shown that a mole of gas occupies 22.4 dm³ at 273 K (0 °C) and 1 atm pressure (these conditions are known as 'standard temperature and pressure'). This is called its **molar volume**. We can use this information to do calculations in terms of volumes of gases (Fig. 4).

 6 a **What volume of sulphur trioxide is produced when 67.2 dm³ sulphur dioxide reacts with oxygen at standard temperature and pressure?**

    b **What mass of sulphuric acid is needed to react with 224 dm³ sulphur trioxide to produce oleum, at standard temperature and pressure?**

Fig. 4 Calculating amounts of gases

Example 1

64 g of sulphur reacts with oxygen gas to produce sulphur dioxide gas. What volume of oxygen is used, and what volume of sulphur dioxide is produced?

By writing out the balanced chemical equation, we get

$S(s)$	$+$	$O_2(g)$	$\rightarrow$	$SO_2(g)$
1 mol		1 mol		1 mol
32 g		22.4 dm³		22.4 dm³

It follows that 64 g of sulphur will react with 44.8 dm³ oxygen to produce 44.8 dm³ sulphur dioxide.

Example 2

What volume of sulphur dioxide (at standard temperature and pressure) will be produced when 1.6 g sulphur react completely with oxygen?

$S(s)$	$+$	$O_2(g)$	$\rightarrow$	$SO_2(g)$
32 g			$\rightarrow$	22.4 dm³
1.6 g			$\rightarrow$	$\dfrac{22.4 \times 1.6}{32}$ dm³
1.6 g			$\rightarrow$	1.12 dm³

So that, 1.6 g sulphur produce 1.12 dm³ oxygen gas.

The amount of a solute

The amount of a sample of a solution, such as sulphuric acid, is easiest to measure in terms of its volume. If we know the concentration of the solution, we can work out how much solute there is in a sample.

Chemists measure the concentration of a solution by stating the amount of solute (in moles) in 1 dm^3 solution. The units are mol dm^{-3}. (Note: 1 dm^3 = 1000 cm^3 = 1 litre.) The concentration of a solution containing 1 mol dm^{-3} of solute is often written as 1M for short.

Similarly, the concentration of a solution containing 2 moles of solute in 1 dm^3 is 2 mol dm^{-3} or 2M. The concentration expressed in mol dm^{-3} is called the **molarity** of the solution (Fig. 5). (In SI units, strictly speaking, concentration should be measured in mol m^{-3}, but in practice mol dm^{-3} are always used.)

 7 a What mass of sodium hydroxide is there in 25 cm^3 of a 0.1M solution?
b 100 cm^3 sulphuric acid solution contains 1.96 g sulphuric acid. What is its molarity?

Fig. 5 Calculations involving molarity

Example 1
Calculate the mass of sulphuric acid in 1 dm^3 of a 0.5M solution.

Molar mass H_2SO_4 = 98 g mol^{-1}
So 1 dm^3 of 1M solution contains 98 g
therefore 1 dm^3 of 0.5M solution will contain 98 × 0.5 g
$$= 49 \text{ g}$$

Example 2
Calculate the amount of sulphuric acid in 100 cm^3 of 2.0M solution.
Amount (mol) = volume (dm^3) × concentration (mol dm^{-3})
$$= 100 × 10^{-3} × 2.0 \text{ mol}$$
$$= 0.2 \text{ mol}$$

Example 3
What mass of sodium hydroxide must be dissolved in 2.5 dm^3 solution to give a 2.0M solution?

Amount (mol) = volume (dm^3) × concentration (mol dm^{-3})
$$= 2.5 × 2.0$$
$$= 5.0 \text{ mol}$$
Molar mass of NaOH = 40 g mol^{-1}
So, mass of NaOH that needs to be dissolved = 5 × 40
$$= 200 \text{ g}$$

Key ideas

- 1 mole of a gas occupies 22.4 dm^3 at standard temperature and pressure.

- The concentration of a solution can be measured in terms of its molarity.

- A 1M solution contains 1 mole of solute in 1 dm^3 of solution.

2.8 The sulphate process

Chris Nejrup inspecting a batch digester in which tioxide ore is reacted with sulphuric acid

8 What mass of titanyl sulphate is produced when 760 tonnes of
   a iron(II) titanate, reacts with excess sulphuric acid?
   b iron(III) titanate reacts with excess sulphuric acid?

The digestion stage produces waste sulphurous gases, such as sulphur dioxide, which are thought to be a cause of acid rain. The waste gases have always been treated to remove some of the sulphur compounds. However, a recently installed gas scrubbing system sprays sodium hydroxide solution over the waste gases to neutralise them. This prevents them from passing into the atmosphere.

Stage one – digestion

'*To get the titanium out of the ilmenite ore we have to heat the finely ground ore with sulphuric acid from the contact process. We carry out this "digestion" of the ilmenite in reinforced concrete or steel reactors lined with lead and acid-resistant bricks.*'

The mixture is heated to start the reaction, which is then very exothermic. The following reactions occur:

$$FeTiO_3(s) + 2H_2SO_4(aq) \rightarrow FeSO_4(aq) + TiOSO_4(aq) + 2H_2O(l)$$

| iron(II) titanate | sulphuric acid | iron(II) sulphate | titanyl sulphate | water |

$$Fe_2(TiO_3)_3(s) + 6H_2SO_4(l) \rightarrow 3TiOSO_4(aq) + Fe_2(SO_4)_3(aq) + 6H_2O(l)$$

| iron(III) titanate | sulphuric acid | titanyl sulphate | iron(III) sulphate | water |

Stage two – reduction

Digesting the ilmenite produces a solid, porous cake containing titanyl sulphate ($TiOSO_4$), iron(II) sulphate ($FeSO_4$), iron(III) sulphate ($Fe_2(SO_4)_3$) and any unreacted ilmenite. It is important to get rid of any iron(III) sulphate that is left in the mixture. Under the conditions in which titanium(IV) oxide is liberated, the iron (III) sulphate forms brown iron(III) hydroxide, which spoils the whiteness of the titanium(IV) oxide. At this stage, therefore, the iron(III) ions are converted to iron(II) ions.

The cake from the digester is dissolved in dilute sulphuric acid to produce a black liquor. This is passed through reduction towers containing baskets of scrap iron. The reaction that occurs is thought to be:
$$Fe_2(SO_4)_3(aq) + Fe(s) \rightarrow 3FeSO_4(aq)$$
The equation for the reduction of iron(III) sulphate to iron(II) sulphate can be written as an ionic equation. An ionic equation tells us the essential chemistry of the reaction (Fig. 6).

1 Rewrite the balanced chemical equation in terms of the ions present:

$$2Fe^{3+} + 3SO_4^{2-} + Fe \rightarrow 3Fe^{2+} + 3SO_4^{2-}$$

2 Cancel the ions that appear on both sides of the equation:

$$2Fe^{3+} + 3SO_4^{2-} + Fe \rightarrow 3Fe^{2+} + 3SO_4^{2-}$$

3 The remaining ions form the ionic equation:

$$2Fe^{3+} + Fe \rightarrow 3Fe^{2+}$$

9 Write ionic equations for the digestion of
a iron(II) titanate,
b iron(III) titanate.

10 Tioxide have a theory that this reaction occurs in two stages: first, scrap iron reacts with sulphuric acid to produce hydrogen gas, and second, the hydrogen gas reacts with iron(III) sulphate to produce iron(II) sulphate and sulphuric acid.
a Write chemical equations for these reactions.
b Write an ionic equation for the conversion of iron(III) sulphate to iron(II) sulphate.

Stage three – settling
The solid residue consists of silicates and other impurities, together with some unreacted ilmenite. It can be removed by letting it settle out of the hot solution and allowing the clean liquor to overflow to the crystallisation section. The residue is filtered and washed to recover titanium which is recycled. The remaining solids are neutralised with chalk before being harmlessly disposed of in a landfill site.

Stage four – crystallisation of iron(II) sulphate
Iron(II) sulphate is less soluble in cold water than in hot. So when the solution from the settling tank is cooled to 30 °C, the iron(II) sulphate crystallises out and is removed by centrifugation. The iron(II) sulphate removed is known as copperas. This is either sold as an iron supplement for animal feedstuffs, or converted to iron(III) sulphate and sold as a water treatment chemical.

Stage five – precipitation
The liquor from the crystalliser is concentrated by heating, and raised to the boiling point. At this temperature the titanyl sulphate reacts to produce titanium(IV) oxide. This precipitates as small crystals.

$$TiOSO_4(aq) + H_2O(l) \rightarrow TiO_2(s) + H_2SO_4(aq)$$

Some iron(II) sulphate remains in the solution and clings to the crystals. This is removed by further washing.

Stage six – filtration to calcination
At the filtration stage any remaining metal sulphates are removed by repeated washing and filtration. The titanium(IV) oxide is then calcined – that is, it is gradually heated to 1000 °C over a period of 16 to 20 hours. This drives off excess water and any remaining sulphuric acid. The calcination kiln operates continuously, with the titanium(IV) oxide moving steadily through it. During the process the titanium(IV) oxide is converted to the correct crystal type and the crystals grow to the correct size.

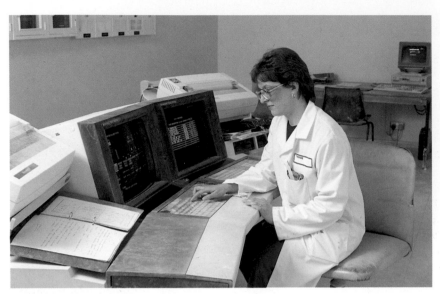

Joanne Lambert works in the central control lab. Part of her job is to monitor the calcination process

'Titanium(IV) oxide may form three different types of crystal, although only two are common. It is important that we produce the correct type of crystal, because they all have different properties when used as pigments. We control the size of crystal being formed by altering the conditions in the kiln, such as air flow and temperature. We regularly take samples from the kiln and analyse them, and adjust the kiln conditions according to the results. The whole process is computerised.'

Calcination, like the digestion stage, produces waste sulphurous gases. These are cooled and any solid particles removed. The sulphurous gases are converted to sulphuric acid in a recently constructed gas cleaning plant. The sulphuric acid is recycled for use in other parts of the plant.

Stage seven – wet treatment

At this stage the titanium(IV) oxide crystals are prepared for their intended use. First they are dry- and wet-milled (ground) to break down any aggregates from the calciners and to reduce the size of the particles even further. Then they are coated with chemicals, the particular compounds chosen depending on the use to which the crystals will be put. For example, one type of coating helps the crystals to mix thoroughly with other paint ingredients, and also protects them from the effects of sunlight.

Finally, the titanium(IV) oxide is washed again, dried and once more milled before being packed into paper or plastic sacks, bulk containers or road tankers. Dust emissions at filling and handling points are controlled by fans and bag filters.

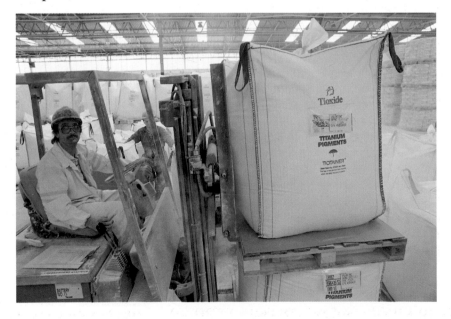

Sacks of titanium(IV) oxide being loaded for delivery

2.9 The gypsum plant

Prior to 1993, the Tioxide factory poured more than 150 000 tonnes of acid directly into the Humber estuary every year (Fig. 7). In 1993, Tioxide built a new treatment plant to convert the waste acid and iron(II) sulphate into gypsum (calcium sulphate). Dave Griffiths is site manager in charge of the gypsum plant.

Dave Griffiths

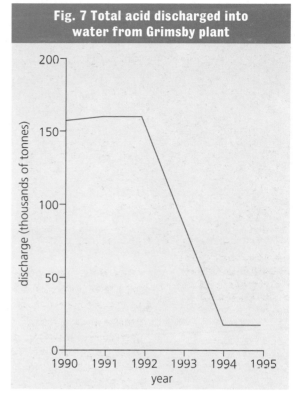

Fig. 7 Total acid discharged into water from Grimsby plant

'We produce two types of gypsum. White gypsum is used to make plasterboard for the building industry. Plasterboard is a "sandwich" of calcium sulphate and cardboard, used to line walls and ceilings. Red gypsum is being used to restore a local old ironstone quarry, which is being developed into a nature park. Both types of gypsum are in great demand by local farmers, who spread them on heavy soils to cut the stickiness of the clay and to break up clods.'

The effluent is treated in two stages. First, the waste sulphuric acid is reacted with local chalk (calcium carbonate) to produce calcium sulphate. The equation for the reaction is:

$$H_2SO_4(aq) + CaCO_3(s) \rightarrow CaSO_4(s) + CO_2(g) + H_2O(l)$$

This calcium sulphate (gypsum) is the major source of raw material for a local plasterboard factory.

The carbon dioxide formed in this process is liquefied on site under high pressure. Most of it is sold to local brewers. Second, the remaining effluent, containing mainly iron(II) sulphate, is reacted with calcium hydroxide to form a mixture of calcium sulphate and iron(II) hydroxide. This is known as red gypsum. The reaction is:

$$FeSO_4(aq) + Ca(OH)_2(s) + H_2O(l) \rightarrow CaSO_4.2H_2O(s) + Fe(OH)_2(s)$$

Elaborate blue and white plasterwork – one of the applications of calcium sulphate

11 Why do you think all of the sulphuric acid waste is not recycled and used at Grimsby?

12 Environmental strategies are expensive. How do you think Tioxide Europe (Grimsby) manages to produce the cheapest titanium(IV) oxide in Europe?

When making gypsum, chemists need to be able to calculate how much acid will react with a known amount of calcium carbonate (Fig. 8).

13 What volume of carbon dioxide gas is produced in the Fig. 8 reaction?

Tioxide relies on several neutralisation reactions to make waste materials harmless. Chemists often carry out neutralisation reactions by titration. This enables them to find the concentration of a solution. Titration is a means of adding, for example, an acid to a base until there is just enough acid to neutralise the base. You can find the concentration of a sample of hydrochloric acid by titrating it against a known volume of sodium hydroxide solution of a known strength (Fig. 9).

Fig. 8 Calculating reactant amounts

Example

What volume of 2M sulphuric acid in needed to react exactly with 1000 g calcium carbonate? What mass of calcium sulphate is produced?

First calculate the volume of sulphuric acid needed.

$$CaCO_3(s) + H_2SO_4(aq) \rightarrow CaSO_4(s) + CO_2(g) + H_2O(l)$$

From the equation,

1 mol	1 mol	$\rightarrow$	1 mol
reacts			

Molar mass of $CaCO_3$ $= 100 \text{ g mol}^{-1}$

So, 1000 g $CaCO_3$ $= \dfrac{1000}{100} \text{ mol } CaCO_3$

         $= 10 \text{ mol}$

From the equation,
10 mol $CaCO_3$ reacts with 10 mol H_2SO_4.

So, 10 mol H_2SO_4 $= 2M \times \text{volume (dm}^3)$

Therefore, volume of 2M H_2SO_4 required $= 5 \text{ dm}^3$

Now find the mass of calcium sulphate produced.

From the equation,
10 mol $CaCO_3$ produces 10 mol $CaSO_4$

Molar mass $CaSO_4$ $= 136$

So, mass of $CaSO_4$ in 10 mol $= 10 \times 136$

         $= 1360 \text{ g}$

Fig. 9 Determining concentration

Example

Suppose 25 cm³ of 0.100 mol dm⁻³ sodium hydroxide solution is neutralised by 19 cm³ hydrochloric acid.

The balanced chemical equation is:
$$HCl(aq) + NaOH(aq) \rightarrow NaCl(aq) + H_2O(l)$$

So, amount of NaOH (mol)

     = volume (dm³) × concentration (mol dm⁻³)

     $= 25 \times 10^{-3} \times 0.100$

     $= 2.5 \times 10^{-3} \text{ mol}$

Now we can calculate the amount of hydrochloric acid that will react with this amount of sodium hydroxide.

From the equation,
1 mol HCl reacts with 1 mol NaOH

So, amount of HCl $= 2.5 \times 10^{-3} \text{ mol}$

Amount HCl (mol)

     = volume (dm³) × concentration (mol dm⁻³)

Or $2.5 \times 10^{-3} = 19 \times 10^{-3} \times \text{concentration}$

Concentration of HCl (mol dm⁻³)

     $= \dfrac{2.5 \times 10^{-3}}{19 \times 10^{-3}}$

     $= 0.132 \text{ mol dm}^{-3}$

14 If 10 cm³ of 0.12 mol dm⁻³ sodium hydroxide solution were neutralised by 9.5 cm³ of hydrochloric acid solution. Calculate the molarity of the hydrochloric acid.

Key ideas

- Ionic equations give the essential chemistry of reactions.

- Unknown molarities can be calculated from acid/base titration data.

2.10 Future strategies

Tioxide has reduced discharges into the Humber estuary (Table 1, Fig. 10). Tioxide's environmental policy also includes strategies to recycle water and reduce energy wherever possible. Their environmental programme is by no means complete. They are currently concentrating on reducing atmospheric emissions, especially of particulate emissions and of sulphurous gases in the digestion and calcination stage. The process of monitoring flora and fauna in the Humber estuary, which was begun many years ago, is now undertaken in conjunction with the National Rivers Authority (NRA). Encouragingly, Tioxide's cleanup initiatives are already beginning to show measurable improvements.

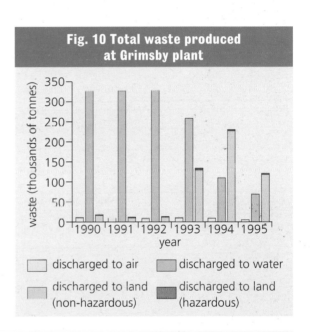

Fig. 10 Total waste produced at Grimsby plant

discharged to air discharged to water

discharged to land (non-hazardous) discharged to land (hazardous)

Table 1 Annual emissions into the river Humber by Tioxide Europe				
	1992	1993	1994	Reduction/%*
Volume/m³	8 000 000	8 400 000	8 500 000	–
Sulphuric acid/tonne	161 000	90 000	7 000	89
Iron/tonne	50 000	42 000	9 000	43
Manganese/tonne	1 500	1 300	960	36
Copper/tonne	7	4	3	54
Lead/tonne	9	5	0.5	94
Titanium (dissolved)/tonne	2 970	2 900	1 900	34

*Comparison of 1994 and 1992 figures.

Discovering elements

A great deal changed between the early 1800s and 1930. In that time electricity, electromagnetism and radioactivity were discovered. Changes in technology influenced advances in chemical theory.

Humphry Davy started his chemical experiments in Bristol, where he experimented with nitrous oxide, often inhaling it himself.

Davy moved to the newly founded Royal Institution in London at the age of 22 and his lectures soon became very popular. During his lifetime he carried out an enormous number of important experiments. Besides using electricity to isolate metallic elements he is also remembered for the development of a miners' safety lamp. He wrote poetry and was friendly with Wordsworth and Coleridge.

Davy discovers potassium

'To form potassium, potash (potassium hydroxide) in a thin piece is placed between 2 discs of platina connected with the extremities of a voltaic apparatus of 200 double plates; it will soon undergo fusion, oxygene will separate at the positive surface and small metallic globules will appear at the negative surface, which consist of potassium. I discovered this metal in the beginning of October 1807.'

Source: Davy, 1812

Emilio Segrè was born in Rome. He had been interested in physics since childhood, but studied engineering at university for four years before changing to physics. He became interested in the newly developing field of atomic physics and moved to the University of California at Berkeley in 1938. He was involved in the Manhattan atomic bomb project at Los Alamos. Like most atomic physicists he worked in a research team. Besides discovering technetium, the first man-made element, he and Perrier also isolated astatine and plutonium-239. Segrè is best known for the discovery of the antiproton, for which he shared the Nobel prize with Owen Chamberlain in 1959.

Segrè discovers technitium

'Every time that physics has offered a new analytical tool to chemistry, the most striking success has been the discovery of new elements... .

In the search for the four missing elements lower than uranium, we have now been able to prepare element 43 and study its properties in detail. The substance was produced in the Berkeley cyclotron, which thus remains for the time the only 'mine' of the element. It was made by bombarding molybdenum with deuterons or with neutrons.'

Source: Segrè, March 1939

Above. A voltaic pile – the 'new' technology used by Davy

Right. The Lawrence cyclotron – the 'new' technology used by Segrè

3.1 Learning objectives

 After working through this chapter, you should be able to:

- **explain** the periodicity of properties of the elements as they are arranged in the Periodic Table;

- **describe** the reactions of Group I metals, Period 3 oxides and Period 3 chlorides with water;

- **describe** the electronic structure of the first 36 elements;

- **describe** an element as s-, p- or d-block;

- **explain** how trends in ionisation energy give evidence for electron arrangement in levels and sub-levels;

- **explain** the terms first ionisation energy and atomic radius;

- **describe** the trends in properties of Period 3 and Group I elements.

3.2 Signs of the times

The discovery of an element is an important event. In 1807 Davy isolated potassium. In 1937 Segrè headed a team that isolated technetium. All were experimenting with the latest technology. However, there was a big difference in the accepted ideas of their times.

In the early 1800s scientists had very little idea about the nature of atoms. They had no easy way of finding accurate atomic masses. Not every element and compound was clearly recognised (e.g. chlorine was thought to be a compound called oxymuriatic acid before Davy found it to be an element). Experimenters believed that:
- an **element** is the simplest substance;

- only a few elements exist;
- some elements and compounds show patterns in their behaviour.

By the 1930s, however, scientists had very accurate ways of determining atomic masses. They accepted the idea of an **atom** with a **nucleus** and they understood radioactivity. They also believed that:
- an element is the simplest substance, but can undergo nuclear transformations;
- many elements existed, as shown by the **Periodic Table**;
- patterns in the behaviour of elements could be predicted from the Periodic Table.

3.3 Reactions of the elements – Group I metals

Davy had been experimenting to see the effects of electricity on some fairly common materials. He saw that an electric current could break down compounds, so he set about trying to decompose potash (potassium hydroxide) and soda (sodium hydroxide).

Davy recognised that there were similarities in the behaviour of some compounds, and by electrolysis managed to isolate elements which he called potassium, sodium, calcium, magnesium, strontium and barium. He also tried to electrolyse alumina, thinking that there was a metallic element in it. He was right in his prediction, but was unable to isolate aluminium because of the very high melting point of aluminium oxide.

Fig 1. Davy's observations of sodium and potassium

Sodium

"When thrown upon water it effervesces violently, but does not inflame, swims on the surface, gradually diminishes with great agitation, and renders the water a solution of soda."

Potassium

"When thrown upon water it acts with great violence, swims upon the surface, and burns with a beautiful light, which is white mixed with red and violet; the water in which it burns is found alkaline, and contains a solution of potassa."

Source: Humphry Davy, 1812

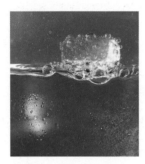

Sodium reacting with water

Initially Davy was unsure how to classify the new elements, but he called them metals because of their shine and the ease with which they conducted electricity and heat. What we now know as the Group I metals, Davy called 'alkali' metals. Davy's original descriptions of their reactions are given in Fig. 1. Unlike Segrè, Davy was not able to explain his discoveries in terms of atoms and chemical equations. Symbols and equations were not yet in use.

Lithium

Lithium was an element unknown to Davy. It reacts slowly with cold water:

$$2Li(s) + 2H_2O(l) \rightarrow + 2LiOH(aq) + H_2(g)$$
lithium hydroxide
solution

Rubidium

Rubidium was unknown to Davy. It reacts even more violently with water than potassium. The hydrogen gas given off catches fire immediately, as in the case of potassium:

$$2Rb(s) + 2H_2O(l) \rightarrow 2RbOH(aq) + H_2(g)$$
rubidium hydroxide
solution

Caesium

Caesium was also unknown to Davy. Unlike other alkali metals, it sinks in water and reacts explosively. This is because of the rapid generation of hydrogen underwater:

$$2Cs(s) + 2H_2O(l) \rightarrow 2CsOH(aq) + H_2(g)$$
caesium hydroxide
solution

There is a pattern in these reactions. Hydrogen and an alkali are always formed. The reactivity of Group I metals increases down the group.

1 Write equations for the reactions of sodium and potassium with water.

2 Suggest why rubidium and caesium were unknown to Davy.

3.4 Reactions of Period 3 compounds

Davy used the small amounts of sodium and potassium he produced to investigate their chemistry. He also studied the oxides (Figs 2 and 3) of what are now called the Period 3 elements. Specifically, how they react with water, **acids** and **alkalis**. Davy often described the taste of the chemicals. His inclination to taste chemicals probably helped to shorten his life.

Oxides

Aluminium oxide shows the properties of both a base and an acid. We say that it is **amphoteric.**

The reaction of silica with alkali indicates that silicon oxide is an acidic oxide. Davy knew that a solution of sulphur dioxide was easily oxidised by air to give oil of vitriol or sulphuric acid. Both sulphur dioxide and sulphur trioxide are acidic gases.

Fig. 2 Reactions of metal oxides

Sodium oxide

"When a little water is added to it, there is a violent reaction between the two bodies"

$$Na_2O(s) + H_2O(l) \rightarrow 2NaOH(aq)$$
alkaline sodium hydroxide solution

Magnesium oxide

"It is scarcely soluble in water, but produces heat when water is mixed with it, and it absorbs a considerable portion of the fluid."

$$2MgO(s) + H_2O(l) \rightarrow Mg(OH)_2(s)$$
magnesium hydroxide

Aluminium oxide

"has no taste or smell, adheres strongly to the tongue, has no action on vegetable colours, is insoluble in water, is soluble in all the mineral acids and in hot solutions of … alkalis"

Source: Humphry Davy, 1812

Fig. 3 Reactions of non-metal oxides

Silicon oxide (silica)

"… can be procured … from common flints, by igniting them in powder, with three or four times their weight of potash, or soda, in a silver crucible"

Phosphorus oxide

"…has no smell; its taste is intensely, but not disagreeably acid. It dissolves in water, producing great heat; and its saturated solution is the consistence of syrup. It … unites to alkalis"

$$P_4O_{10}(s) + 6H_2O(l) \rightarrow 4H_3PO_4(aq)$$
phosphoric(V) acid

Sulphur dioxide

"… is obtained when sulphur burns in oxygen with a beautiful violet flame. It reddens vegetable blues, and gradually destroys most of them. It is absorbed by water; this fluid takes up about 30 times its bulk, and gains a nauseous subacid taste."

$$SO_2(g) + H_2O(l) \rightarrow H_2SO_3(aq)$$
sulphuric(IV) acid
$$SO_3(g) + H_2O(l) \rightarrow H_2SO_4(aq)$$
sulphuric(VI) acid

Source: Humphry Davy, 1812

Chlorides

Sodium chloride

Its properties were so well known that Davy did not mention that sodium chloride dissolves in water, with no further reaction.

Magnesium chloride

Davy was unable to purify magnesium chloride. It dissolves in water, with no further reaction.

Aluminium chloride

Solid aluminium chloride fumes with water to form aluminium hydroxide and hydrogen chloride gas:

$$AlCl_3(s) + 3H_2O(l) \rightarrow Al(OH)_3(s) + 3HCl(g)$$

Silicon chloride

Silicon chloride reacts rapidly with water to form a hydrated form of silica and a solution of hydrochloric acid:

$$SiCl_4(l) + 2H_2O(l) \rightarrow SiO_2(s) + 4HCl(aq)$$

Davy did not know about the reactions of aluminium chloride and silicon chloride, because aluminium and silicon had not been isolated. Figure 5 summarises the properties of Period 3 compounds (page 30).

Fig. 4 Reaction of a chloride

Phosphorus chloride

"Its properties are very peculiar. It is a snow-white substance. It is very volatile, and rises in a gaseous form at a temperature much below that of boiling water … It acts violently upon water, which it decomposes. Its phosphorus combines with the oxygen, producing phosphoric acid, and its chlorine with hydrogen forms muriatic [hydrochloric] acid."

$$PCl_5 + 4H_2O(l) \rightarrow H_3PO_4(aq) + 5HCl(aq)$$

Source: Humphry Davy, 1812

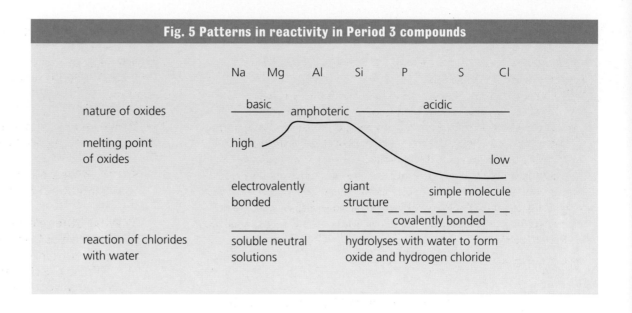

Fig. 5 Patterns in reactivity in Period 3 compounds

Na Mg Al Si P S Cl

nature of oxides — basic — amphoteric — acidic —

melting point of oxides — high / low

electrovalently bonded — giant structure — simple molecule — covalently bonded

reaction of chlorides with water — soluble neutral solutions — hydrolyses with water to form oxide and hydrogen chloride

3.5 Patterns in reactions

Davy's work helped to identify patterns in the reactions of certain oxides and chlorides with water. The oxides change from being alkaline (sodium and magnesium) to amphoteric (aluminium) to acidic (silicon, phosphorus and sulphur). Similarly, the reaction of the chlorides with water changes from being unreactive (sodium and magnesium) to forming basic oxides (aluminium) to forming acidic oxides (silicon and phosphorus).

The reason for these patterns is the nature of the bonding in the compounds. This information was not accessible to Davy, but patterns such as these led to the development of the **Periodic Table** (Fig. 6).

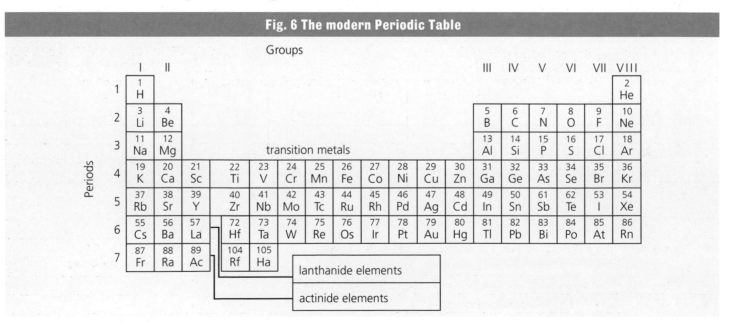

Fig. 6 The modern Periodic Table

Groups

	I	II											III	IV	V	VI	VII	VIII
1	1 H																	2 He
2	3 Li	4 Be											5 B	6 C	7 N	8 O	9 F	10 Ne
3	11 Na	12 Mg				transition metals							13 Al	14 Si	15 P	16 S	17 Cl	18 Ar
4	19 K	20 Ca	21 Sc	22 Ti	23 V	24 Cr	25 Mn	26 Fe	27 Co	28 Ni	29 Cu	30 Zn	31 Ga	32 Ge	33 As	34 Se	35 Br	36 Kr
5	37 Rb	38 Sr	39 Y	40 Zr	41 Nb	42 Mo	43 Tc	44 Ru	45 Rh	46 Pd	47 Ag	48 Cd	49 In	50 Sn	61 Sb	62 Te	53 I	54 Xe
6	55 Cs	56 Ba	57 La	72 Hf	73 Ta	74 W	75 Re	76 Os	77 Ir	78 Pt	79 Au	80 Hg	81 Tl	82 Pb	83 Bi	84 Po	85 At	86 Rn
7	87 Fr	88 Ra	89 Ac	104 Rf	105 Ha													

Periods

lanthanide elements

actinide elements

30

1. The elements, if arranged according to their atomic weights, exhibit an evident periodicity of properties.

2. Elements which are similar as regards their chemical properties have atomic weights which are either of nearly the same value (e.g. platinum, iridium, osmium) or which increase regularly (e.g. potassium, rubidium, caesium).

3. The arrangement of the elements, or of groups of elements in order of their atomic weights corresponds to their so-called valencies as well as, to some extent, to their distinctive chemical properties – as is apparent among other series in that of lithium, beryllium, boron, carbon, nitrogen, oxygen and fluorine.

4. We must expect the discovery of many yet unknown elements, for example, elements analogous to aluminium and silicon, whose atomic weight would be between 65 and 75.

Source: Dmitri Mendeleev, 1889

insistence that the table be arranged to show 'repeating patterns', or periodicity, meant that some gaps were left. These gaps were to be filled by, as yet, undiscovered elements.

3 Which group of elements is missing from Mendeleev's Periodic Table?

4 Which element was Mendeleev talking about in statement 4?

5 What other elements would we recognise as being like platinum, iridium and osmium – having similar properties because of similar atomic mass?

Development of the Periodic Table

Credit for developing the modern Periodic Table is often given to the Russian chemist Dmitri Mendeleev, but he was by no means the only person to develop key ideas in this area. He recognised the contributions of De Chancourtois, Newlands and Meyer.

Mendeleev's first version of the Periodic Table was published by the Russian Chemical Society in the spring of 1869. He produced a second, improved version in 1871 (Fig. 7). Mendeleev arranged the known elements in order of atomic weight and put them into groups that had similar physical and chemical properties. His

The Periodic Table provided a very powerful tool for chemists. It allowed them to explore and predict patterns in the reactions and behaviour of elements. Unfortunately not all elements seemed to fit in exactly the right place, because Mendeleev's table was based on atomic mass (see Chapter 1). The modern Periodic Table is based on atomic number. The idea of atomic number was the result of the advances made in atomic theory at the beginning of the 20th century.

The trends in properties of elements are related to the position of the element in the Periodic Table.

Row	Group I --- R_2O	Group II --- RO	Group III --- R_2O_3	Group IV RH_4 RO_2	Group V RH_3 R_2O_5	Group VI RH_2 RO_3	Group VII RH R_2O_7	Group VIII --- RO_4
1	H = 1							
2	Li = 7	Be = 9.4	B = 11	C = 12	N = 14	O =16	F = 19	
3	Na = 23	Mg = 24	Al = 27.3	Si = 28	P = 31	S = 32	Cl = 35.5	
4	K = 39	Ca = 40	-- = 44	Ti = 48	V = 51	Cr = 52	Mn = 55	Fe = 56, Co =59, Ni = 59, Cu' = 63
5	(Cu = 63)	Zn = 65	-- = 68	-- = 72	As = 75	Se = 78	Br = 80	
6	Rb = 85	Sr = 87	?Yt = 88	Zr = 90	Nb = 94	Mo = 96	-- = 100	Ru = 104, Rh = 104, Pd = 106, Ag = 108
7	(Ag = 108)	Cd = 112	In = 113	Sn = 118	Sb = 122	Te = 125	I = 127	
8	Cs = 133	Ba = 137	?Di = 138	?Ce = 140	--	--	--	----

Fig. 7 Part of Mendeleev's Periodic Table of 1871

3.6 Development of atomic theory

When Davy started his work the notion of an atom was not clear. In 1808 John Dalton proposed his model of an atom – an indivisible particle that cannot be created or destroyed. This idea was not accepted by all chemists at the time. Dalton proposed that atoms or 'ultimate particles' of different elements had different sizes and therefore different masses. He also produced a set of atomic masses for some elements.

Dalton was the first chemist to give symbols to atoms of different elements (Fig. 8). This idea was refined by the Swedish chemist Berzelius in 1813, and forms the basis of today's notation. He suggested that one 'volume' of an element should be represented by the initial letter of its Latin name written as a capital. Where two elements had the same initial letter, the non-metal was given the single letter and a second letter was added for the symbol of the metal (e.g. C and Cu, F and Fe).

At this time there was no notion of protons, electrons and neutrons. Further refinement of ideas about atoms did not come until the beginning of the 20th century. Ideas on the structure of atoms came from experiments in which electricity was passed through gases at very low pressure. From these experiments, J.J. Thomson suggested all atoms contain oppositely charged sub-atomic particles. His idea of an atom was a sphere of uniform positive charge within which rings of electrons rotated. After Thomson published his ideas experiments showed he was not entirely correct.

Ernest Rutherford – a New Zealander working under Thomson's supervision – later observed that when a beam of alpha particles, which have positive charge, was aimed at a very thin metal foil, some were deflected (Fig. 9).

Hans Geiger and Ernest Marsden studied this very carefully. They found that although most alpha particles were either not deflected or only deflected slightly, a very small number bounced back towards the particle source. Rutherford described this as being as if you had fired a 15-inch shell at a piece of tissue paper and it had come back and hit you (Fig. 10). This important finding led Rutherford to suggest that the atom had an extremely small

Fig. 8 Daltons list of elements

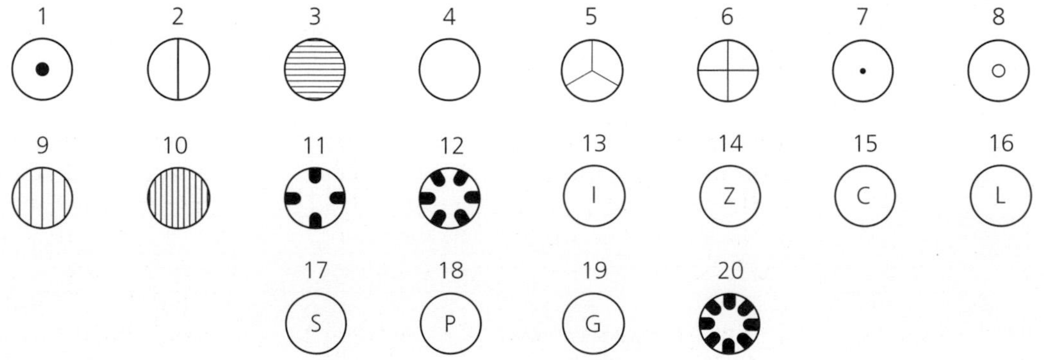

1 Hydrogen	6 Sulphur	11 Strontites	16 Lead
2 Azote	7 Magnesia	12 Barytes	17 Silver
3 Carbone or charcoal	8 Lime	13 Iron	18 Platina
4 Oxygen	9 Soda	14 Zinc	19 Gold
5 Phosphorus	10 Potash	15 Copper	20 Mercury

Fig. 9 Rutherford's experiment

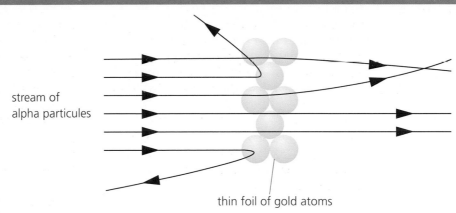

Positively charged particles called alpha particles were aimed at a piece of gold foil. The foil was only a few atoms across. Atoms were then pictured as balls of evenly spread electrical charges. It therefore came as a surprise when about 1 in every 1000 alpha particles was deflected through a large angle, sometimes up to 180 degrees.

stream of alpha particules

thin foil of gold atoms

Fig. 10 Rutherford's analogy

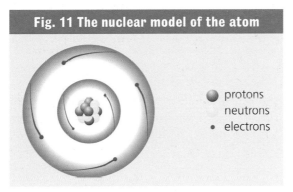

Fig. 11 The nuclear model of the atom

- protons
- neutrons
- electrons

centre which was positively charged and so deflected the incoming alpha particles. He called this centre the **nucleus**, and indicated that the positive charge was balanced by negatively charged electrons revolving around the nucleus at a considerable distance. This model (Fig. 11) is used by chemists today.

In this model all the positive charge is concentrated in a tiny nucleus. The unexpected deflections in Rutherford's experiment were due to the positive alpha particles approaching the positive nucleus and being electrically repelled. This model cannot have all the characteristics of the real atom. It does not show that the electrons are in constant motion or give a clear idea of scale. If this figure was drawn to scale, a nucleus this size would require an atom ten times larger than a classroom.

3.7 Electron energy levels

Rutherford's theory was a major step in atomic theory, but it was not complete. It did not explain why electrons stayed in orbit around the nucleus, rather than spiralling in attracted by the positive charge.

This puzzle was solved by Niels Bohr, a Danish physicist who worked for a time with Thomson and Rutherford. Bohr proposed that electrons can only move in specific orbits around the nucleus and that each orbit has its own **energy level**. This makes it impossible for electrons to occupy 'in between' orbits, making it equally impossible for electrons to lose, or gain, energy gradually. The electrons can only have sudden jumps in energy.

Evidence to support Bohr's theory came from the atomic spectra of elements. Robert Bunsen and Gustav Kirchoff had devised a spectroscope to examine the flame colours of metal salts. A prism spread out the light from the flames revealing, not a continuous spectrum of colour, but individual coloured lines. They found that each metal had a characteristic set of lines.

Bohr suggested that these lines

represented electrons jumping to lower orbits and losing a precise amount of energy in the form of light (Fig. 12). The energy required for one jump corresponds to a line in the element's spectrum. Energy levels get closer together the further they are from the nucleus. An electron will also jump to a higher orbit if it is given the right amount of energy in the form of light – this is seen in *absorption* spectra. When an electron is given sufficient energy to remove it from the influence of the nucleus, the spectral lines become a continuum.

Fig. 12 Energy levels and electrons

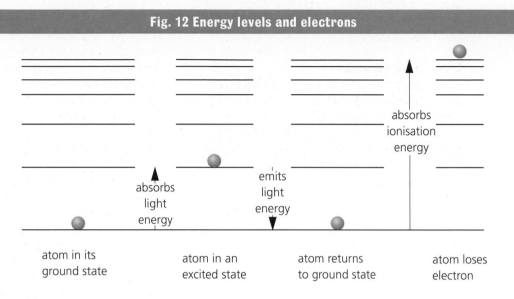

atom in its ground state atom in an excited state atom returns to ground state atom loses electron

Electrons in an atom can only exist at certain energy levels. An atom can be *excited* when an electron jumps to a higher energy level by absorbing the right amount of energy in the form of light. The electron will later drop back, returning the atom to its *ground state*, by emitting the same amount of energy as light. The amount of energy determines the wavelength of the light.

3.8 The importance of atomic number

Moseley obtained experimental results of great value. He was destined for a brilliant career but died in World War I at the age of 27

Soon after Rutherford proposed his ideas for the structure of the atom, Henry Moseley, one of his students at the Cavendish Laboratory, examined the X-ray spectra of a large number of elements. Moseley wanted to explore Rutherford's ideas more fully. He discovered that every element is characterised by a number, N, which determines its X-ray spectrum. This number, called the **atomic number**, is related to the number of positive charges in the nucleus of the element. In other words, the atomic number of an element is the number of **protons** in its atom.

Moseley recognised that for the vast majority of elements, placing them in order of atomic number gives the same pattern as placing them in order of atomic mass. Mendeleev's Periodic Table did not need to be amended much to produce the modern form of the Periodic Table. Moseley also identified that there were three missing elements with atomic numbers 43, 61 and 75.

Segrè and Perrier know these ideas about the Periodic Table and atomic structure. These important ideas and the development of experimental atomic physics made the discovery of element 43 – technetium – possible.

3.9 Patterns and periodicity

Chemists use periodicity and atomic theory to explain some of the physical and chemical properties of elements. Davy was unable to explain the patterns of his observations in terms of the nature of atoms and bonding. Today we can explore many features of elements from their position in the Periodic Table.

Electronic structure

The arrangement of electrons in an atom determines the chemical behaviour of the element. The number of electrons in a neutral atom is the same as the number of protons in its nucleus, i.e. the same as the atomic number. Stripping the outermost electrons from am atom gives useful information. If an electron is given sufficient energy to remove it from the influence of the nucleus, the atom becomes a positively charged ion:

$$X \rightarrow X^+ + e^-$$

The energy required to remove 1 mole of the outermost electrons from 1 mole of an element is called the **first ionisation energy** of the element (Table 1).

Table 1 shows these patterns:
- The first ionisation energy for Group I elements is always much smaller than the second and third. This indicates that the first outer electron is easy to remove, but that the next two electrons are much harder to remove. This suggests that the first electron is alone in the outer energy level.
- The first ionisation energy decreases down the group. This is because the outermost electrons become more *shielded* from the attractive positive charge on the nucleus. The shielding is provided by the negative electrons occupying the innermost energy levels (Fig. 13). This decrease in ionisation energy explains why Group I metals become more reactive down the group.

Table 1 Selected ionisation energies of Group I elements/kJ mol⁻¹					
	Lithium (Li)	Sodium (Na)	Potassium (K)	Rubidium (Rb)	Caesium (Cs)
first ionisation energy	520	496	419	403	376
second ionisation energy	7298	4563	3051	2632	2420
third ionisation energy	11815	6913	4412	3900	3300

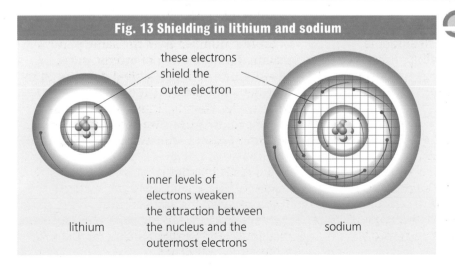

Fig. 13 Shielding in lithium and sodium

these electrons shield the outer electron

inner levels of electrons weaken the attraction between the nucleus and the outermost electrons

lithium

sodium

6 Look back at the descriptions of the reactions of lithium to caesium with water. How would you explain to Humphry Davy why potassium is more reactive than sodium?

7 Lithium to caesium are Group I metals and the first of the s-block elements. The other group of s-block elements is the Group II metals. Use the data pages to examine the first, second and third ionisation energies of beryllium to barium. What patterns can you find?

There are also patterns in ionisation energy across a period of elements (Fig. 14). Two features of Fig. 14 are important:

- There is a general trend of increasing ionisation energy across the period. An electron becomes more difficult to remove as the energy level fills up. This is because there is an increasing number of protons in the nucleus, which increases the attraction on the outer electrons.
- There are troughs in the graph at boron and oxygen. This is related to **sub-levels** being full at beryllium and half-full at nitrogen.

Fig. 14 Graph of first ionisation energy against atomic number

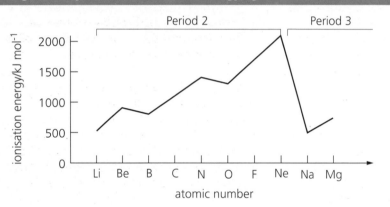

 8 Use the information in the data section to plot a graph of first ionisation energies of sodium to argon. What patterns are there?

Table 2 Electron configurations

Element	Electron configuration		
hydrogen	$1s^1$		
helium	$1s^2$ (full level)		
lithium	$1s^2$	$2s^1$	
beryllium	$1s^2$	$2s^2$ (full sub-level)	
boron	$1s^2$	$2s^2$	$2p^1$
carbon	$1s^2$	$2s^2$	$2p^2$
nitrogen	$1s^2$	$2s^2$	$2p^3$ (half-full sub-level)
oxygen	$1s^2$	$2s^2$	$2p^4$
fluorine	$1s^2$	$2s^2$	$2p^5$
neon	$1s^2$	$2s^2$	$2p^6$ (full level)

Electron configuration

Electrons are arranged in levels (1,2,3, etc.) and sub-levels (s,p,d). Level 1 has a single s sub-level. Level 2 has s and p sub-levels. Level 3 has s, p and d sub-levels. The s sub-level can hold up to two electrons in one orbital. The p sub-level can hold up to six electrons in three orbitals. The d sub-level can hold up to ten electrons in five orbitals. To indicate 3 electrons in the p sub-level, level 2, we write: $2p^3$. The complete electron configurations of hydrogen to neon are shown in Table 2.

 9 Write the electron configurations for the elements sodium to argon.

The elements boron to fluorine are known as p-block elements, because the p sub-level is partially filled. The d-block elements have incomplete d sub-levels. For example, the electron configurations of scandium and titanium are:

scandium: $1s^2\ 2s^2\ 2p^6\ 3s^2\ 3p^6\ 3d^1\ 4s^2$

titanium: $1s^2\ 2s^2\ 2p^6\ 3s^2\ 3p^6\ 3d^2\ 4s^2$.

 10 Write the electron configurations for the elements vanadium to zinc.

Atomic radius

Atoms are extremely small. The radius of an atom is about 10^{-10} m. Rutherford and his team were able to show that the radius of the nucleus of copper is less than 1.2×10^{-14} m.

The atomic radius of an element is the distance from the centre of the nucleus to the outermost electrons. The patterns in atomic radius are related to those in ionisation energy.

- The **atomic radius** increases down a group. This is because there are increasing numbers of full levels of electrons.
- The atomic radius decreases across a period. This is because the effective attractive charge on electrons in the same level increases, pulling the outer electrons slightly closer to the nucleus as the level fills up.

Fig. 15 Atomic radii (in nm) and relative sizes

Li	Be	B	C	N	O	F	Ne
0.134	0.125	0.080	0.077	0.075	0.073	0.071	0.160
Na	Mg	Al	Si	P	S	Cl	Ar
0.154	0.145	0.130	0.118	0.110	0.102	0.099	0.190

11 Why do neon and argon have larger atomic radii than the other elements in the same period (Fig. 15)?

Electronegativity

Elements which lose outer electrons easily are described as electropositive. Caesium is the most **electropositive** element. Elements which gain electrons easily are called **electronegative**. Fluorine is the most electronegative element. Electronegativity:

• increases across a period;
• decreases down a group.

The trend from metal to non-metal across a period is indicated by the changes in electronegativity. The change from metal to non-metal is also shown by trends in melting points (Table 3). Metals have high melting points because of metallic

Davy noted the violent reaction when a very electropositive element combines with a very eleronegative element – "Potassium burns spontaneously in chlorine with intense brilliance"

bonding. Non-metals have high melting points if they form **giant structures** and low melting points if they form simple molecules.

Compounds which contain an electropositive element and an electronegative element such as sodium chloride are electrovalently bonded. Compounds which contain elements with similar electronegativities, such as silicon oxide are covalently bonded. Covalently bonded compounds containing elements in the middle of the period are often giant structures, e.g. silicon oxide. Covalently bonded compounds of electronegative elements, e.g. sulphur dioxide, are often small molecules. This is reflected in their melting points.

12 Suggest why ceramics are made from materials which have a high content of silicon oxide.

Segrè and his team predicted the physical properties and chemical reactions of technetium from its position in the Periodic Table. They expected it to form several oxides with high melting points, just like the other d-block elements (see Chapter 9). They were able to show some of these properties but not all. Just as Davy had only been able to isolate a small quantity of potassium, so only a very small quantity of technetium was initially obtained in the cyclotron.

Many other scientists, besides those mentioned here, made very important contributions to developing atomic theory and periodicity.

		Table 3					
		Melting points of Period 3 elements/K					
Metals			Non-metals				
Na	Mg	Al	Si	P	S	Cl	Ar
371	923	933	1680	317	392	172	83.8

Key ideas

• Elements with similar properties are in columns in the Periodic Table. Important properties are atomic radius, electromagnetivity and melting point.

• Atoms of elements contain a very small positively charged nucleus. Electrons orbit

the nucleus in energy levels; full levels and full sub-levels are stable arrangements.

• Trends in ionisation energy in the periodic Table give evidence for electronic energy levels.

Bonding and semiconductors

Computers are everywhere today. They play an important part in our society. They are used in factories, supermarkets, libraries, doctors' surgeries, cinema box offices and cars, to name just a few examples. Computers run the communications systems that link the world into a 'global village'. Computers are fun too: millions of people turn to their home computers for a huge range of entertainment. We are living in an electronic age. But the computer is barely 50 years old.

Integrated circuits are the key to the powerful and incredibly fast computers of today. These machines may be only as big as a fair-sized paperback, but each can store the equivalent of a whole shelf-full of books. And the storage capacity of computers is increasing at a dramatic rate.

Above. The first electronic computer, Colossus, was used to decipher German code messages during World War II. Colossus relied on valves, as did its American counterpart, ENIAC (Electronic Numerical Indicator and Calculator). This machine could store the equivalent of about 100 words. Early computers used radio valves as amplifiers, detectors or switches. The valves were large, and used a lot of power. They got very hot

Left. In modern computers valves have been replaced by transistors, which are far smaller, cheaper and much less power-hungry. In a transistor, three or more electrical contacts are made with a block of semiconducting material. Transistors can be assembled on tiny wafers ('microchips') of silicon, together with minute electronic devices such as capacitors and resistors, to form integrated circuits

4.1 Learning objectives

After working through this chapter, you should be able to:

- **explain** the nature of metallic, covalent and ionic bonds;

- **describe** the electron configurations of simple molecules using dot-and-cross diagrams;

- **explain** the properties of a substance in terms of the bonding in its molecules;

- **explain** why some covalent bonds are polar by using electronegatvity values.

4.2 Metallic bonding

Transistors are the result of the discovery of **semiconductors** – materials which are insulators at low temperatures and conductors at high temperatures. The electrical conductivity of semiconductors increases as the temperature rises, unlike metals, which conduct electricity well at all temperatures, and most non-metals which are insulators. The electrical conductivity of a substance – whether it is a conductor, a semiconductor or an insulator – is a direct result of the type of bonding that links its atoms.

Metals are good conductors of electricity. In most electronic devices, metals are used to carry electric current. Tin-plated copper wire is used in the circuitry of modern computers. The fine wiring connecting the silicon chips is usually gold or aluminium.

Metals conduct electricity, because the electrons in the highest energy level of a metal atom can leave their nucleus quite easily. The orbits of these outer electrons overlap, with the overlapping extending

throughout the metal. The electrons, which are all free to move through the metal, form a sea of negative charge surrounding the positive metal ions (cations). They no longer belong to one particular atomic nucleus. They are said to be **delocalised** (Fig. 1). If a potential difference is applied across a metal, the delocalised electrons will move towards the positive terminal – a current flows.

1 Suggest why the metal cations do not push each other apart.

Thermionic valve (top), transistor (centre) and microchip (right)

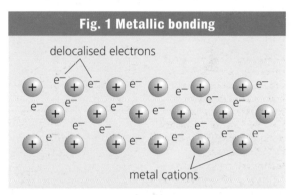

Fig. 1 Metallic bonding

delocalised electrons

metal cations

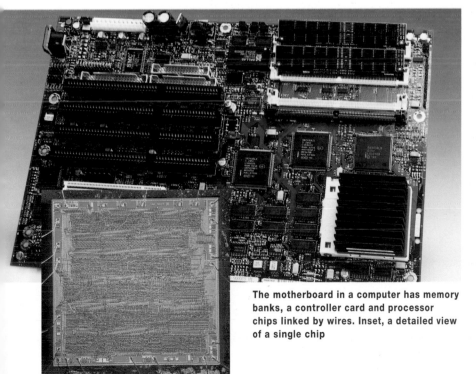

The motherboard in a computer has memory banks, a controller card and processor chips linked by wires. Inset, a detailed view of a single chip

All the electrical circuits that control the stage lighting rely on the electrical conductivity of metals

4.3 Covalent bonding

When non-metal atoms join together, they form chemical bonds called **covalent bonds**. Covalent bonds form when electrons in the highest energy levels are shared between two atoms. A hydrogen molecule contains a covalent bond (Fig. 2).

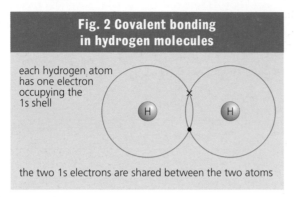

Fig. 2 Covalent bonding in hydrogen molecules

each hydrogen atom has one electron occupying the 1s shell

H   H

the two 1s electrons are shared between the two atoms

Each hydrogen atom in the hydrogen molecule has two electrons in its outer shell. This is the electron configuration of helium (a noble gas). It is a stable arrangement: noble (inert) gases are very unreactive. The pair of shared electrons forms a **single covalent bond**. The bonding can be shown in a **dot-and-cross diagram**, in which the dots and crosses represent electrons:

$$H \overset{\bullet}{\underset{\times}{}} H$$

Dot-and-cross diagrams don't imply that there are two different kinds of electron. All electrons are identical. Dots and crosses just make it easier to show where the different electrons come from.

Hydrogen molecules do not conduct electricity. A substance cannot conduct electric current unless it contains electrons that are free to carry the charge. The electrons in hydrogen are 'locked' into the covalent bond, and are not free to move.

There is direct evidence to support the existence of covalent bonds. When X-rays strike a molecule or a crystal, they are diffracted by the electrons it contains. Using computers, the density of the

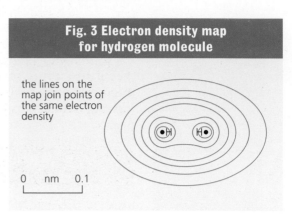

Fig. 3 Electron density map for hydrogen molecule

the lines on the map join points of the same electron density

0   nm   0.1

electrons can be determined at different places within the molecule/crystal. The results are recorded on an **electron density map** (Fig. 3). The highest electron density is around and between the two nuclei; this is where the electrons are most likely to be found. Covalent bonds are strong bonds.

The atoms in iodine molecules are covalently bonded (Fig. 4). In an iodine molecule, each iodine atom has eight electrons in its outermost energy level: seven of its own, and one that is shared with the other iodine atom. This configuration is the same number as the noble gas neon. It is a stable electronic configuration.

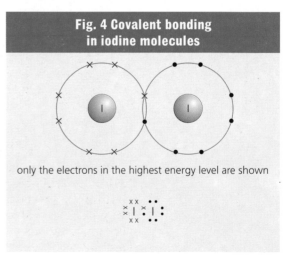

Fig. 4 Covalent bonding in iodine molecules

only the electrons in the highest energy level are shown

Carbon is also covalently bonded (Fig. 5). Each carbon atom in diamond is covalently bonded to four other carbon atoms. Because the electrons in a covalent bond are regions of higher negative charge, they repel each other. The four bonds therefore lie as far apart as possible, forming a tetrahedral (pyramidal) structure (Fig. 6).

Fig. 5 Covalent bonding between carbon atoms

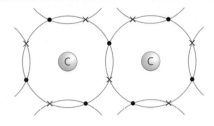

the dot-and-cross diagram shows one bond only

Fig. 6 Tetrahedral arrangement of carbon electrons

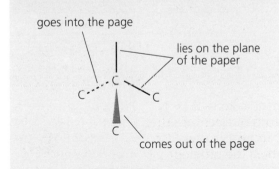

Iodine and diamond (carbon), like hydrogen, will not conduct electricity, because their electrons are not free to move. They are electrical insulators. Insulators are very important in the construction of computers. Carbon (diamond) has excellent insulating properties, which make it suitable for use in the specialised silicon chips used in spacecraft.

Fig. 7 Covalent bonding in methane

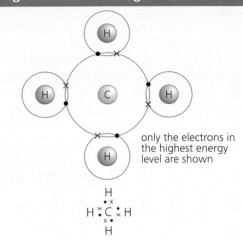

only the electrons in the highest energy level are shown

Covalent bonding also occurs between different atoms, such as carbon and hydrogen atoms in methane (Fig. 7). In this molecule, the carbon atom has eight electrons in the highest energy level (the same as neon) while the hydrogen atoms each have two (like helium). Both atoms have the same electronic configurations as a noble gas.

2 Draw dot-and-cross diagrams to show covalent bonding in
   a ammonia
   b water.

In carbon dioxide, four electrons are shared in each covalent bond; two from the carbon atom and two from an oxygen atom (Fig. 8). This gives both carbon and oxygen the electron configuration of a noble gas. The arrangement is called a **double covalent bond**.

Fig. 8 Covalent bonding in carbon dioxide

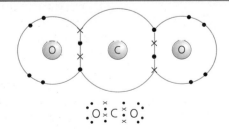

3 Draw a dot-and-cross diagram to show the bonding in ethene, (CH$_2$=CH$_2$).

4 Triple bonds also exist. Draw a dot-and-cross diagram to show the triple bond in ethyne, (CH≡CH).

Covalent bonding can exist between metals and non-metals. When ammonia vapour mixes with aluminium fluoride vapour, a white solid with the formula NH$_3$AlF$_3$ is formed:

$$
\begin{array}{ccc}
\text{H} & & \text{F} \\
\text{H:N:} & + & \text{Al:F} \\
\text{H} & & \text{F}
\end{array}
\longrightarrow
\begin{array}{ccc}
\text{H} & & \text{F} \\
\text{H:N:Al:F} \\
\text{H} & & \text{F}
\end{array}
$$

Both the electrons shared between the aluminium atom and the nitrogen atom come from the nitrogen atom. The formula of the compound is often written as

$$
\begin{array}{ccc}
\text{H} & & \text{F} \\
| & & | \\
\text{H---N} & \longrightarrow & \text{Al---F} \\
| & & | \\
\text{H} & & \text{F}
\end{array}
$$

where the arrow denotes the origin of the shared electrons. This type of bond is called a **dative covalent bond** or a **coordinate bond**.

In covalent substances, whether they contain single, double or coordinate bonds, there are no electrons free to move about. This means that the substances do not usually conduct electricity. The insulating covers over silicon chips inside computers are made of ceramics. Ceramic materials contain covalently bonded atoms.

Far right. Ceramic insulating materials, used with electrical cables, are covalently bonded and do not conduct electricity

4.4 Ionic bonding

Covalently bonded substances are not the only insulators. Solid crystalline salts such as sodium chloride and copper sulphate are non-conductors too. The bonding in sodium chloride is **ionic** (Fig. 9).

Since the sodium atom loses one electron, it has an overall positive charge. It is called a sodium **ion**, written Na$^+$. The chlorine atom gains an electron to become a chloride ion (Cl$^-$). It has an overall negative charge. The oppositely charged ions form a **lattice** of ions, in the solid state held together by the electrical attraction between the opposite charges (Fig. 10).

No sodium chloride molecules exist as such: the molecular formula NaCl represents the ratio of sodium ions to chloride ions.

All ionic compounds contain ionic bonds (Table 1), which are relatively strong as the ions are held firmly in place by electrostatic attraction. This is why solid ionic crystals are insulators, and have high melting points. If the crystals are melted or dissolved in water the ions are then free to move about. This is why ionic compounds can conduct electricity when molten, or dissolved in water. The properties of covalent and ionic substances are quite different (see Table 2; page 44).

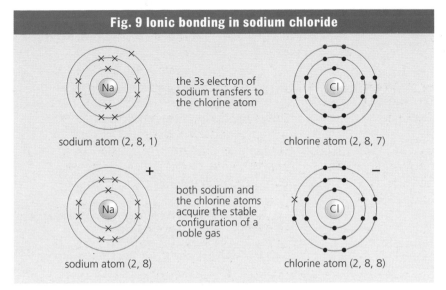

Fig. 9 Ionic bonding in sodium chloride

the 3s electron of sodium transfers to the chlorine atom

sodium atom (2, 8, 1)

chlorine atom (2, 8, 7)

+

both sodium and the chlorine atoms acquire the stable configuration of a noble gas

sodium atom (2, 8)

chlorine atom (2, 8, 8)

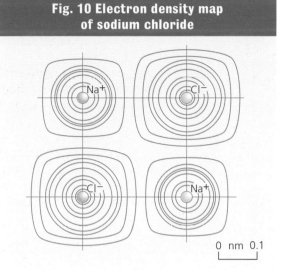

Fig. 10 Electron density map of sodium chloride

0 nm 0.1

Q 5 Draw dot-and-cross diagrams to show the ionic bonding in
a potassium oxide, K₂O
b sodium nitride, Na₃N
c iron(III) oxide, Fe₂O₃.

The ability of ionic substances to conduct electricity when molten or in solution is used in many industrial processes: electroplating, extracting metals such as aluminium, magnesium and calcium, purifying copper, manufacturing chlorine, hydrogen, sodium chlorate(I) (bleach) and potassium chlorate(V) (used in matches and fireworks), and many others.

Rack of copper-plated sheets being removed from an electroplating bath during the first stage in the preparation of flexible electronic circuits

Table 1 Some ionically bonded compounds		
Name	Molecular formula	Dot-and-cross diagram
calcium fluoride	CaF₂	
magnesium oxide	MgO	
sodium oxide	Na₂O	

43

Table 2 Comparison of ionic and covalent substances

	Ionic bonding	Covalent bonding
Formation	Metal elements combine with non-metallic elements to form ionic compounds; the metal atom forms the positive ion and the non-metallic atom forms the negative ion, e.g. Na$^+$Cl$^-$	Non-metallic elements combine, forming covalent bonds; the number of electrons in the highest energy level equals the maximum number of bonds that can be formed
Bond strength	Ionic bonds are strong bonds	Covalent bonds are strong bonds
Structure	Ionic compounds have giant ionic structures, containing millions of ions	Covalent substances may be individual molecules, molecular structures or giant atomic structures

Melting point and boiling point	Because of the strong bonding in ionic compounds, they have high melting points and high boiling points	Individual molecules such as CO_2 have negligible forces of attraction between the molecules. They have low melting and boiling points.
		  Molecular structures, such as that of iodine, also have weak intermolecular forces and low melting and boiling points.
		  Giant atomic structures, such as that of diamond, contain only strong covalent bonds, and have high melting and boiling points

Conduction of electricity	Ionic compounds are insulators in the solid state, and conductors in solution or when molten	Covalent substances do not usually conduct electricity
Solubility	Most ionic compounds are soluble in water and insoluble in organic solvents such as alcohol	Most covalent substances are insoluble in water and soluble in organic solvents

Graphite: the odd one out

Graphite is an **allotrope** of carbon. (Allotropes are different forms of the same element.) Graphite is a non-metal but it conducts electricity. Graphite has a giant structure, made up of sheets of carbon atoms with clouds of **delocalised** electrons between the sheets. Since these electrons are free to move when a potential difference is applied, it is a good conductor of electricity (Fig. 11). Graphite components are used in brushes on electric motors, in dry batteries and in many other electrical appliances.

Fig. 11 Cross-section of graphite

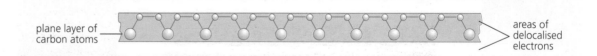

plane layer of carbon atoms

areas of delocalised electrons

Key ideas

- Metallic bonding consists of a lattice of metal cations surrounded by delocalised electrons.

- Non-metals form covalent bonds in which shared electrons are usually located between the two nuclei.

- Compounds of metals with non-metals contain ionic bonds. In ionic bonds, electrons are donated from the metal atom to the non-metal atom.

4.5 Bond polarisation

**Fig. 12
Electron distribution
in H_2 and HF molecules**

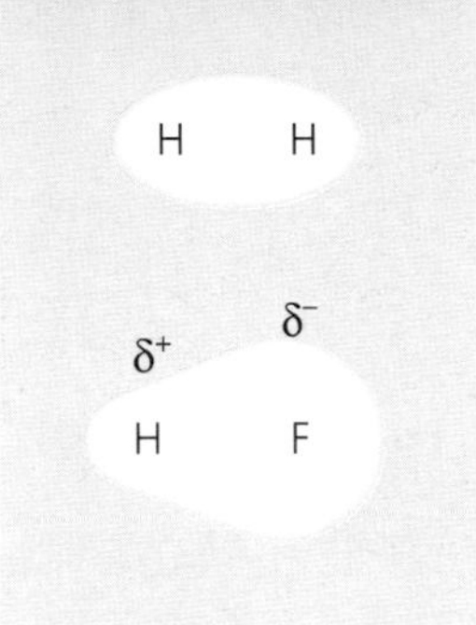

In a covalent bond between two hydrogen atoms, the density of the electrons is distributed evenly between the hydrogen atoms (Fig. 12). In a covalent bond between hydrogen and fluorine, the electrons are drawn towards the fluorine atom (Fig. 12).

This is because fluorine attracts electrons more strongly than hydrogen, and so distorts the electron cloud. The ability of an atom to attract electrons is called its **electronegativity**. Fluorine is more electronegative than hydrogen. Electronegativity is shown by the symbols δ^+, meaning a small positive charge, and δ^-, a small negative charge (δ is the Greek letter delta). It is written as

$$\overset{\delta+ \quad \delta-}{H—F}$$

A molecule such as hydrogen fluoride, in which the electron cloud between the atoms is asymmetrical, is described as a **polar** molecule.

Electronegativities cannot be measured directly. Linus Pauling devised a scale which gives a numerical value to the power of an atom to attract electrons (Table 3). Fluorine is the most electronegative element. The metals at the bottom of Group I are the least electronegative elements.

Table 3 Electronegativities for the elements of Periods 1, 2 and 3

H							He
2.1							–
Li	Be	B	C	N	O	F	Ne
1.0	1.5	2.0	2.5	3.0	3.5	4.0	–
Na	Mg	Al	Si	P	S	Cl	Ar
0.9	1.2	1.5	1.8	2.1	2.5	3.0	–

6 Why are there no values for the noble gases in Table 3?

7 Plot a graph of the electronegativity of the first 18 elements against atomic number Z.

8 Electronegativities of atoms increase across a period because of the increasing positive charge of the nuclei. Explain why electronegativity decreases down a group.

Predicting the nature of bonds

We can use electronegativities to predict the type of bonding present (Fig. 13). Compounds with wholly ionic or wholly covalent bonds are extreme types; most compounds are intermediate, showing polarisation to some degree.

9 Write down the type of bonding you would expect in
 a lithium fluoride, LiF
 b magnesium chloride, $MgCl_2$
 c chlorine oxide, Cl_2O
 d nitrogen gas, N_2
 e carbon dioxide, CO_2

Fig. 13 Electron distribution in hydrogen fluoride molecules

Predicting the nature of bonds

- Bonds between atoms with widely different electronegativities will be ionic.
- Bonds between atoms with the same electronegativities will be covalent and non-polar.
- Bonds between atoms with slightly different electronegativities will be covalent and slightly polar, unless both atoms are metals.
- Bonds between two metal atoms will be metallic bonds.

Key ideas

- Electronegativity is a measure of the power of an atom to attract electrons.
- Electronegativies are measured on the Pauling scale.

- Many covalent bonds have distorted electron clouds because of the differences in the electronegativities of the bonding atoms.

4.6 Semiconductors

Silicon (as SiO₂) is readily available in sand

The world of computing was revolutionised almost overnight by the invention of the transistor in 1947. Its three inventors, Shockley, Bardeen and Brattain, were awarded the Nobel prize in 1956 for their ingenuity. The transistor relied on one of the commonest of all elements – silicon.

Silicon is a non-metal, and is normally an insulator. Silicon atoms have two 3s electrons and two 3p electrons available for bonding. Like carbon, silicon atoms are linked by covalent bonds (Fig. 14) to form giant atomic structures (Fig. 15).

When silicon is insulating, electrons remain in **energy levels** 1, 2 and 3 (Fig. 16). Silicon is a semiconductor, capable of conducting charge at higher temperatures. If silicon is to conduct an electric current, one or more electrons must move to a higher energy level and leave the atom in order to conduct charge.

The electrons in insulating materials need a lot of energy to move away from their normal energy level. Electrons in conducting materials need much less energy to do this. Semiconducting materials are midway between insulating and conducting materials (Fig. 17).

Fig. 14 Covalent bonding in silicon

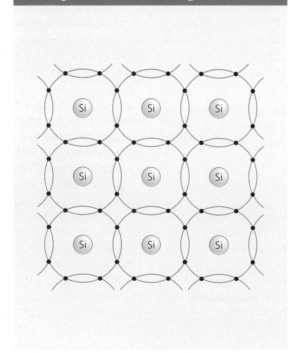

Fig. 15 Giant atomic structure of silicon

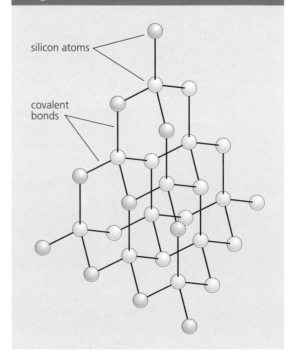

silicon atoms

covalent bonds

Fig. 16 Electron configuration of silicon

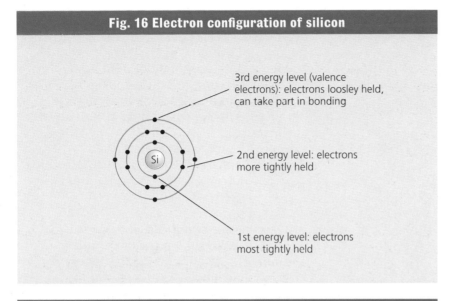

Fig. 18 Doping silicon with phosphorus

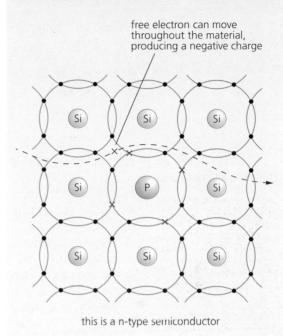

this is a n-type semiconductor

Fig. 17 Electron energy levels in metals, semiconductors and insulators

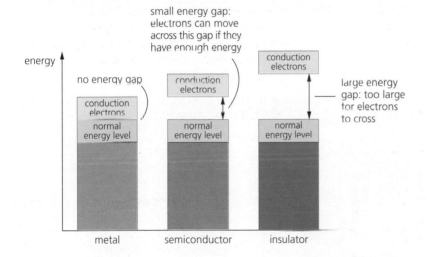

When a semiconductor is heated, the electrons in the highest energy level gain enough energy to move away from their normal energy level. The material becomes a conductor. This is not very convenient in an electronic device, since conduction then depends on temperature. An alternative way to alter the way in which a semiconductor conducts electricity is to 'dope' the semiconductor with impurities.

Doping

There are two ways of doping a semiconductor. One is by adding a Group V element. Phosphorus, for example, has five electrons available for bonding. When phosphorus is added to silicon, four of the five are used to make covalent bonds with silicon. The fifth electron can move throughout the system, carrying an electric current (Fig. 18); the material becomes negatively charged. Semiconductors doped with Group V elements are called **n-type** semiconductors ('n' for negative).

A second way to dope semiconductors is to add a Group III element. Indium, is a Group III element, and has three electrons available for bonding. All three can be used in covalent bonds with silicon atoms. This leaves a 'hole' – a missing electron, in effect; the material becomes positively charged. Another electron from another bond can move into the hole (Fig. 19 on the next page). The current flows by electrons jumping from hole to hole. This kind of doped silicon is called a **p-type** semiconductor ('p' for positive).

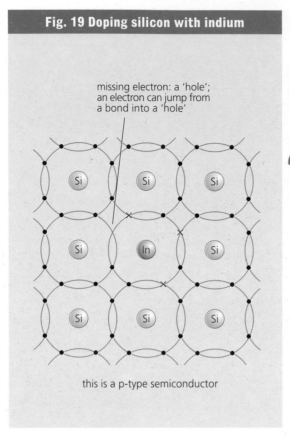

Fig. 19 Doping silicon with indium

missing electron: a 'hole';
an electron can jump from
a bond into a 'hole'

Si Si Si

Si In Si

Si Si Si

this is a p-type semiconductor

Putting an n-type semiconductor next to a p-type semiconductor creates a 'p–n' junction, which will allow the current to pass in only one direction. Transistors commonly consist of three layers of silicon: p–n–p or n–p–n. They control the movement of electric current through the silicon chip.

10 Explain how a 'p–n' junction works in terms of the movement of electrons.

Transistor switches are used in every computer. When a piece of data – a number, a letter or a punctuation mark such as a comma – is entered into a computer it is changed into binary form. That is, it is given a number, called a bit, which is written using only the two numbers 0 and 1. Transistor switches are set to a pattern of on/off settings in which a '1' corresponds to an 'on' setting and '0' to 'off'. In this form the piece of information becomes a pattern of electric currents, and can be held in a computer's memory.

4.7 The future

Control room at Houston
Space NASA

A silicon chip the size of a child's fingernail can now hold more than four million transistors in a single integrated circuit. The smaller the device, the faster it can respond, because the electrons have shorter distances to move. Computer technologists are wondering how small circuits can become before their physical ability is affected by their size. As more and more circuit elements are packed on to silicon chips, integrated circuits will eventually reach the point where these elements are made out of only a handful of atoms. At this level, matter obeys different rules. Some scientists think that the computers of the future will be based on individual atoms – 'quantum computers'.

5 Real and ideal gases

'Travelling out into space, and looking back at planet Earth, gave me the greatest thrill of my life. Earth is crowded, often it's dirty and it's probably steadily warming up, but it is our home.'

Could we settle on any other planet within our solar system? Some astronomers think that this idea is not too far-fetched. What would be needed to change the planet Mars, say, in such a way that humans could live there comfortably? – to 'terra-form' it, as they call it. Although it would take many thousands of years to terra-form Mars, theoretically the process just might be possible.

The planet Mars, taken by Viking Orbiter 2, from over 418 174 km away. Could humans live there?

5.1 Learning objectives

After working through this chapter, you should be able to:

- **explain** how conditions of temperature and pressure affect the state of a substance;

- **calculate** the condition of a particular gas using the ideal gas equation;

- **recall** that the ideal gas equation only holds for some gases under particular conditions;

- **describe** the nature of intermolecular bonding in non-polar substances in terms of van der Waals forces;

- **describe** van der Waals forces as temporary dipole–dipole interactions;

- **recall** that covalent bonds between atoms of different electronegativity will have polar character;

- **describe** the nature of intermolecular forces between molecules with permanent dipoles;

- **describe** hydrogen bonding in water and other compounds;

- **explain** the comparative strengths of covalent and intermolecular bonds;

- **describe** some of the anomalous properties of water that stem from hydrogen bonding, including its high boiling point;

- **describe** how the shape of a covalently bonded molecules is determined by bonding and non-bonding pairs of electrons;

- **describe** bonding in crystals as ionic, molecular or giant atomic.

5.2 Looking at planets

Table 1 Basic data for some planets							
	Terrestrial planets				Outer planets		
	Mercury	Venus	Earth	Mars	Jupiter	Saturn	Uranus
mean distance from Sun/10^8 km	0.579	1.082	1.496	2.279	7.783	14.27	28.7
orbital period around the Sun/years	0.241	0.615	1.0	1.88	11.86	29.46	84.01
rotational period/hours	1406	5832	23.93	24.62	9.84	10.23	15.5
mass/10^{26} g	3.30	48.7	59.8	6.42	18 990	5686	866
mean density/g cm^{-3}	5.42	5.25	5.52	3.94	1.31	0.69	1.58
relative surface gravity (Earth = 1)	0.37	0.88	1	0.38	2.64	1.15	1.17
equatorial surface temperature day:night/K	720:95	750:749	298:280	250:185			
relative atmospheric pressure (Earth = 1)	10^{-15}	9	1	0.007			

If humans were ever to consider colonising a distant planet, they would have to start by finding out about conditions there. A great deal of planetary data has been collected (Tables 1 and 2).

The atmosphere on Earth is unusual in that it contains a sizeable proportion of oxygen and only a little carbon dioxide. The concentrations of these gases in the Earth's atmosphere are controlled by means of rapid recycling in biological processes. These include photosynthesis in green plants, which produces oxygen and uses up carbon dioxide. If there were no life on Earth, any atmospheric oxygen would be rapidly used up in oxidation reactions of materials in the planet's crust. On other planets it is solely chemical processes which determine the composition of the atmosphere. The atmospheres of Mars and Venus, for instance, are almost entirely made up of carbon dioxide, with small amounts of nitrogen and argon.

The surface temperatures and pressures of the terrestrial planets are different. The densities of their atmospheres are also different, partly because of gravitational forces. The behaviour of gases in these atmospheres, at different temperatures and pressures, depends to some extent on their bonding.

1 Why are the densities of the outer planets lower than those of the inner planets?

2 Table 2 gives data for the less abundant gases in terms of parts per million, rather than percentages. From the table, work out the percentages of
   a sulphur dioxide in the atmosphere of Venus,
   b carbon dioxide in the Earth's atmosphere.

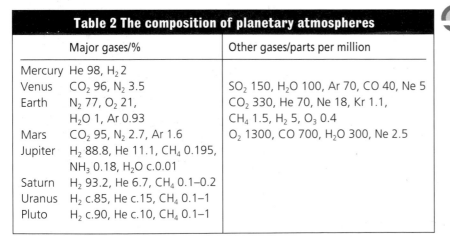

Table 2 The composition of planetary atmospheres		
	Major gases/%	Other gases/parts per million
Mercury	He 98, H_2 2	
Venus	CO_2 96, N_2 3.5	SO_2 150, H_2O 100, Ar 70, CO 40, Ne 5
Earth	N_2 77, O_2 21, H_2O 1, Ar 0.93	CO_2 330, He 70, Ne 18, Kr 1.1, CH_4 1.5, H_2 5, O_3 0.4
Mars	CO_2 95, N_2 2.7, Ar 1.6	O_2 1300, CO 700, H_2O 300, Ne 2.5
Jupiter	H_2 88.8, He 11.1, CH_4 0.195, NH_3 0.18, H_2O c.0.01	
Saturn	H_2 93.2, He 6.7, CH_4 0.1–0.2	
Uranus	H_2 c.85, He c.15, CH_4 0.1–1	
Pluto	H_2 c.90, He c.10, CH_4 0.1–1	

5.3 Planetary atmospheres

The atmospheres of planets are mostly made up of atoms or very small molecules. We can predict how a given volume of any of these gases will behave when temperature and pressure are changed. An **ideal gas** is one that fits the following model:

1 The gas is made up of identical particles in continuous random motion.
2 The particles are 'pointlike' – they are considered to have zero volume.
3 The particles do not react when they collide.
4 Collisions between particles are elastic, i.e. the total kinetic energy of the particles after a collision is the same as before.

No gas fits this model exactly. Some gases, however, do behave predictably over a limited range of temperatures and pressures. In practice, hydrogen, nitrogen, oxygen and the inert gases (also called nobel gases) are the gases that behave most like ideal gases (Fig. 1).

Robert Boyle was one of the first chemists to study the behaviour of gases systematically. He noticed that the higher the pressure of a gas, the smaller is its volume. He put forward his ideas in 1662 in the following statement:

at constant temperature, the volume of a fixed mass of gas is inversely proportional to the applied pressure.

This theory has proved to be true in so many cases that it is now known as Boyle's Law. It can be written mathematically:

when T is constant, $p \times V = $ constant

A century or so later, the Frenchman Jacques Charles (an enthusiastic balloonist) studied temperature effects on gases. In particular hydrogen interested him, because it was used in balloons. Charles published his results in 1787:

at constant pressure the volume of a fixed mass of gas is proportional to its temperature, or, when p is constant, $V = $ constant $\times T$

Fig. 1 Movement of particles in an ideal gas and a real gas

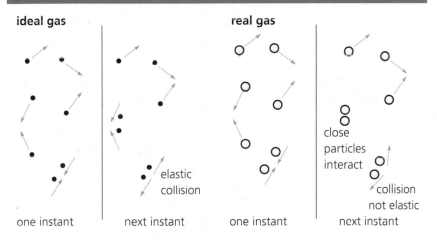

ideal gas   **real gas**

elastic collision

one instant   next instant

close particles interact

collision not elastic

one instant   next instant

The early balloonists used the low density of hydrogen to lift their craft from the ground; only after a series of disastrous fires did their attention turn to helium as a safer if more expensive alternative

51

The equation for Charles' Law implies that at a certain very low temperature the volume of any sample of gas will be zero. Experiments show that volumes of gases when plotted against temperature (Fig. 2) extrapolate to zero at the same temperature. This temperature is –273.15 °C. The Kelvin temperature scale takes this temperature as 0 K, the temperature at which an ideal gas occupies zero volume. When you do calculations using gas laws, remember always to use temperatures in kelvins.

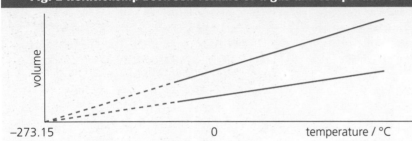

Fig. 2 Relationship between volume of a gas and temperature

Boyle's Law and Charles' Law can be combined into a single **ideal gas equation**. To do that, one more piece of information is helpful. This stems from the work of Avogadro, who in 1811 published his hypothesis (now recognised as a law) stating that

equal volumes of different gases at the same temperature and pressure contain equal number of particles.

It follows that the molar volume, the volume occupied by one mole of a gas, is the same for all gases at the same temperature and pressure (Fig. 3).

At standard temperature (273 K) and standard pressure (1.01×10^5 Pa) one mole of a gas occupies 22.4 dm^3 (see Chapter 2). When the pressure and temperature are constant, the volume of a gas is proportional to the number of moles of the gas present, or:

when p and T are constant, $V = \text{constant} \times n$

where n = number of moles of the gas.

The **ideal gas equation** combines all this information about gases in one equation:

$$pV = nRT$$

R is the same for every gas and is called the **molar gas constant**. It has the value 8.314 J K^{-1} mol^{-1}.

 3 Show how the three equations
$pV = \text{constant}$
$V = \text{constant} \times T$
$V = \text{constant} \times n$
can be combined to give the ideal gas equation.

4 Show how the units of R come to be J K^{-1} mol^{-1}.

The Martian atmosphere
We can use the ideal gas equation to compare some aspects of the atmospheres on different planets. This information could help space centres to plan for the colonisation of planets other than Earth.

Fig. 3 Molar volume of gases

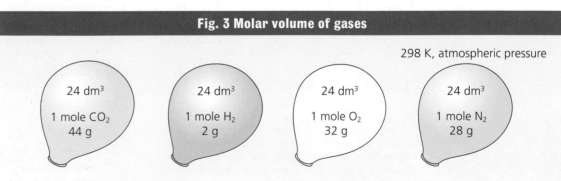

298 K, atmospheric pressure

| 24 dm^3 | 24 dm^3 | 24 dm^3 | 24 dm^3 |
| 1 mole CO$_2$ 44 g | 1 mole H$_2$ 2 g | 1 mole O$_2$ 32 g | 1 mole N$_2$ 28 g |

We can start by working out the number of particles per cubic centimetre in the Earth's atmosphere and in the atmosphere of Mars. Begin with the Earth's atmosphere. We will imagine for the moment that air is an ideal gas. Standard atmospheric pressure is 1.01×10^5 Pa; the daytime temperature is 298 K (25 °C), and the volume of 1 cubic centimetre is 1×10^{-6} m^3.

It is important to use the correct units, and use them consistently. In this case we use SI units of Pa and m^3, for pressure and volume. If you measure pressures in atmospheres and volumes in cm^3, or if you use a mixture of units, you cannot use the value of the gas constant given here:

$p = 1.01 \times 10^5$ Pa, $V = 1 \times 10^{-6}$ m^3, $T = 298$ K, $R = 8.314$ J K^{-1} mol^{-1}

Using the equation $pV = nRT$,
$(1.01 \times 10^5) \times (1 \times 10^{-6}) = n \times (8.314 \times 298)$

Or $n = \dfrac{(1.01 \times 10^5) \times (1 \times 10^{-6})}{(8.314 \times 298)}$
$= 4.08 \times 10^{-5}$

In other words, the number of moles of air in 1 cm^3 is 4.08×10^{-5} mol. We can use the Avogadro constant L to calculate how many particles this is (see Chapter 2, page 17 to remind yourself of such calculations):

Number of particles = number of moles × Avogadro constant (nL)
$= 4.08 \times 10^{-5} \times 6.022 \times 10^{23}$
$= 2.46 \times 10^{19}$

Now consider the atmosphere on Mars: Atmospheric pressure on Mars is $0.007 \times 1.01 \times 10^5$ Pa; the daytime temperature is 250 K, and the volume of 1 cubic centimetre is 1×10^{-6} m^3

$p = 7.07 \times 10^2$ Pa, $V = 1 \times 10^{-6}$ m^3, $T = 250$ K, $R = 8.314$ J K^{-1} mol^{-1}

Using $pV = nRT$ again,
$(7.07 \times 10^2) \times (1 \times 10^{-6}) = n \times (8.314 \times 250)$
Or, $n = \dfrac{(7.07 \times 10^2) \times (1 \times 10^{-6})}{(8.314 \times 250)}$
$= 3.40 \times 10^{-7}$

The number of particles in one cubic centimetre of atmosphere on Mars is
$= (3.40 \times 10^{-7}) \times (6.022 \times 10^{23})$
$= 2.05 \times 10^{17}$

This shows that in the Martian atmosphere there are only about one-hundredth as many particles per cubic centimetre as there are in the Earth's atmosphere. This is equivalent to the particle density in the Earth's atmosphere about 32 km above sea level! (The summit of Mount Everest is just 8.85 km above sea level.)

Climbers on the upper slopes of Everest have difficulties in functioning in the low concentrations of oxygen in the rarefied atmosphere – oxygen in cylinders can help them

5 Calculate the particle density, in particles per cubic centimetre, of the atmosphere of Venus.

In these calculations we have assumed that Earth and Mars have only ideal gases in their atmospheres. Although this assumption isn't really true, the calculations do give us some idea of how the two particle densities compare.

The calculation is more inaccurate for the atmosphere on Mars than for Earth. This is because the Martian atmosphere is mostly carbon dioxide, whereas that of the Earth is mostly nitrogen. Carbon dioxide behaves less ideally than nitrogen does. As we will see, the forces between carbon dioxide molecules are stronger than those between nitrogen molecules.

5.4 Using the ideal gas equation

If we know two of the variables in the ideal gas equation, we can calculate the other one. For instance, we can use it to determine the volume of a mass of gas under different conditions of temperature and pressure.

If humans were to survive on Mars, they would need a sufficient supply of oxygen. This could be transported in cylinders from Earth or generated from chemical reactions. The oxygen might be produced by electrolysing water. (The water would need to contain an electrolyte such as an inorganic acid, as otherwise it would not conduct electricity.)

$$2H_2O(l) \rightarrow 2H_2(g) + O_2(g)$$

The reactions at the electrodes are:

cathode: $4H^+ (aq) + 4e^- \rightarrow 2H_2(g)$
anode: $4OH^-(aq) \rightarrow 2H_2O(l) + O_2(g) + 2e^-$

How much oxygen would a human on Mars need? We can work out how much water would be needed to give sufficient oxygen to support respiration. Buildings on Mars would need to be pressurised to about Earth's atmospheric pressure (1.01×10^5 Pa) and heated to about 298 K to be comfortable for humans.

Let's assume that a compact Martian dwelling occupies the same volume as a small classroom – say 4 m × 4 m × 2.5 m = 40 m³. We would want about 20% of the gas in this dwelling to be oxygen – the equivalent of 8 m³. We can use the ideal gas equation to work out how many moles of oxygen this is.
$p = 1.01 \times 10^5$ Pa, $V = 8$ m³, $T = 298$ K, $R = 8.314$ J K^{-1} mol^{-1}

Rearranging the ideal gas equation
$$n = \frac{pV}{RT}$$

$$= \frac{1.01 \times 10^5 \times 8}{8.314 \times 298}$$
$$= 326 \text{ moles}$$

From the electolysis equations, we can see that one mole of oxygen is formed from the electrolysis of two moles of water. So 652 moles of water would be needed to provide 8 m³ of oxygen.
The mass of water needed
= no. of moles × r.m.m. of water
= 326 × 18 g
= 5868 g
This is nearly 6 kg or 6 dm³. The hydrogen generated from the electrolysis could be used as fuel, or it could be released into the Martian atmosphere.

The water would produce 652 moles of hydrogen. What volume would this occupy, if released into the Martian atmosphere?

$p = 0.007 \times 1.01 \times 10^5$ Pa, $n = 652$ mol, $T = 250$ K, $R = 8.314$ J K^{-1} mol^{-1}

Rearranging the ideal gas equation

$$V = \frac{nRT}{p}$$
$$= \frac{652 \times 8.314 \times 250}{0.007 \times 1.01 \times 10^5}$$
$$= 1920 \text{ dm}^3$$

This means that 16 m³ of hydrogen produced at Earth's temperature and pressure would occupy 1920 m³ at Martian temperature and pressure. Notice that in this calculation we could have compared the volume of the hydrogen on Earth with the volume on Mars without calculating the number of moles. Some of the terms would cancel:

$$\frac{p_1V_1}{T_1} = nR = \frac{p_2V_2}{T_2}$$

For this example: $p_1 = 1.01 \times 10^5$ Pa, $V_1 = 16$ m³, $T_1 = 298$ K
$p_2 = 0.007 \times 1.01 \times 10^5$ Pa, $T_2 = 250$ K

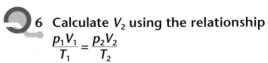 6 Calculate V_2 using the relationship
$$\frac{p_1V_1}{T_1} = \frac{p_2V_2}{T_2}$$

5.5 Ideal and non-ideal gases – bonding

No gas is ideal because, among other things, the particles of a real gas will always occupy a finite volume. Some gases, such as the inert gases and non-polar diatomic gases, will behave like ideal gases at relatively low pressures and relatively high temperatures. Under these conditions, any interaction between the particles is at its lowest.

Nitrogen, the most abundant gas in Earth's atmosphere, will obey the ideal gas equation under normal atmospheric conditions. Nitrogen is a diatomic gas, in which the atoms are held together by strong covalent bonding. In an ideal gas there is no interaction between particles. In nitrogen there is very weak **intermolecular bonding** resulting from **temporary dipoles** set up in nitrogen molecules.

At any instant in a nitrogen molecule the electron density may not be symmetrical. For a moment, this makes one part of the molecule very slightly more negatively charged than another part. This temporary dipole can induce another dipole in a neighbouring nitrogen molecule. There is very weak attraction, called **van der Waals forces**, between these temporary dipoles (Fig. 4). Van der Waals forces vary between one-hundredth and one-tenth of the typical covalent bond energies.

Carbon dioxide, which makes up most of the Martian atmosphere, is a non-polar molecule.

Molecules with a **permanent dipole**, such as carbon monoxide, form slightly stronger intermolecular bonds (Fig. 5).

There will also be interaction between carbon dioxide molecules through weak van der Waals forces. Because carbon dioxide molecules are larger and have more electrons than nitrogen molecules, however, the van der Waals forces will be slightly stronger than in nitrogen. Carbon dioxide will obey the ideal gas equation only at low pressures and high temperatures.

 7 Why do conditions of low pressure and high temperature allow real gases to behave like ideal gases?

Fig. 4 Van der Waals forces in nitrogen

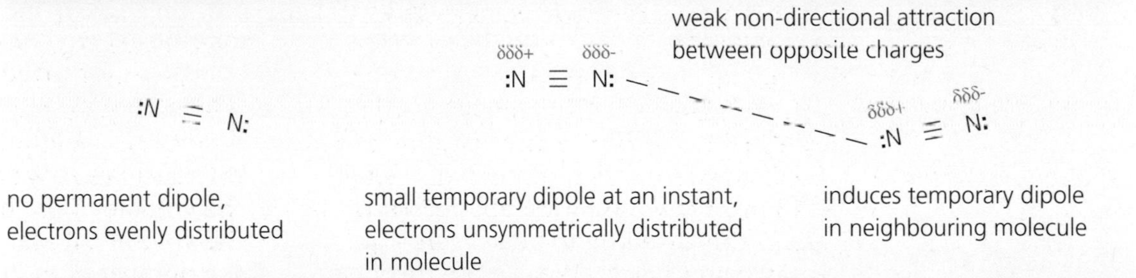

$\delta\delta\delta+$ $\delta\delta\delta-$
:N ≡ N: ⟍   weak non-directional attraction between opposite charges

:N ≡ N:

$\delta\delta\delta+$ $\delta\delta\delta-$
:N ≡ N:

no permanent dipole, electrons evenly distributed

small temporary dipole at an instant, electrons unsymmetrically distributed in molecule

induces temporary dipole in neighbouring molecule

Fig. 5 Dipole–dipole attractions in carbon monoxide

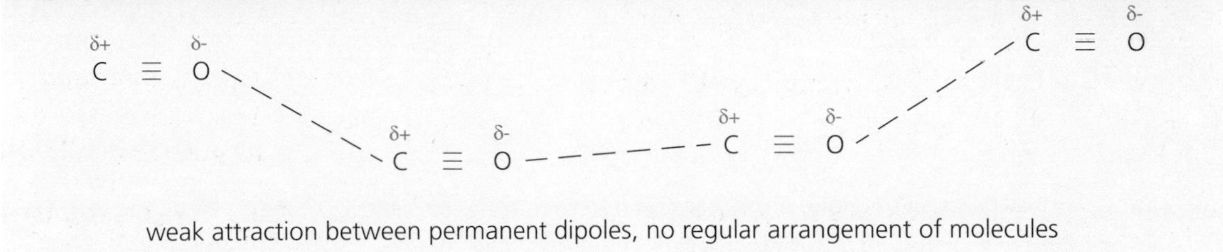

$\delta+$ $\delta-$
C ≡ O

$\delta+$ $\delta-$
C ≡ O

$\delta+$ $\delta-$
C ≡ O

$\delta+$ $\delta-$
C ≡ O

weak attraction between permanent dipoles, no regular arrangement of molecules

Key ideas

- The ideal gas equation, $pV = nRT$, can be used to calculate how simple gaseous atoms and molecules behave under differing atmospheric conditions.

- Real gases best obey the ideal gas equation at high temperature and low pressure.

5.6 Problems in terra-forming Mars

Not only has the Martian atmosphere a much lower particle density than Earth's; it also has a composition that would require considerable change before Mars could be colonised. One of the important features of Earth, in being able to support life, is the co-existence of water in its three different states – solid, liquid and gas. This is not the situation on Mars or Venus, although water exists on both planets. To understand this it is helpful to examine the bonding within and between water molecules.

Bonding within water molecules

Water is covalently bonded, through a 1s electron on each hydrogen and two 2p electrons on oxygen. Two **lone (non-bonding) pairs** of electrons remain on the oxygen atom. The bonding and non-bonding electrons on the oxygen atom repel each other. This results in a bent-planar shape for the molecule (Fig. 6). This is one example of the way in which the shapes of covalent molecules depend on their electronic structures (Fig. 7).

 8 Why is carbon dioxide non-polar, even though the carbon–oxygen bonds are both polar? Sketching the bonding in carbon dioxide and its molecular shape may help you.

Bonding between water molecules

Hydrogen and oxygen have different electronegativities (see Chapter 3, page 37). This makes the hydrogen–oxygen bond polar. The water molecule also has a permanent dipole because of its shape.

The permanent dipoles in neighbouring molecules attract each other. This attraction between water molecules is called **hydrogen bonding** (Fig. 8). Hydrogen bonding happens in other compounds too. Wherever hydrogen is bonded covalently to a strongly electronegative element, such as fluorine, oxygen or nitrogen, hydrogen bonds can form between the molecules. Hydrogen bonds between molecules are about one-tenth the strength of covalent bonds within molecules. Van der Waals forces are also present in hydrogen-bonded compounds.

 9 a In which of the following compounds would you expect hydrogen bonding to occur? hydrogen fluoride HF, ammonia NH_3, methane CH_4, hydrazine N_2H_4, hydrogen cyanide HCN, ethanol C_2H_5OH.
b Draw the shapes of these molecules and show the intermolecular bonding.

Fig. 6 Bonding in water molecules

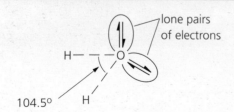

lone pairs of electrons

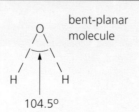

bent-planar molecule

104.5°

104.5°

less than normal tetrahedral bond angle; repulsion between lone pair and lone pair is greater than that between lone pair and bonding pair

Fig. 7 Shapes of molecules

The shape of a covalent molecule is determined by the repulsion between bonding and non-bonding electron pairs within it.

In the methane molecule, there are four bonding pairs (four single covalent bonds). The four bonding pairs all repel each other with equal force, resulting in a regular tetrahedral structure with an H—C—H bond angle of 109.5°:

109.5°

regular tetrahedron

In ammonia there are three bonding pairs and one non-bonding pair. Repulsion between non-bonding and bonding pairs is greater than between two bonding pairs. The H—N—H bond angle in ammonia is thus smaller (107°) than in methane. The shape of the molecule is described as trigonal pyramidal.

107°

trigonal pyramid

In the water molecule there are two bonding pairs and two non-bonding pairs (Fig. 6). Repulsion between two non-bonding electron pairs is greater than that between a non-bonding and a bonding pair. The bond angle in water is smaller again (104.5°).

In hydrogen chloride there is one bonding pair, together with three non-bonding pairs. The molecule is linear, that is, the bond angle is 180°:

180° $H—\overset{\delta+}{}\overset{\delta-}{Cl}$

linear molecule

Some other covalent molecules do not have four electron pairs on the central atom. Boron trifluoride, BF_3, for example, has three:

120°   trigonal planar

In the phosphorus pentachloride molecule there are five bonding pairs on the central phosphorus atom:

90°   120°

trigonal bipyramid

and the sulphur atom in sulphur hexafluoride, SF_6, has six:

90°   90°

octahedron

Fig. 8 Hydrogen bonding between water molecules

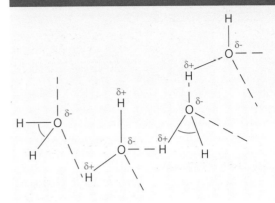

Water on Earth

Hydrogen bonding is the reason behind some of the important and unusual properties of water.

In ice, hydrogen bonding holds the water molecules further away from each other than they are in liquid water. This makes ice less dense than liquid water (0.92 g cm^{-3} compared with 1 g cm^{-3}). That is, water expands when it freezes. Most other liquids contract when they solidify. Water has its maximum density at 4 °C.

This property of water is one reason why Earth can support life. As the temperature of the Earth's surface drops below the freezing point of water, the water on the surface of a lake or pond freezes. The ice formed not only floats but also acts as a good insulator for the warmer water underneath. If water was like most other liquids the ice would sink as it formed, more ice would be formed and the whole lake could freeze solid. Lakes would freeze

Ice floats on the surface of a lake; if ice sank in liquid water, no aquatic life could survive in a hard winter

Fig. 9 Aquatic survival on Earth

if ice were denser than water

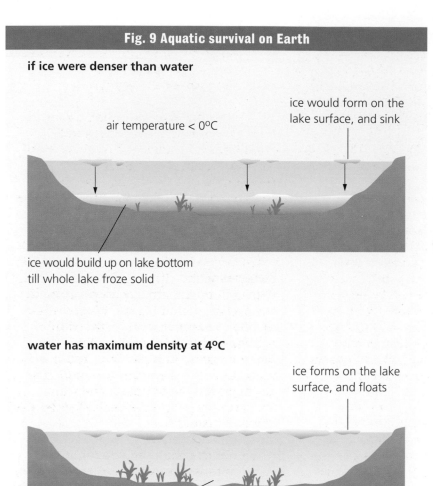

air temperature < 0°C

ice would form on the lake surface, and sink

ice would build up on lake bottom till whole lake froze solid

water has maximum density at 4°C

ice forms on the lake surface, and floats

temperature at lake bottom does not fall below 4°C

Table 3 Thermochemistry of some hydrides

	Boiling point/°C (at standard atmospheric pressure)	Standard enthalpy change of vaporisation /kJ mol^{-1}
water	100	40.7
hydrogen sulphide	–	18.7
hydrogen selenide	–	19.3
hydrogen telluride	–	23.2
hydrogen fluoride	20	–
hydrogen chloride	–85	–
hydrogen bromide	–67	–
hydrogen iodide	–35	–
hexane	69	28.4
heptane	99	32.5

under rather than *over*. There would be no ice-skating, and all aquatic life would be frozen in ice (Fig. 9).

Most compounds with small molecules, such as water, exist as gases under Earth's conditions of temperature and pressure. Water has a higher boiling point than most other compounds with small molecules (Table 3); so too have ammonia and hydrogen fluoride. The hydrogen bonding between molecules also makes the enthalpy change of vaporisation high.

10 Plot a graph of the boiling points of halogen hydrides against their periods in the Periodic Table. Explain the shape of the graph.

11 Why is it more dangerous to put your hand in steam at 100 °C, than in gaseous heptane (petrol) at just above its boiling point (99 °C)? How is this related to intermolecular bonding?

In solid water (ice) the hydrogen bonds hold the molecules in a regular pattern. When ice crystals start to form they are tiny hexagons. The nature of the hydrogen bonding at the edges of the hexagons encourages crystal growth in a single plane and at the six points of the hexagon. It is hydrogen bonding which is responsible for the beautiful shapes of snowflakes.

The six-armed structure of snowflakes

Solid carbon dioxide being emitted from a fire extinguisher – lowering the pressure of a gas and rapidly increasing the volume reduces the temperature

At the normal temperatures and pressures on the Earth's surface, all three phases of water – solid, liquid and gaseous – can exist. This is not so on Mars or Venus. The phase diagram for water (Fig. 10) indicates the conditions under which each phase will be present. At high temperature and low pressure water will be in a gaseous state. At high pressure and low temperature water will be a solid. When a liquid boils, its vapour pressure is the same as the atmospheric pressure.

The lines in a phase diagram show the conditions under which two phases are in equilibrium with each other. The point at which all these lines meet is called the **triple point**. At the particular conditions of the triple point all three phases can co-exist. Conditions on Earth vary, of course, but they are not far from the triple point of water.

12 What phases of water would we expect to find on Mars, given its surface temperature and atmospheric pressure?

A phase diagram for carbon dioxide (Fig. 11) can help us to understand conditions on planets such as Venus and Mars. In this phase diagram, the solid–liquid line slopes the other way to that in the water diagram. This is because carbon dioxide behaves 'normally' when cooled: when it turns from a liquid to a solid, it contracts. You will not see liquid carbon dioxide on Earth, however. This is because the conditions of temperature and pressure in the Earth's atmosphere lie in the bottom part of Fig. 11. When carbon dioxide gas is cooled on Earth, without applying pressure, it forms solid carbon dioxide instead of liquefying. You may have seen this when carbon dioxide fire extinguishers are operated. The white 'smoke' they give out is finely divided solid carbon dioxide.

13 Clouds have been seen in the atmosphere of Venus, where the pressure is about 5×10^3 Pa and the temperature 240 K. Could these clouds be droplets of liquid carbon dioxide?

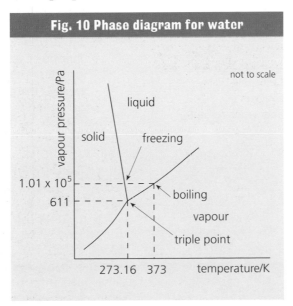

Fig. 10 Phase diagram for water

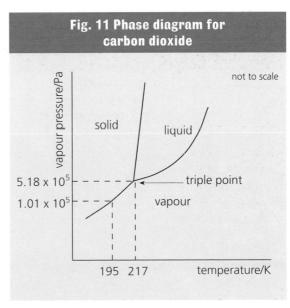

Fig. 11 Phase diagram for carbon dioxide

Key ideas

- Intermolecular bonding between covalent molecules takes one of three forms:
1 interactions between temporary dipoles in non-polar molecules – van der Waals forces;
2 interactions between permanent dipoles in polar molecules;
3 hydrogen bonding in between molecules containing hydrogen bonded to an electronegative element.

- Hydrogen bonding accounts for the anomalous properties of water: temperature-induced density changes, high melting and boiling point and high enthalpy of vaporisation.

5.7 Crystals and solutions

Fig. 12 Crystalline solids

Simple molecular solids
In iodine crystals, for example, covalently bonded iodine molecules are held in place by weak van der Waals forces:

van der Waals forces between molecules hold the molecules in a regular array

regular arrangement of (I–I) molecules

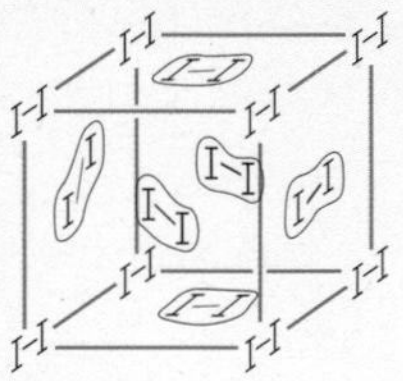

Giant ionic crystals
Sodium chloride is an example. It forms cubic crystals:

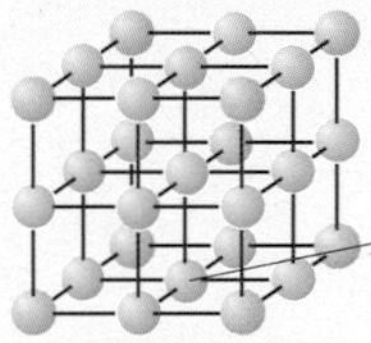

face of unit cube

Giant atomic crystals
Carbon forms two kinds of crystal, both of which are lattices of atoms. One kind is diamond, in which each carbon atom is covalently bonded to four other carbon atoms:

carbon atom tetrahedrally bonded to four other carbon atoms

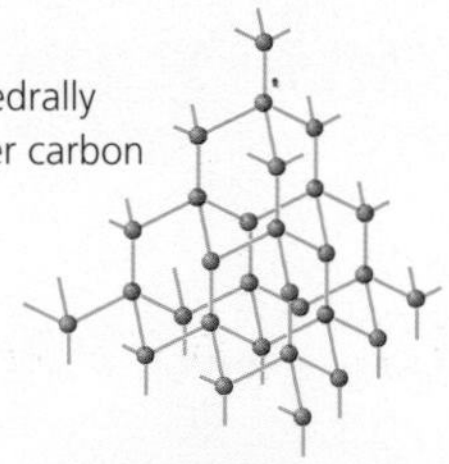

In the other kind, graphite, each carbon atom is covalently bonded to three other carbon atoms in one plane. Van der Waals forces act between the planes of carbon atoms:

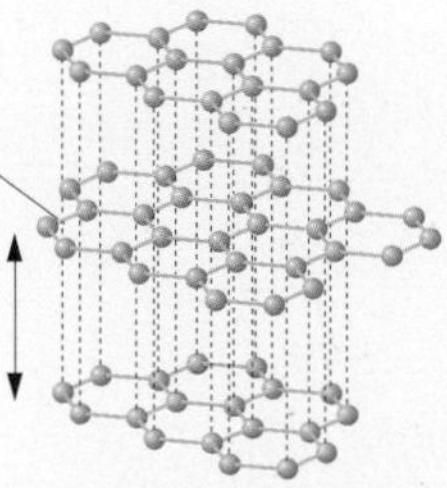

0.142 nm (C—C single covalent)

distance between layers 0.335 nm

Metallic crystals
For details of metallic bonding see Chapter 4, page39.

Ice and solid carbon dioxide are molecular solids. In ice, the water molecules are held in a regular pattern by hydrogen bonding (Fig. 8). In other simple molecular solids such as carbon dioxide, iodine and sulphur, there are only weak van der Waals forces between the molecules (Fig. 12).

A crystal is a regular array of atoms, molecules or ions. We see and use many crystalline solids on Earth, but not all are simple molecular solids. Many are either covalently bonded or ionically bonded giant structures.

14 a What properties of solid sulphur indicate that it is a simple molecular solid?
b Sulphur can form needle-shaped crystals (monoclinic sulphur). Show how S_8 rings of sulphur atoms are arranged in monoclinic sulphur.

There are enormous quantities of liquid water on Earth. Water is vital for life. Our bodies, like those of most other living organisms, contain a very high percentage of water.

One of the most important properties of water in organisms is that it is an excellent solvent, capable of dissolving a wide range of compounds. One reason is the polar nature of its molecule. Many compounds that are soluble in water form ionically bonded crystals. When water comes into contact with a crystal face, the polar water molecule is attracted to the charged ions (Fig. 13). Energy is needed to separate oppositely charged ions in the crystals (**lattice energy**) and to break the hydrogen bonds between the water molecules. This energy is recovered in the formation of bonds between the individual ions and the water molecules which surround them in solution (**hydration energy**).

Some ionically bonded crystals do not dissolve in water. This is because the lattice energy of the particular crystal is higher than the hydration energy of the ions.

Most covalently bonded compounds do not dissolve in water. Again, energy considerations are the reason. The polar water molecules are not attracted by the non-polar covalent molecules. Since no energy is released by bond formation, none is available for breaking the hydrogen bonds between water molecules. These compounds usually do dissolve in non-polar covalently bonded solvents however. This is because the intermolecular van der Waals forces are similar in both solute and solvent.

15 Glucose ($C_6H_{12}O_6$) forms molecular crystals. Explain why glucose and other simple carbohydrates will dissolve in water.

Fig. 13 Ionic crystal dissolving in water

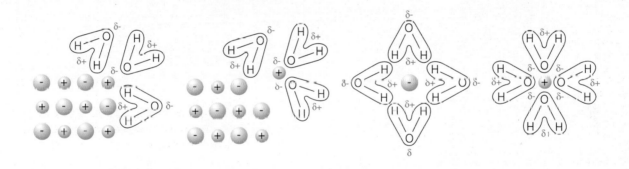

5.8 Is terra-forming Mars possible?

We have seen how different the atmospheres of Mars and Venus are from Earth's. In the world of science fiction, humans have colonised many planets. What would really be needed to terra-form Mars?

A NASA scientist, Chris McKay, considers that the process could be undertaken in two steps. The first step would be to raise the temperature of the Martian surface at about 0 °C. This could be done by building factories on Mars that would churn out greenhouse gases – CFCs and carbon dioxide. These gases are chosen because there are massive reserves of carbon dioxide in the Martian polar regions, and because Martian soils contain carbon, fluorine and chlorine. Chris McKay considers that if an initial temperature rise of 4 °C was induced in this way, it would trigger a runaway greenhouse effect. This would raise the temperature of the planet by about 55 °C over a couple of hundred years.

The inhospitable surface of the planet Mars, as seen from the spacecraft Viking 2

In the second step, organisms living on water and trace elements would use sunlight to photosynthesise, so removing carbon dioxide from the atmosphere and raising its oxygen content to a level at which humans could breathe. But this stage would take around 100 000 years!

There are many uncertainties in such a scheme. We do not even know whether Mars has sufficient reserves of carbon dioxide, water and nitrogen – molecules that contain the elements considered most essential for life.

 16 **Do you think it is ethical to change the climate on another planet? Should we put money into research and development which may enable us to colonise another planet?**

Key ideas

- The shapes of covalent molecules are determined by forces between bonding and non-bonding electron pairs on central atoms. The magnitude of the repulsive forces are in the order:

non-bonding/non-bonding > non-bonding/bonding > bonding/bonding.

- Crystals can be classified as ionic, molecular or giant atomic.

- Water will dissolve many ionic crystals.

Energy from fuels

'Cars in Brazil run on either alcohol fuel or petrol. At my filling station I sell both. Motorists have many reasons for choosing the type of fuel they use. As long as they go on buying fuel from me, I don't mind which they choose!'

'Many people are hungry in Brazil. Land used to grow sugar cane for ethanol doesn't produce any food. Only the richest fifth of the population have cars. We just need our land to grow food for our children.' ▶

This petrol attendant in Brazil is filling the car with ethanol fuel

In 1975, Brazil set up the world's biggest programme for the production of an alternative fuel, the 'Proalcool' scheme. Brazil does not have enough reserves of oil to be self-sufficient, but it does have a

climate that is ideal for growing sugar cane. Today, ethanol (an alcohol) produced from sugar cane is used to power about one-third of Brazil's 12 million cars. In the US, in 1990, about 20 billion litres of ethanol were produced from American corn (maize) to support the US gasohol programme. Not all Brazilians support the use of ethanol as a motor fuel, however.

Why did Brazil embark on this controversial experiment? What benefits did the Brazilian government expect to come from the huge investment it has made in sugar cane farming? And anyway, is ethanol as efficient a motor fuel as petrol? We need to look at some of the issues surrounding the use of ethanol as an alternative to petrol.

6.1 Learning objectives

After working through this chapter, you should be able to:

- **explain** the energy changes associated with exothermic and endothermic reactions;

- **recall** the definition of the standard enthalpy change of combustion;

- **determine** enthalpies of combustion values experimentally;

- **recall** the definition of the standard enthalpy of formation;

- **calculate** enthalpies of reactions using standard enthalpy of formation values;

- **work out** the stabilities of compounds from their standard enthalpies of formation;

- **calculate** enthalpies of reaction using Hess's law;

- **calculate** enthalpies of reactions using bond enthalpies.

6.2 Fossil fuels: the problems

A finite resource

The Industrial Revolution was powered for nearly two centuries on coal. Today, the world's economy depends almost entirely on crude oil. Oil, natural gas and coal are **fossil fuels**. But it took millions of years to turn decaying forests and swamps into oil and coal. And, less than three centuries after people began to use them heavily, we are already hearing the question, 'What happens when the oil runs out?' Fossil fuels cannot be replaced at the rate at which we are consuming them. They are a finite resource – one day they could be exhausted.

If we are to continue relying on carbon and its compounds as energy sources, then we need to develop technology based on non-fossil carbon. Carbon sources are readily available in plants (the **biomass**). We need to develop renewable fuels – fuels from plants that can be grown and harvested over a short time span, so that they are continuously available.

Brazil is one country that has succeeded in doing this. Brazil's Proalcool programme depends on growing large quanties of sugar cane. Ethanol, used as a motor fuel (Fig. 1), is produced from sugar cane by **fermentation**. The process is similar to that used in brewing or winemaking.

'Recycling' carbon dioxide

Many researchers believe that the increasing use of fossil fuels is responsible for the steady rise in carbon dioxide levels in the atmosphere over the last two or three centuries. Carbon dioxide is believed to be the main cause of global warming through the greenhouse effect. Traffic is a major source of carbon dioxide: the average car produces four times its own mass of carbon dioxide every year. Both petrol and ethanol produce carbon dioxide when they burn.

However, ethanol is produced from biomass. Plants take in, or 'fix', carbon from atmospheric carbon dioxide during photosynthesis. When ethanol produced from sugar cane is burnt as a fuel, the same mass of carbon is released back to the atmosphere (Fig. 2). The overall balance is maintained. We cannot replace fossil fuels, but we can replace the sugar cane.

Fig. 1 Ethanol fuel and gasohol

'straight' ethanol fuel

5% water

95% ethanol

gasohol fuel

80% petrol

20% ethanol

Fig. 2 The fuel cycle

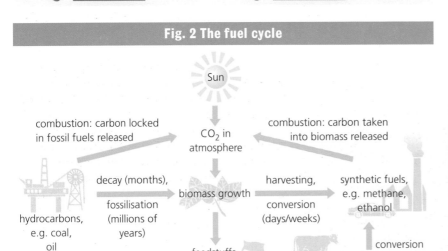

Sun

combustion: carbon locked in fossil fuels released

CO_2 in atmosphere

combustion: carbon taken into biomass released

decay (months),

fossilisation (millions of years)

biomass growth

harvesting, conversion (days/weeks)

synthetic fuels, e.g. methane, ethanol

hydrocarbons, e.g. coal, oil

feedstuffs

conversion animal wastes

People in Bangladesh already have to cope with major floods, global warming could make the situation worse

6.3 Energy from fuels

How do octane and ethanol compare as fuels? Crude oil is a mixture of hydrocarbons, ranging from very small molecules such as methane, CH_4, to large molecules containing 50 or more carbon atoms. Petrol, which is extracted from crude oil in a refinery, is a mixture of middle-sized molecules – from pentane, C_5H_{12}, to undecane, $C_{11}H_{24}$. What happens to a middle-sized molecule, octane (C_8H_{18}), when it reacts with oxygen in the cylinder of a car engine? The equation for the reaction is

$$2C_8H_{18}(g) + 25O_2(g) \rightarrow 16CO_2(g) + 18H_2O(g)$$
octane   oxygen   carbon dioxide   water

The products of the reaction leave the engine via the exhaust pipe, and the engine gets hot. That is, the reaction mixture – the **system** – gives out energy (in the form of heat), which is taken up by the **surroundings** – broadly speaking, the engine of the car and the atmosphere. Chemists say that the reaction is **exothermic** (Fig. 3).

Fig. 3 Energy changes for the combustion of octane

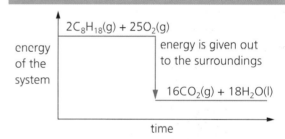

Ethanol reacts with oxygen as follows:

$$C_2H_5OH(g) + 3O_2(g) \rightarrow 2CO_2(g) + 3H_2O(g)$$
ethanol   oxygen   carbon dioxide   water

This reaction, like the burning of petrol, is highly exothermic: energy is released from the reaction system and is transferred to the surroundings.

The energy content of the reacting substances is called the **enthalpy** of the system. There is no way of measuring individual enthalpies directly, but we can measure the heat energy that is transferred in a chemical reaction, which is called the enthalpy change of the reaction. **Enthalpy changes** are given the symbol ΔH (Δ is the Greek capital letter delta, and means 'a change in'). They are measured in kilojoules per mole (kJ mol^{-1}).

Firefighter Red Adair was asked to put out the oil wells set alight in Kuwait by the Iraqi troops at the end of the Gulf War

In some reactions, energy is transferred *from* the surroundings *to* the reactants. These are called **endothermic** reactions.

Brandy burning in flambé cookery – an exothermic reaction

The formation of ethyne, C_2H_2, from the elements carbon and hydrogen is an example of an endothermic reaction (Fig. 4.).

Fig. 4 Energy changes for the formation of ethyne

energy of the system

$C_2H_2(g)$

$2C(s) + H_2(g)$

energy is taken in from the surroundings

time

Key ideas

• Chemical reactions are accompanied by an exchange of energy.

• In exothermic reactions, energy is transferred *from* the reactants *to* the surroundings.

• In endothermic reactions, energy is transferred *to* the reactants *from* the surroundings.

• The energy transferred in a reaction is called the enthalpy change of the reaction.

6.4 Measuring enthalpy changes

Enthalpy changes of reactions depend on the conditions of the reaction – for example, the temperature and the concentration (or pressure, where either the reactants or the products are gaseous). So if we want to compare enthalpy changes, we must measure them under the same reaction conditions. Enthalpy values are usually given for reactions taking place under standard conditions; chemists worldwide agreed that **standard conditions** are a reaction temperature of 298 K (25 °C) and a pressure of 1 atmosphere.

We also need to give the state of the reactants; in practice, enthalpy values are always given for reactants that are in the state that is normal to them under standard conditions. For example, if we are

measuring the enthalpy change of burning carbon in oxygen to form carbon dioxide, we must use solid carbon (graphite) and gaseous oxygen. Standard conditions are denoted by the superscript $^{\ominus}$. An enthalpy change at standard conditions has the symbol $\Delta H^{\ominus}$.

When ethanol or petrol reacts with oxygen, the reaction is an example of combustion. The enthalpy change of a combustion reaction is called the **standard enthalpy change of combustion**, $\Delta H_c{}^{\ominus}$. It is defined as

the energy transferred when one mole of a substance is completely burnt in oxygen under standard conditions.

In combustion reactions energy is usually given out, so $\Delta H_c{}^{\ominus}$ is negative (the reaction is exothermic).

Measuring standard enthalpy changes of combustion

Simple apparatus (Fig. 5) can be used to obtain approximate values for enthalpy changes of combustion.

Fig. 5 Measuring enthalpy change for combustion of ethanol

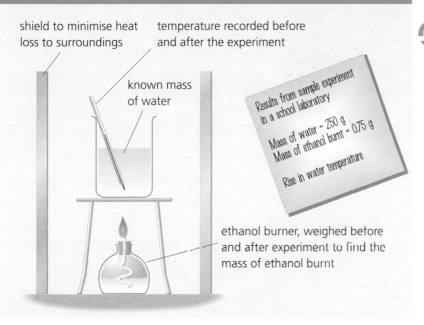

shield to minimise heat loss to surroundings

temperature recorded before and after the experiment

known mass of water

Results from sample experiment in a school laboratory

Mass of water = 250 g
Mass of ethanol burnt = 0.75 g

Rise in water temperature

ethanol burner, weighed before and after experiment to find the mass of ethanol burnt

Fig. 6 Calculating enthalpy change for combustion of ethanol

Heat energy transferred during experiment (J) =
mass of water (g) × specific heat capacity of water (Jg^{-1} K^{-1}) × temperature change (°C)

The specific heat capacity of a substance is *the amount of heat energy required to raise the temperature of 1 g of the substance by 1 K (or 1 °C)*. The specific heat capacity of water is 4.18 Jg^{-1} K^{-1}.

So heat energy transferred = 250 × 4.18 × 20 J
= 20 900 J or 20.9 kJ

The molecular mass of M_r ethanol is 46 g

So, moles of ethanol burnt = $\dfrac{0.75}{46}$
= 0.0163 mol

Enthalpy of combustion = $\dfrac{20.9}{0.0163}$ kJ mol^{-1}
= 1282 kJ mol^{-1}

Because heat is transferred to the surroundings, ΔH_c is negative.

So $\Delta H_c = -1282$ kJ mol^{-1}.

We can use the results in Figure 5 to calculate a figure for the enthalpy change of combustion for ethanol (Fig. 6). The enthalpy of combustion for the reaction can be written as:

$$C_2H_5OH(l) + 3O_2(g) \rightarrow 2CO_2(g) + 3H_2O(l)$$
$$\Delta H_c^{\ominus} = 1282 \text{ kJ mol}^{-1}$$

1 a The standard enthalpy change of combustion for ethanol is 1367 kJ mol^{-1}. Suggest why the experimental value is lower.

b Burning 0.67 g of methanol raises the temperature of 200 g of water by 16 °C. Is methanol a better fuel than ethanol in terms of enthalpy content?

Enthalpy changes of combustion can be determined much more accurately using a bomb calorimeter (Fig. 7). In this apparatus a fuel (or food) is fired by an electrically heated wire in an oxygen atmosphere, the fuel burns and the temperature change in the surrounding water bath is monitored. Insulation reduces energy loss to the surroundings. Fuel engineers use the bomb calorimeter to find the energy values of fuels, and food scientists use it to calculate the energy values of foods.

Fig. 7 Bomb calorimeter

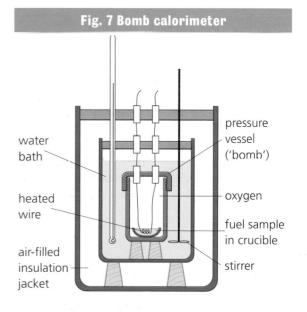

water bath

pressure vessel ('bomb')

heated wire

oxygen

fuel sample in crucible

air-filled insulation jacket

stirrer

Standard enthalpy changes of combustion can be found in most data books. Some are included in the data pages at the back of this book. The tables give the standard enthalpy change of combustion of octane as –5470.2 kJ mol^{-1} – more than four times that of ethanol. Does this mean that octane is four times as good a fuel as ethanol?

Fuels are not sold in moles, but by litres. Moles of different substances contain the same number of particles (see Chapter 2). Octane molecules (M_r = 114) are larger than ethanol molecules, so one litre of octane contains fewer molecules than one litre of ethanol. The litre of octane does produce more heat energy when it burns (Table 1), but the difference is not as great.

An active person needs energy from food

Table 1 Heating values of fuels	
Fuel	Heating value/kJ dm^{-3}
ethanol	21.09
unleaded petrol	32.16

6.5 Calculating standard enthalpy changes of reaction

We do not need to rely only on experimental data to find the enthalpy change for a reaction. There is a theoretical approach using **standard enthalpy of formation** values.

Standard enthalpy of formation (symbol $\Delta H_f^{\ominus}$) is defined as

the energy absorbed when one mole of a substance is formed from its elements in their standard states.

For example, the standard enthalpy of formation of ethanol is the energy absorbed when 46 g of ethanol is formed from solid carbon (graphite), gaseous oxygen and gaseous hydrogen. (In reality, this reaction does not occur.) It takes zero energy to form an element from its 'elements'. It follows that the $\Delta H_f^{\ominus}$ of all elements must be zero. This gives a common 'base line' from which the enthalpies of formation of compounds can be measured. Enthalpies of formation are given in data books, and some are at the back of this book. Using these values, we can calculate the standard enthalpy of combustion of ethanol (Fig. 8). (Remember, enthalpy values do not measure the energy *content* of chemicals. They measure the *changes* in energy that occur during a chemical reaction.)

Fig. 8 Calculating enthalpy change of combustion using enthalpy of formation

1 Write out the equation.
$C_2H_5OH(l) + 3O_2(g) \rightarrow 2CO_2(g) + 3H_2O(l)$

2 Write the $\Delta H_f^{\ominus}$ value for each substance under its formula in the equation.
$C_2H_5OH(l) \quad + \quad 3O_2(g) \rightarrow \quad 2CO_2(g) \quad + \quad 3H_2O(l)$

–277.1   0   2 × –393.5   3 × –285.8
Multiplying out gives,
–277.1   0   –787   –857.4

3 Total $\Delta H_f^{\ominus}$ (reactants) + ΔH(reaction) = total $\Delta H_f^{\ominus}$ (products)
So –277.1 + ΔH(reaction) = –787 + –857.4
Rearranging ΔH(reaction) = –1644.4 – –277.1 kJ mol^{-1}
$\Delta H_c^{\ominus}$ (ethanol)   = –1367.3 kJ mol^{-1}

---

 2 **Use a data book to calculate the ΔH_c of octane from the ΔH_f values for the reactants and products.**

6.6 Using enthalpy changes of formation

The $\Delta H_f^\ominus$ of a compound can also be useful for predicting the stability of a compound. Most compounds are formed exothermically from their elements. The compounds that are formed have a lower energy level than their constituents and are therefore more stable. Octane is such a compound. You could think of energy levels in terms of positions on a ladder. Your most stable position is standing at the bottom of the ladder; as you climb the ladder, you feel less and less stable. Octane is 'lower down the ladder' than its constituent elements carbon and hydrogen (Fig. 9).

A few compounds, such as ethyne, are formed endothermically (look back at Fig. 4). You can think of ethyne as being higher up the ladder than the elements carbon and hydrogen (Fig. 9).

When ethyne (acetylene) burns in oxygen large amounts of heat are released which can be used to weld metal

Fig. 9 Stabilities of ethyne and octane

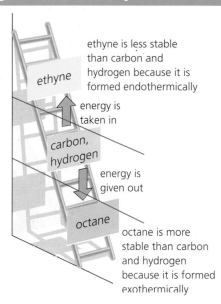

ethyne is less stable than carbon and hydrogen because it is formed endothermically

energy is taken in

energy is given out

octane is more stable than carbon and hydrogen because it is formed exothermically

Ethyne has a higher energy level than its constituents. So why doesn't it decompose into its elements? It does, but *very*, slowly – so slowly that ethyne is quite stable at low temperatures and can be stored for some time. In the presence of a catalyst or at high temperatures, however, it decomposes quite readily. $\Delta H_f^\ominus$ predictions on stability tell us nothing about whether the reaction is fast or slow. They are a guide only. The study of **reaction kinetics** tells us about reaction rates (see Chapter 16).

Key ideas

- The standard enthalpy change of combustion of a substance, $\Delta H_c^\ominus$, is the energy transferred when one mole of the substance is burnt in oxygen under standard conditions.

- Standard enthalpy changes of combustion, $\Delta H_c^\ominus$, can be determined experimentally.

- The standard enthalpy of formation, $\Delta H_f^\ominus$, of a substance is the energy absorbed when one mole of the substance is formed from its elements under standard conditions.

- The standard enthalpy of formation, $\Delta H_f^\ominus$, of a substance can be used to calculate the standard enthalpy change of a reaction.

- The standard enthalpy of formation, $\Delta H_f^\ominus$, can be used to predict the relative stabilities of compounds.

6.7 Overall energy balance

'I'm concerned about the overall energy balance of using ethanol to run cars. It's hard to tell whether the energy put into ethanol production is more or less than the energy we can get from ethanol fuel. I'm not sure we get back all we put in.'

Pure ethanol is not used as a fuel in most countries. The raw materials (sugar cane, corn) are more often used as foods. Large-scale ethanol production requires sugar cane to be grown and harvested. This means that energy is required for making and running tractors, and for making and transporting fertilisers and pesticides. Factories have to be built. The fermentation mixture has to be kept at a constant temperature, so heat energy has to be transferred to the system; separation of ethanol from the mix by fractional distillation requires still more energy. Many economists would sympathise with Rosita's concerns. On the other hand, the solid wastes left from the fermentation mix can be used as animal feed or as fuel, and the liquid wastes make good fertiliser. A positive energy balance is possible, but only if agricultural processes are carefully designed (Fig. 10).

Until 1992 ethanol fuel cost less than petrol in Brazil. Petrol taxes were high, so the government subsidised the Proalcool programme to reduce Brazil's dependence on imported oil. The World Bank estimated that ethanol was economic if sugar cane cost less than about £9 a tonne, and crude oil stayed above £20 a barrel.

Cut sugar cane being transported to the factory in Brazil

Q 3 Why do the economics of ethanol production depend on the price of crude oil?

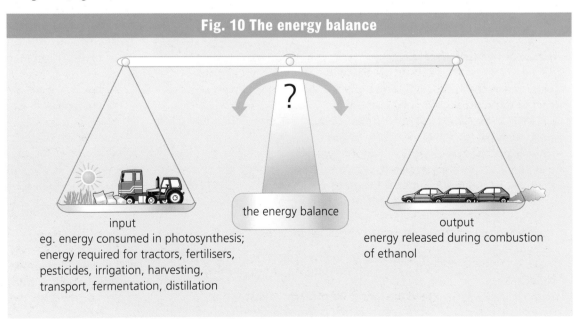

Fig. 10 The energy balance

input
eg. energy consumed in photosynthesis; energy required for tractors, fertilisers, pesticides, irrigation, harvesting, transport, fermentation, distillation

the energy balance

output
energy released during combustion of ethanol

6.8 Hess's law

Calculating the energy inputs of ethanol production is difficult. We can, however, calculate the amount of energy consumed during photosynthesis. Photosynthesis is the process by which green plants utilise sunlight energy to make sugars, like glucose from carbon doxide and water. Sugars can then be fermented to produce ethanol.

To calculate the standard enthalpy change of the photosynthesis reaction we will use **Hess's law**. This law is an application of the law of conservation of energy. It states that

the total standard enthalpy change of a chemical reaction is always the same, whatever the route by which the reaction takes place.

This provides us with a way of calculating unknown enthalpy changes by using known enthalpy changes (Fig. 11).

Figure 11 shows that plants take in 2802 kJ of energy from sunlight for every mole of glucose they produce. The glucose made during photosynthesis is converted to sucrose. After harvesting the sugar cane, the sucrose is fermented to produce ethanol. One mole of glucose produces 2 moles of ethanol.

 4 Write an equation to show how 1 mole of glucose produces 2 moles of ethanol during fermentation.

The standard enthalpy change of combustion for ethanol is 1367 kJ mol^{-1}. Burning 2 moles of ethanol in a car engine will produce 2734 kJ of energy.

Using Hess's law

Hess's law can be used in many ways. It can be used to find the standard enthalpy of combustion of ethanol (Fig. 12).

 5 Use Hess's law to calculate the enthalpy of combustion for octane.

Fig. 11 Calculating the standard enthalpy of photosynthesis

1 Write out the equation.

2 Write down the constituent elements underneath. Add arrows to the reactants and the products, to complete the triangle (an energy cycle). Balance all equations.

$$\Delta H_1$$
$$6CO_2(g) + 6H_2O(l) \longrightarrow C_6H_{12}O_6(aq) + 6O_2(g)$$
$$\Delta H_2 \qquad \qquad \Delta H_3$$
$$6C(s) + 6H_2(g) + 9O_2(g)$$

3 We want to find ΔH_1. From Hess's law, we know that the overall energy change in going from the constituent elements to glucose must be the same as the energy change in going from the elements to carbon dioxide and water and then to glucose. So we can write:

$\Delta H_2 + \Delta H_1 = \Delta H_3$ Or $\Delta H_1 = \Delta H_3 - \Delta H_2$

From the equation,

$\Delta H_2 = 6[\Delta H_f^{\ominus}(\text{carbon dioxide}(g))] + 6[\Delta H_f^{\ominus}(\text{water}(l))]$

Using $\Delta H_f^{\ominus}$ values from tables, we have

$\Delta H_2 = 6[-393.5] + 6[-285.8]$ kJ mol^{-1}

$\quad = -2361 + -1714.8$ kJ mol^{-1}

$\quad = -4075.8$ kJ mol^{-1}

We can also look up ΔH_3, the enthalpy of formation of glucose from its elements:

$\Delta H_3 = \Delta H_f^{\ominus}(\text{glucose}(s)) = -1273.3$ kJ mol^{-1}

Therefore,

$\Delta H_1 = -1273.3 - (-4075.8)$ kJ mol^{-1} = +2802.5 kJ mol^{-1}

Fig. 12 Calculating the standard enthalpy of combustion of ethanol

1 Write the energy cycle.

$$\Delta H_1$$
$$C_2H_5OH(l) + 3O_2(g) \longrightarrow 2CO_2(g) + 3H_2O(l)$$
$$\Delta H_2 \qquad \qquad \Delta H_3$$
$$2C(s) + 3H_2(g) + 3O_2(g)$$

2 As before, we can write:

Rearranging $\Delta H_2 + \Delta H_1 = \Delta H_3$

$\Delta H_1 = \Delta H_3 - \Delta H_2$

Using $\Delta H_f^{\ominus}$ values from tables, we have

$\Delta H_3 = 2[\Delta H_f^{\ominus}(\text{carbon dioxide}(g))] + 3[\Delta H_f^{\ominus}(\text{water}(l))]$

$\quad = 2[-393.5] + 3[-285.8]$ kJ mol^{-1}

$\quad = -787 + -857.4$ kJ mol^{-1}

$\quad = -1664.4$ kJ mol^{-1}

Also from tables,

$\Delta H_2 = \Delta H_f^{\ominus}(\text{ethanol})$

$\quad = -277.1$ kJ mol^{-1}

$\Delta H_1 = -1664 - (-277.1)$ kJ mol^{-1}

$\quad = -1367.3$ kJ mol^{-1}

6.9 Bond enthalpy calculations

Another way to calculate the enthalpy change of a reaction is to consider which bonds are broken and which are made, and what the associated enthalpy changes are. For example, methane (CH_4) contains four C–H bonds. Suppose that methane is broken down into its five constituent atoms (**dissociated**); we can write the enthalpy change as follows:

$$CH_4(g) \rightarrow C(g) + 4H(g) \quad \Delta H = +1662 \text{ kJ mol}^{-1}$$

Breaking four C–H bonds requires 1662 kJ of energy. This implies that the average enthalpy for each C–H bond is:
$E(\text{C–H}) = 413 \text{ kJ mol}^{-1}$

The symbol E stands for **bond energy term**, or **bond enthalpy**. Values for some bond enthalpies are given at the back of this book. Bond enthalpies depend on the environment of the bond within a molecule (Table 2).

Table 2	
Bond enthalpies: the C–F bond/kJ mol^{-1}	
C–F bond in CF_4	485
C–F bond in CH_3F	452

We can work out the standard enthalpy of combustion of ethanol by looking at bond enthalpies. Energy is taken in by the reactants when bonds are broken, and given out when bonds are made (Fig. 13). From Fig. 13 the energy used to break bonds is given by:

5 $E(\text{C–H})$	= 5 × 413 =	2065
1 $E(\text{C–C})$	=	347
1 $E(\text{C–O})$	=	358
1 $E(\text{O–H})$	=	464
3 $E(\text{O=O})$	= 3 × 498 =	1494
Total		= 4728 kJ mol^{-1}

The energy released when bonds are made is given by:

6 $E(\text{O–H})$	=	2784
4 $E(\text{C=O})$	=	3220
Total enthalpy change		
		= 6004 kJ mol^{-1}

Therefore, the standard enthalpy of combustion of ethanol
= 4728 – 6004 kJ mol^{-1}
= –1276 kJ mol^{-1}

6 a Use standard bond enthalpy values to calculate the enthalpy of combustion of octane.
b Compare your result with the value given in the data pages.

Fig. 13 Bond enthalpies for combustion of ethanol

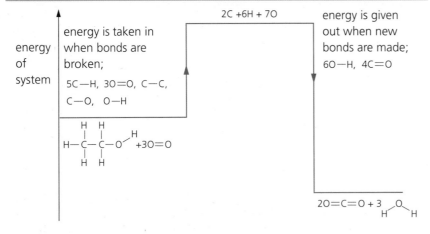

energy of system

energy is taken in when bonds are broken;

5C—H, 3O=O, C—C, C—O, O—H

2C +6H + 7O

energy is given out when new bonds are made; 6O—H, 4C=O

Key ideas

- Hess's law can be used to find enthalpy changes of reactions.

- The standard bond enthalpy is the energy associated with a particular bond.

- Standard bond enthalpies can be used to calculate enthalpy changes of reactions.

- Breaking bonds requires energy.

- Making bonds requires energy.

6.10 Ethanol fuel and the motor car

'I'm very concerned about the filth that traffic pours into the air. Ethanol fuel is much cleaner than petrol. It produces less carbon monoxide and there's no pollution by antiknock additives such as tetraethyllead or benzene. (see Table 3)'

Ethanol fuel can be used in spark ignition engines (normal car engines) and in diesel engines. Engines have to be modified before they can be used with straight hydrated ethanol (5% water, 95% ethanol), because the fuel is corrosive. For example, the inside of the fuel tank has to be coated with tin and the fuel lines need to be coated with nickel over copper. All the adaptations required cost about £300 per car. Carburettors have to be fitted with wider inlet valves to allow more fuel into the engine cylinder. The increased fuel consumption is compensated for by compressing the fuel mixture more. Ethanol fuels are less likely than petrol to cause 'knock' in the engine at high compression.

Gasohol fuel (in Brazil 20% ethanol, 80% gasoline) can be used in normal petrol engines, and the fuel needs no added antiknock agent.

Table 3 Emissions from 1.4 litre Ford engine/g km^{-1}			
Emission (exhaust)	Petrol	Gasohol (10% ethanol)	Hydrated ethanol
hydrocarbons	2.07	1.50	1.56
carbon monoxide	30.86	12.89	10.62
nitrogen oxides	1.16	1.79	1.04
Source: Ford (Brazil)			

6.11 Proalcool: what next?

The future of Brazil's Proalcool programme is to some degree uncertain. It will depend on:
- improving productivity of ethanol (researchers estimate that new strains of sugar cane could increase productivity by 10%);
- environmental issues (Sao Paulo has 1.2 million gasohol cars and 1.1 million ethanol cars. Changing to petrol fuel could increase carbon dioxide emissions by 120%, hydrocarbon emissions by 100% and nitrogen oxide emissions by 10%);
- economics (the world price of crude oil is crucial, and affects the economic viability of ethanol fuel);
- the political situation in Brazil can change very quickly.

Controlling equilibria

'I'm always busy! Morning to night, people come here to buy food. As Cairo grows, the markets get more crowded. Sometimes I think: all over the world there are markets like mine, selling food to people who for one reason or another can't grow their own. More and more people ...'

The population of the world has risen dramatically in the last fifty years. Food production has risen enormously, as well. Farmers are growing their crops more efficiently, and fertiliser use has increased (Fig. 1).

Food production and consumption are not distributed evenly, however. The richer countries consume a greater proportion. The effects of wars, politics and climatic catastrophes mean that large numbers of people still survive on barely adequate diets. The development of artificial fertilisers is one contribution to increased food production.

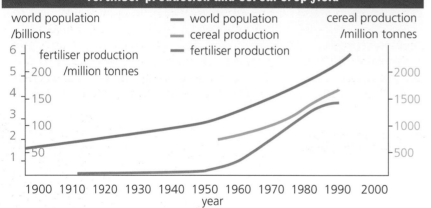

7.1 Learning objectives

After working through this chapter, you should be able to:

- **describe** a dynamic equilibrium reaction as reversible, with both forward and back reactions;

- **explain** why dynamic equilibria only occur in closed systems;

- **derive** the equilibrium constant expression for a homogeneous equilibrium;

- **work out** the effect of changing the temperature on an equilibrium position and equilibrium constant;

- **work out** the effect of changing the concentration on equilibrium reactions in solution;

- **work out** the effect of changing the pressure on equilibrium reactions in the gaseous phase;

- **explain** the principles underlying the Haber process in terms of the balance between equilibrium yield and rates of reaction.

7.2 Are fertilisers essential?

Staple crops such as wheat, rice and potatoes supply most of the world's food energy needs. These crops are processed to make suitable foods or used as animal feed. As crops grow they take nitrogen compounds out of the soil, and use them to build up amino acids and proteins inside the plants. Different crops take up (or fix) nitrogen from the soil at different rates (Table 1).

Crop yields are related to the level of available nitrogen in the soil. If fields are used intensively, the nitrogen compounds being removed must be replaced, or yields will fall. Nitrogen is plentiful; it makes up 78% by volume of the Earth's atmosphere. But the bond between the nitrogen atoms is very strong, so nitrogen gas is unreactive. Plants cannot fix nitrogen from the air.

Nitrogen changes its chemical form in soil and in plants (Fig. 2). The balance of nitrogen in the soil depends on many reactions. Some add nitrogen to the soil, others remove it (Fig. 3).

Micro-organisms are involved in some of these reactions. Some soil micro-organisms can break the N–N bond and convert atmospheric nitrogen into nitrogen compounds that plants can use. Others break down the proteins of dead plants and animals into compounds that pass into the soil. These compounds are recycled by the next generation of growing plants.

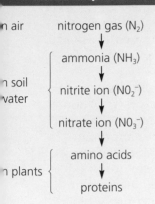

Fig. 2 Nitrogen movement from air to plants

In air: nitrogen gas (N_2)

In soil water:
ammonia (NH_3)
↓
nitrite ion (NO_2^-)
↓
nitrate ion (NO_3^-)

In plants:
amino acids
↓
proteins

Table 1 Nitrogen fixation by crops

Crop	Average annual yield/tonnes ha^{-1}	Nitrogen fixed/kg ha^{-1}
wheat	7	130
barley	6	100
oats	6	100
potatoes	50	150
sugar beet	45	200
kale	50	224

Note: 1 hectare (ha) is 10 000 m^2 or 0.01 km^2

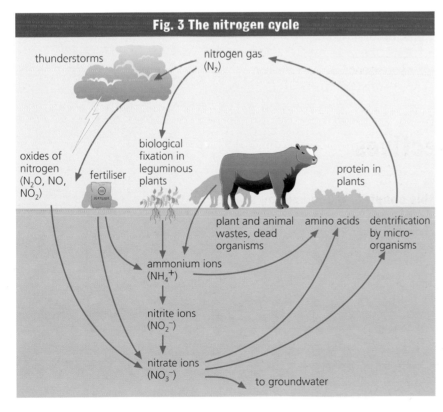

Fig. 3 The nitrogen cycle

thunderstorms

nitrogen gas (N_2)

oxides of nitrogen (N_2O, NO, NO_2)

fertiliser

biological fixation in leguminous plants

protein in plants

plant and animal wastes, dead organisms

amino acids

dentrification by micro-organisms

ammonium ions (NH_4^+)

nitrite ions (NO_2^-)

nitrate ions (NO_3^-)

to groundwater

The roots of peas and beans have nodules in which there are nitrogen-fixing bacteria. The bacteria can absorb nitrogen and convert it to nitrates

For as long as humans have been cultivating crops, they have used animal manures to make soils more fertile. As the explosive rise in the world's population led to a soaring demand for farm products, however, these nitrogen sources became insufficient to meet the needs of increasingly intensive agriculture. Gardeners, 'organic' farmers and many subsistence farmers in developing countries continue to use manures to supplement nitrogen levels.

Minerals containing nitrogen can be used as inorganic fertilisers. Their nitrogen content is in the form of ammonium ions (NH_4^+) or nitrate ions (NO_3^-). Like manures, these fertilisers can supply other essential elements for plant growth, including potassium and phosphorus.

There are naturally occurring deposits of sodium nitrate in the Earth's crust. One, known as Chile saltpetre, was used not only as a fertiliser, but also as a raw material for making explosives. In the early 1900s authorities around the world recognised that these deposits would be exhausted fairly rapidly. It became important to find an alternative source of nitrogen.

Ammonium salts and nitrates can be made from ammonia gas (NH_3). The compound has been known since ancient times, by its smell at least, as a constituent of manures and rotting animal remains. Ammonia was first isolated by the English chemist Joseph Black in 1756. However, no one knew how to make it both cheaply and in large quantities.

The most obvious source of nitrogen for making ammonia is air. Unfortunately, it is not easy to convert nitrogen gas to ammonia. In 1904, the chemist Fritz Haber set out to find out how to do it on an industrial scale. His understanding of the reversible nature of some chemical reactions helped him.

Haber's work, outlined in this chapter, was laborious but his success was dramatic. Within ten years Germany, on the brink of World War I, had all the ammonia it needed for munitions, and cheap fertilisers as well. British scientists did not begin working on ammonia manufacture until 1917, encouraged by the Prime Minister Lloyd George. But they met with no great success until after the war was over. Two engineers then offered to sell the German company BASF's secrets to the British firm Brunner Mond; a sale that led to the building of the first ammonia plant on Teesside. Brunner Mond later merged with other companies to become ICI: ammonia is still made on Teesside to this day.

Explosives can be used in a controlled way; here a motorway bridge is being demolished

Fritz Haber, 1905

7.3 Reversible and irreversible reactions

Most nitrates decompose on heating. For example, ammonium nitrate, a common fertiliser made from ammonia, decomposes as follows:

$$2NH_4NO_3(s) \rightarrow 2H_2O(g) + N_2O(g)$$
$$\text{nitrogen(I) oxide}$$

The single-headed arrow in this equation indicates that *all* the ammonium nitrate decomposes, and that you can't get it back again by trying to make nitrogen(I) oxide react with water. The reaction is effectively irreversible.

On the other hand, many reaction mixtures contain both the reactants and the products of the reaction, however long is allowed for the reaction to go to completion. For example, a gas jar of nitrogen dioxide gas (NO_2) always contains some dinitrogen tetroxide, N_2O_4. Dinitrogen tetroxide is a dimer of nitrogen dioxide. (A dimer is two molecules joined together.) We can write what happens like this:

$$2NO_2(g) \rightleftharpoons N_2O_4$$
$$\text{brown} \qquad \text{colourless}$$

The double-headed arrow in the equation is important. It indicates that the reaction is **reversible**. In a **closed system**, both forward and backward reactions happen at the same time. We say that the reactants and products are in **dynamic equilibrium**.

We can think of a sealed syringe of nitrogen dioxide as a closed system. In the syringe, some nitrogen dioxide molecules combine to form dinitrogen tetroxide. Some dinitrogen tetroxide molecules dissociate to form nitrogen dioxide. When the system reaches equilibium, these two reactions happen at the same rate, and the concentrations of nitrogen dioxide and dinitrogen tetroxide stay constant (Fig. 4).

Fig. 4 Competing reactions at equilibrium

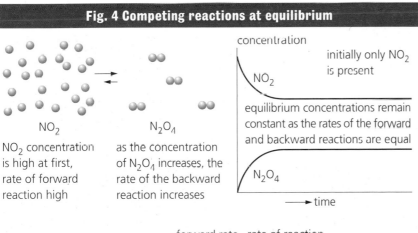

NO$_2$ concentration is high at first, rate of forward reaction high

as the concentration of N_2O_4 increases, the rate of the backward reaction increases

concentration

initially only NO_2 is present

NO_2

equilibrium concentrations remain constant as the rates of the forward and backward reactions are equal

N_2O_4

time

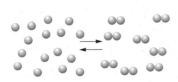

at equilibrium the rates of the forward and backward reactions are the same

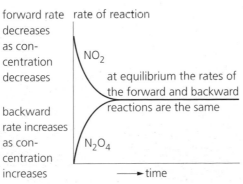

forward rate decreases as concentration decreases

backward rate increases as concentration increases

rate of reaction

NO_2

at equilibrium the rates of the forward and backward reactions are the same

N_2O_4

time

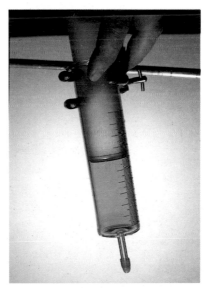

A sealed gas syringe containing nitrogen dioxide and dinitrogen tetroxide at equilibrium

Fig. 5 Effect of removing a component from equilibrium system

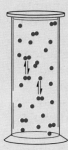
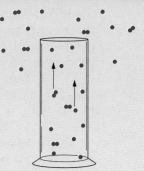

in a sealed container, the system is at equilibrium

N_2O_4 is formed from NO_2 at the same rate that NO_2 is formed from N_2O_4

when the container is opened, NO_2 leaves the mixture as it diffuses out

NO_2 no longer forms N_2O_4 at the same rate that N_2O_4 dissociates

in the open system, the reaction mixture is no longer at equilibrium

Reactions can only reach equilibrium in a closed system. If any of the reactants or products can leave the system, the concentration of that component changes and the equilibrium is destroyed (Fig. 5).

1 **In which of the following is there a dynamic equilibrium?**

  a **An unopened bottle of fizzy lemonade.**
  b **A bottle of fizzy lemonade with the top left off.**
  c **A sealed gas jar containing bromine vapour and bromine liquid.**
  d **Bromine vapour and bromine liquid in an open gas jar.**

In some equilibria all the components are in the same phase. For example, in the nitrogen dioxide–dinitrogen tetroxide equilibrium both components are gases. This is an example of a **homogeneous equilibrium**. In a **heterogeneous equilibrium** the components are in different phases. Fritz Haber used a heterogeneous equilibrium reaction to make hydrogen for the manufacture of ammonia:

$$C(s) + H_2O(g) \rightleftharpoons CO(g) + H_2(g)$$
coke   steam

Key ideas

- Equilibria occur in closed systems.

- Chemical equilibria are dynamic. Forward and back reactions occur at the same rate at equilibrium.

- In homogeneous equilibria the components are all in the same phase.

- In heterogenous equilibria the components are in different phases.

7.4 Industrial fixation of nitrogen

When Haber started his research, several methods of making ammonia and nitrates had been invented. However, they were all costly in terms of energy and raw materials. Haber was interested in the most efficient way of making nitrogen compounds from the nitrogen in air. He looked at the production of nitrogen oxides by sparking together a mixture of nitrogen and oxygen – a first step towards nitric acid. The German chemical company BASF became interested in his work, and agreed to fund research on ammonia synthesis. This allowed Haber to proceed without financial worries, while BASF stood to benefit from any commercial applications that resulted.

Haber began to study the reaction between nitrogen and hydrogen to form ammonia. He knew this reaction was reversible:

$$N_2(g) + 3H_2(g) \rightleftharpoons 2NH_3(g)$$

He also knew that the position of equilibrium lay well towards the reactants: at 1000 °C, with iron as a catalyst, the reaction mixture contained only 0.0005–0.0012% of ammonia (Fig. 6).

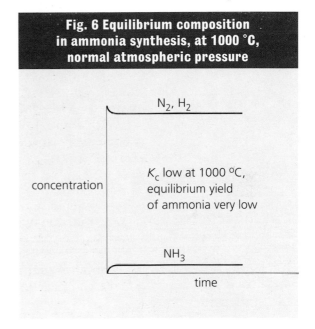

Fig. 6 Equilibrium composition in ammonia synthesis, at 1000 °C, normal atmospheric pressure

N_2, H_2

concentration

K_c low at 1000 °C, equilibrium yield of ammonia very low

NH_3

time

7.5 Equilibrium constants

Haber wasn't discouraged by this incredibly small yield. He knew enough about equilibrium reactions to be sure that he could improve the yield, if he changed the reaction conditions.

In a homogeneous equilibrium, the composition of the reaction mixture at equilibrium can be described by an expression called an **equilibrium constant** (symbol K_c). This relates the concentrations of reactants and products.

For the homogeneous equilibrium

$$mA(l) + nB(l) \rightleftharpoons pC(l) + qD(l)$$

the equilibrium constant is given by

$$K_c = \frac{[C(l)]^p \, [D(l)]^q}{[A(l)]^m \, [B(l)]^n}$$

where the square brackets indicate concentrations *at equilibrium* in mol dm^{-3}.

We can write the equilibrium constant for the synthesis of ammonia as

$$K_c = \frac{[NH_3(g)]^2}{[N_2(g)] \, [H_2(g)]^3}$$

The units for this equilibrium constant are mol^{-2} dm^6.

The size of K_c indicates the composition of the reaction mixture at equilibrium. A large K_c means that the concentrations of products are high: the reaction goes most of the way to completion. A small K_c means that the concentrations of products are low: K_c for ammonia synthesis at 1000 °C is very small indeed.

2 a Write the expression for the equilibrium constant for the nitrogen dioxide equilibrium

$$N_2O_4\,(g) \rightleftharpoons 2NO_2(g)$$

b What are its units?

You will often see the equilibrium in question 2 written the other way round. It does not matter from which side the equilibrium is approached: at the same temperature and pressure, the concentrations in the equilibrium mixture will be exactly the same (Fig. 7). But you do have to be clear what equation you are using when you work out expressions for K_c.

 3 a Write the expression for the equilibrium constant for the reaction written

$$2NO_2(g) \rightleftharpoons N_2O_4(g)$$

b What are its units?

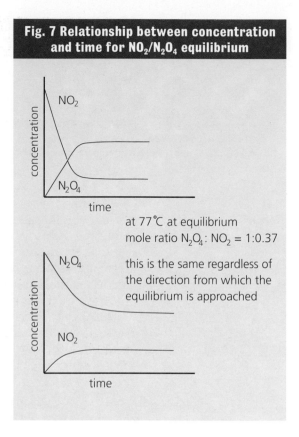

Fig. 7 Relationship between concentration and time for NO₂/N₂O₄ equilibrium

at 77°C at equilibrium mole ratio $N_2O_4 : NO_2 = 1:0.37$

this is the same regardless of the direction from which the equilibrium is approached

7.6 Effects of temperature on equilibria

If the temperature is changed, the value of the equilibrium constant changes. For the reaction in question 2, for example, K_c at 327 °C is many thousand times as large as it is at room temperature.

 4 What colour would you expect to see in this reaction mixture
a at 25 °C?
b at 327 °C?

Haber knew that the equilibrium constant for the ammonia synthesis was small at high temperatures, yet he went on using a temperature of 1000 °C. The research was as follows. While the value of the equilibrium constant indicates the position of equilibrium, it doesn't tell us how long the reaction mixture takes to get there. Many equilibrium reactions are very slow to reach equilibrium, although a

suitable catalyst may speed them up. The catalyst has no effect on the equilibrium constant. Similarly, information about the rate of a chemical reaction tells us nothing about the *position* of equilibrium for that reaction. Haber's problem was that he needed to get a good yield of ammonia *at a reasonable rate*. Unless he used a high temperature, the reaction was far too slow.

Haber carried out a set of experiments to find equilibrium constants for the reaction

$$N_2(g) + 3H_2(g) \rightleftharpoons 2NH_3(g)$$

under different initial reaction conditions. Using his experimental data and knowledge of equilibria, he could then predict the reaction conditions that would give the best yield of ammonia. Some sample results are given in Table 2. Clearly, if the operating pressure stays the same,

Table 2 Relationship between K_c for the N_2/H_2 equilibrium and temperature	
Temperature/°C	K_c/mol^{-2} dm^6
25	4.05×10^8
127	4.39×10^3
227	59.8
327	4.03
427	0.256
527	2.98×10^{-2}
627	5.45×10^{-3}
827	4.08×10^{-4}

temperature will encourage the dissociation of ammonia, so the yield decreases.

 5 **Look back at the effect of temperature on the equilibrium constant of the nitrogen dioxide–dinitrogen tetroxide equilibrium (page 80). Which reaction is exothermic: the dissociation of dinitrogen tetroxide or the dimerisation of nitrogen dioxide?**

increasing the temperature decreases the yield of ammonia.

We can explain this change in equilibrium constant with temperature if we look at the energy changes in the reaction (see Chapter 6). The reaction for the production of ammonia is **exothermic**:

$$N_2(g) + 3H_2(g) \rightarrow 2NH_3(g) \quad \Delta H^\ominus = -92.4 \text{ kJ mol}^{-1}$$

This means that the reverse reaction is **endothermic**. Increasing the temperature encourages the reaction that needs to take in energy. In this case increasing the

Le Châtelier's principle

The effect of temperature on equilibrium reactions is an example of the action of Le Châtelier's principle, formulated in 1888 by the French chemist Henri Le Châtelier. Haber knew the principle well.

Le Châtelier's experiments had established that

when an equilibrium reaction mixture is subject to a change in conditions, the composition of the mixture adjusts to counteract the change.

The 'change in conditions' can refer to a change in temperature (Fig. 8), pressure or concentration.

Fig. 8 Effects of temperature on an equilibrium mixture

- Changing the temperature changes the equilibrium constant.

- Increasing the temperature encourages the endothermic process.

- Decreasing the temperature encourages the exothermic process.

Key ideas

- An equilibrium constant expression can be written for any equilibrium.

- Increasing the temperature changes the equilibrium constant and encourages the endothermic reaction.

7.7 Gaseous equilibria and the Haber process

If the gases in the syringe on page 77 are compressed the colour changes

In a homogeneous gas phase reaction, pressure changes can affect the equilibrium position but *not* the equilibrium constant. Again, Le Châtelier's principle helps to explain what happens. Look again at the equilibrium

$$2NO_2(g) \rightleftharpoons N_2O_4(g)$$

If the reaction mixture is compressed, the colour changes. The mixture loses some of its brown colour, indicating more dinitrogen tetroxide has been formed (Fig. 9). This is another example of Le Châtelier's principle in action.

When the pressure is increased, all concentrations rapidly increase (Fig. 10). The reaction then reaches a new equilibrium position. The individual concentrations of the reactants and products adjust as necessary to keep K_c unchanged.

 6 In the nitrogen dioxide–nitrogen tetroxide equilibrium, what colour change would you see if the pressure is reduced? Give reasons for your answer.

7 What changes would you expect to see in equilibrium composition if the pressure is increased in the following reactions?
a $2SO_2(g) + O_2(g) \rightleftharpoons 2SO_3(g)$
b $H_2(g) + I_2(g) \rightleftharpoons 2HI(g)$

Fig. 9 Effects of pressure on an equilibrium mixture

- Increasing the pressure encourages the process that leads to fewer molecules in the reaction mixture.

- Increasing the pressure encourages the process that tends to reduce the pressure.

Fig. 10 Effect of pressure on equilibrium position for a gaseous reaction

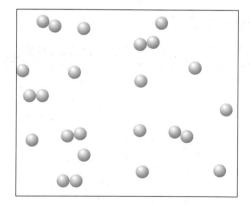

equilibrium conditions
NO₂   N₂O₄
at same rate

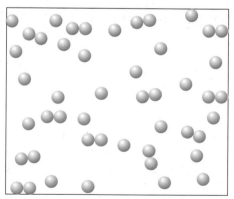

pressure increase results in more molecular collisions, higher concentrations of both NO₂ and N₂O₄

affects equilibrium position ⟶

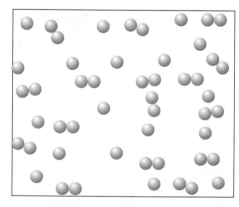

at the new equilibrium position there is more N₂O₄, less NO₂; the ratio $[NO_2]^2:[N_2O_4]$ is the same as at the initial equilibrium

Haber explained the effect of increasing pressure on ammonia synthesis in this way:

'To begin with, it was clear that a change to the use of maximum pressure would be advantageous. It would improve the point of equilibrium and probably the rate of reaction as well. The compressor which we then possessed allowed gas to be compressed to 200 atmospheres.'

The equation for the synthesis of ammonia shows that 4 molecules of the reactants produce 2 molecules of ammonia. We can see why Haber expected an increase in pressure to increase the yield of ammonia. His problem now was how to balance conflicting conditions to get a reasonable yield of ammonia (Fig. 11).

With his assistant Robert le Rossignol, Haber carried out many experiments to find the optimum conditions on a laboratory scale, using a range of temperatures, pressures and catalysts. Eventually, they found suitable conditions for ammonia synthesis using small-scale apparatus. They then had to scale up ammonia production for industrial manufacture. They needed two things: a reasonable yield of ammonia, and a reasonable rate of reaction. They found that the best conditions to meet

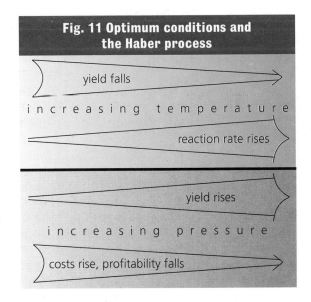

Fig. 11 Optimum conditions and the Haber process

yield falls

i n c r e a s i n g   t e m p e r a t u r e

reaction rate rises

yield rises

i n c r e a s i n g   p r e s s u r e

costs rise, profitability falls

these requirements were:
- a nitrogen:hydrogen mole ratio of 1:3;
- a temperature of 500–600 °C;
- a pressure of around 200 atmospheres;
- an osmium catalyst.

A pressure of 200 atmospheres presented some technical problems. It's about what the pressure on the base of a brick wall would be if the wall were about one and a half kilometres high!

7.8 Commercial ammonia manufacture

Haber and le Rossignol's small ammonia plant persuaded BASF to fund scaling up the process to a manufacturing level. Carl Bosch, a BASF chemical engineer, managed to solve the technical problems presented by the pressure required. Compressing and circulating gases at very high pressures required some very inventive technology. At 200 atmospheres pressure, hydrogen diffuses into steel, destroying its strength.

Bosch ingeniously solved this problem by separating its parts, mainly by designing a novel double-walled reactor (Fig. 12). He also developed an alternative catalyst to the expensive osmium. Bosch found a catalyst containing iron as the active substance.

A fracture in a steel pipe caused by hydrogen attack

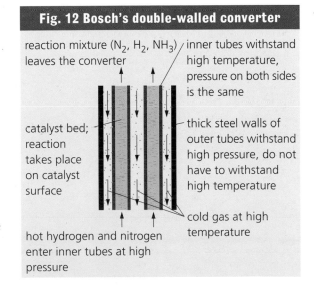

Fig. 12 Bosch's double-walled converter

reaction mixture (N_2, H_2, NH_3) leaves the converter

inner tubes withstand high temperature, pressure on both sides is the same

catalyst bed; reaction takes place on catalyst surface

thick steel walls of outer tubes withstand high pressure, do not have to withstand high temperature

hot hydrogen and nitrogen enter inner tubes at high pressure

cold gas at high temperature

Even under the optimum reaction conditions, however, the reaction mixture contained only about 15% ammonia. After extraction of the ammonia, the unreacted nitrogen and hydrogen were recycled.

Haber was awarded the Nobel prize for chemistry in 1918, Bosch received the same prize in 1931. These awards recognised the enormous social impact of the work.

Developing the Haber–Bosch process

Bosch's plant could produce 30 tonnes of ammonia a day; modern plants produce about 50 times as much. The high energy costs of the process have been reduced, and the cheapest sources of raw materials are used. Bosch used the reactions between steam and red-hot coke (carbon) to produce hydrogen:

$$C(s) + H_2O(g) \rightarrow CO(g) + H_2(g) \quad \Delta H^{\ominus} = + 131.3 \text{ kJ mol}^{-1}$$

An equilibrium is set up:

$$CO(g) + H_2O(g) \rightleftharpoons CO_2(g) + H_2(g) \quad \Delta H^{\ominus} = - 41.2 \text{ kJ mol}^{-1}$$

More recently natural gas, methane, has proved an alternative source of hydrogen. When methane is passed with steam over a nickel catalyst at 750 °C, a process called steam reforming, the following reactions happen:

$$CH_4(g) + H_2O(g) \rightleftharpoons CO(g) + 3H_2(g) \quad \Delta H^{\ominus} = + 206.1 \text{ kJ mol}^{-1}$$

$$CH_4(g) + 2H_2O(g) \rightleftharpoons CO_2(g) + 4H_2(g) \quad \Delta H^{\ominus} = + 164.9 \text{ kJ mol}^{-1}$$

The $\Delta H^{\ominus}$ values quoted for these equilibria are for the forward reaction in each case.

 8 a **Why is the steam reforming of methane carried out at a high temperature?**
  b **What will be the best pressure conditions for a high yield of hydrogen in the reaction mixture?**

The whole process is a continuous one, with the gas mixture constantly recirculating through the system (Fig. 13).

Fig. 13 Ammonia manufacturing process

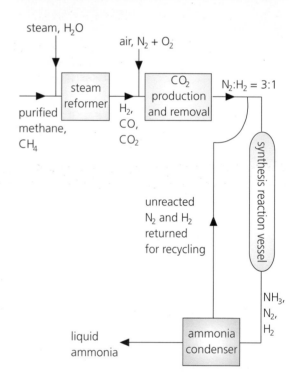

7.9 Effect of concentration on liquid-phase equilibria

Equilibria in the liquid phase are not affected by changes in pressure, but they are affected by changes in concentration.

In manufacturing plants ammonia is separated from the other gases by cooling the mixture and condensing out liquid ammonia (Fig. 13). Another way of separating ammonia from a reaction mixture is by dissolving it in water. Ammonia dissociates in water, forming a weakly alkaline solution:

$$NH_3(aq) + H_2O(l) \rightleftharpoons NH_4^+(aq) + OH^-(aq)$$

Ammonia can take part in other dynamic equilibria in solution. For example, it can form complexes with copper ions:

$$Cu^{2+}(aq) + 4NH_3(aq) \rightleftharpoons Cu(NH_3)_4^{2+}(aq)$$
pale blue   deep blue

Fig. 14 Effect of increasing reactant concentration on an equilibrium

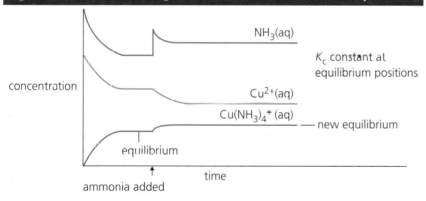

NH₃(aq)

K_c constant at equilibrium positions

Cu²⁺(aq)

Cu(NH₃)₄⁺ (aq)

new equilibrium

concentration

equilibrium

time

ammonia added

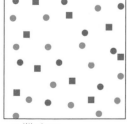

equilibrium
- Cu²⁺
- NH₃
- complex

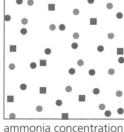

ammonia concentration increased; rate of reaction rises as the number of collisions involving ammonia increases

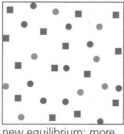

new equilibrium: more complex, less copper, more ammonia

Changing the concentrations of the chemicals in these equilibrium reactions changes the composition of the equilibrium mixture but – as with pressure changes in gas reactions – not the equilibrium constant. This is another example of Le Châtelier's principle in action.

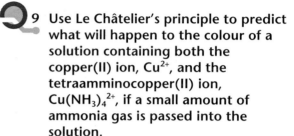

9 Use Le Châtelier's principle to predict what will happen to the colour of a solution containing both the copper(II) ion, Cu²⁺, and the tetraamminocopper(II) ion, Cu(NH₃)₄²⁺, if a small amount of ammonia gas is passed into the solution.

When ammonia gas is added to the equilibrium mixture in question 9, the volume of the solution does not change. So the concentration of ammonia rises. This temporarily increases the rate of the reaction in which the ammonia is consumed (Fig. 14). Provided the temperature does not change, the equilibrium constant remains the same.

By Le Châtelier's principle, increasing the concentration of one of the components in an equilibrium mixture alters the equilibrium position in such a way as to counteract the increase.

10 What will happen in the following reaction at equilibrium

$$CH_3COOH(l) + C_2H_5OH(l) \rightleftharpoons CH_3COOC_2H_5(l) + H_2O(l)$$

a if ethanol is added to the reaction mixture?
b if ethyl ethanoate is added to the reaction mixture?
c if ethyl ethanoate is removed from the reaction mixture?

7.10 Improving fertilisers

Over 80% of ammonia produced is used to make fertilisers. Ammonia reacts with acids such as nitric, phosphoric and sulphuric acids to make the corresponding salts, which are used on a large scale as inorganic fertilisers (Fig. 15).

Fertiliser use in the UK has declined in the past few years, partly because less land is used for growing crops, and partly because fertilisers are being used more efficiently. Less fertiliser is used per hectare, but the same good crop yields are being obtained. In some areas, too, there is disquiet that over-use of fertilisers may pollute the groundwater.

11 Why is using more fertilisers not an answer to the shortage of food in some parts of the world?

Plants can absorb both ammonium ions and nitrate ions. Ammonium ions are changed by micro-organisms into nitrite and then to nitrate ions. Nitrate ions move more easily through soil water than ammonium ions do, and if not absorbed by plants can leach into groundwater and rivers. BASF – still involved in fertiliser research and production today – are working on an improved fertiliser (BASAMMON) which stabilises ammonium ions and discourages the nitrate formation. This development should help the efficiency of fertilisers and reduce nitrate pollution. Like Haber, BASF's research team were helped by their detailed knowledge of chemical equilibria.

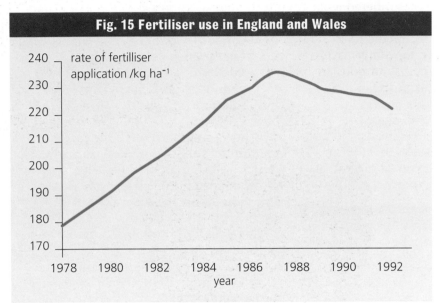

Fig. 15 Fertiliser use in England and Wales

rate of fertiliser application /kg ha^{-1}

year

Key ideas

- Increasing the pressure on a gas reaction encourages the reaction that reduces the number of molecules present.

- Increasing the concentration of a component in an equilibrium encourages the reaction that removes this component.

- A catalyst does not affect an equilibrium position or equilibrium constant.

Controlling pH

'Everyone's hair is different – dark or fair, coarse or fine, greasy or dry, curly or straight. But everyone likes their hair to look well-groomed and beautifully healthy and glossy. In my hairdressing salon we help them to get the look they want by offering all kinds of shampoos, lotions, creams and sprays for sale, as well as our cutting, styling and hair colouring services.'

Have you ever wondered what chemicals your hair stylist is massaging into your hair and scalp? What do the ingredients in shampoos and conditioners do? Many advertisements proudly claim that their shampoos are 'pH balanced', but what do they mean? And what is this mysterious stuff that grows on all our heads on which we lavish so much worry and care – and money?

Care of the Hair

The beauty of the hair depends on the care bestowed on it. The ordinary modern man, who takes his morning bath regularly, rarely neglects to place the bath-sponge on the top of his head. This wash suffices to keep the hair clean. But in many cases washing leads to a dry state of the hair, if it is not dressed immediately after with some oily preparation. As a rule brilliantine suffices.

Shampooing Preparations

These should contain a little free alkali and soap and are best when recently prepared.
Beat up the yolk of a fresh egg, mix with it rose water (10 ozs) and add:

Liquid soap	$\frac{1}{2}$ oz
Potassium carbonate	$2\frac{1}{2}$ scruples
Solution of ammonia	1 drachm
Perfume	a sufficiency

(1oz = 28.25g, 1 drachm = 3.88g, 1 scruple = 1.3g)

do you want shiny, healthy hair? do you want admiring glances?

Then use our mild herbal shampoo. **Especially formulated for you to use as often as you need.**

Herbal Shampoo

Wet hair and gently massage the shampoo into hair and scalp. Rinse thoroughly and repeat as necessary. Contains biodegradable detergents. Has not been tested on animals.

INGREDIENTS
Water, sodium lauryl sulphate, cocaidopropyl betaine, sodium chloride, perfume, dimethicone copolyol, citric acid, preservative (2-bromo-2-nitropropane-1,3-diol).
COLOURS
(E102, Acid Blue 1)

8.1 Learning objectives

After working through this chapter, you should be able to:

- **describe** an acid as a proton donor;

- **describe** a base as a proton acceptor;

- **recall** that strong acids and strong bases are fully ionised in water;

- **explain** pH in terms of hydrogen ion concentration;

- **calculate** the hydrogen ion concentration of a solution from its pH;

- **calculate** the pH of a strong acid from its concentration;

- **recall** that water is weakly ionised;

- **calculate** the pH of a solution of a strong base from its concentration, using the ionic product of water;

- **recall** that weak acids and weak bases are partially ionised in solution;

- **recall** that the pH of solutions of a salt depends upon the relative strengths of the corresponding acid and base;

- **derive** an expression for the dissociation constant of a weak acid;

- **describe** a buffer as a solution resistant to changes in pH.

8.2 The nature of hair

Hair consists mainly of a protein called α-keratin. The helical keratin molecules are twisted together in slender bundles, which are arranged side by side in microfibrils. The microfibrils lie together in strands called macrofibrils. A single hair is made up of many macrofibrils (Fig. 1).

Both eighteenth-century arisocrats and twentieth-century youth express their personality through bizarre and exaggerated hairstyles

Fig. 1 Structure of a hair

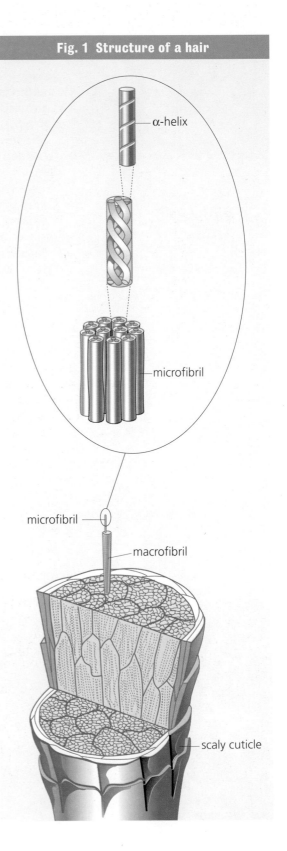

α-helix

microfibril

microfibril

macrofibril

scaly cuticle

Fig. 2 Bonding in protein molecules

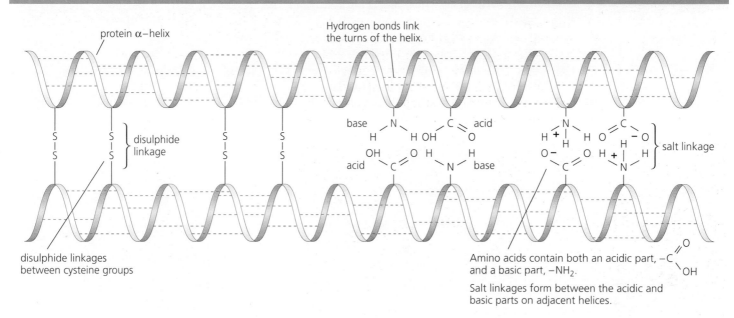

protein α−helix

Hydrogen bonds link the turns of the helix.

disulphide linkage

base ... acid

acid ... base

salt linkage

disulphide linkages between cysteine groups

Amino acids contain both an acidic part, $-C\overset{O}{\underset{OH}{}}$ and a basic part, $-NH_2$.

Salt linkages form between the acidic and basic parts on adjacent helices.

Like all proteins, keratin is a polymer of amino acids. Amino acids are organic acids which have both $-NH_2$ and $-COOH$ groups in their molecules. The helix is kept in shape by **hydrogen bonds** between the amino acids (Fig. 2). (Hydrogen bonding is dealt with in Chapter 5.)

The microfibrils are joined to each other by three types of **intermolecular bonding** (Fig. 2):

- hydrogen bonding – the same type as that holding the α-helix in position;
- salt linkages – an acid group from an amino acid on one keratin molecule interacting with a basic group on the next;
- disulphide bonds – linkages between two molecules of the sulphur-containing amino acid cysteine in adjacent keratin helices.

When the hair is wet, water gets between the microfibrils and breaks the hydrogen bonds. This is why wet hair can be stretched much more easily than dry hair (Fig. 3). Wetting the hair breaks the salt linkages too. These also break when the hair is heated – for example, with a hair-dryer.

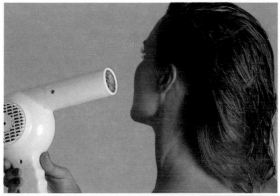

Blow-drying wet hair restores the hydrogen bonds, making sure they re-form in the right position

Fig. 3 Effect of breaking hydrogen bonds in the α-helix

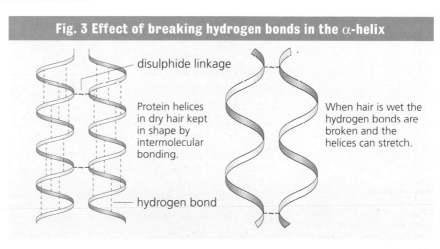

disulphide linkage

Protein helices in dry hair kept in shape by intermolecular bonding.

When hair is wet the hydrogen bonds are broken and the helices can stretch.

hydrogen bond

Both the hydrogen bonds and salt linkages re-form when the hair is cool and dry. Careful styling using blow-drying or setting will make these bonds re-form so that the hair takes up a new shape, although this is only temporary.

When hair is permed, some of the disulphide bonds are broken, and allowed to re-form in different positions (Fig. 4).

Again, this allows the hair to take up a different shape; most people want it to wave or curl. This time the change of shape is permanent. The perm lotion contains a **reducing agent**, which breaks the disulphide bonds. The 'neutraliser' that is put on the hair when perming is complete contains an **oxidising agent**, which re-forms the disulphide bonds.

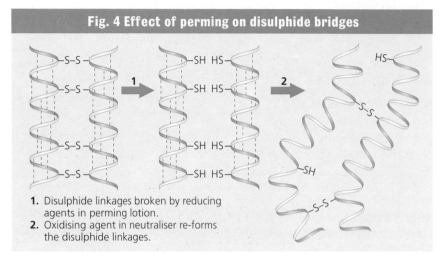

Fig. 4 Effect of perming on disulphide bridges

1. Disulphide linkages broken by reducing agents in perming lotion.
2. Oxidising agent in neutraliser re-forms the disulphide linkages.

Many people have their straight hair permed in order to make it curly. Similarly, breaking the disulphide bonds in curly hair allows it to be permanently straightened

8.3 Chemicals for cleaning

Most people wash their hair several times a week, sometimes once or twice a day. So what goes into the shampoo they use is important. A good shampoo will:
• clean hair well;
• leave hair in good condition;
• produce a pleasant lather that rinses out easily;
• be safe to use;
• leave hair smelling fragrant.

Cosmetic scientists have to balance these different requirements in formulating shampoos and other hair care products, always bearing in mind the effect that these products will have on the structure of hair.

Everyone's skin produces sweat, grease and oil, and this collects on hair, together with dust and dirt from the atmosphere. Cleaning these deposits off the hair is one of the most important tasks for a shampoo. But not all chemicals which remove grease

can be used in shampoos! One of the most effective chemicals for removing grease is sodium hydroxide, used in oven cleaners. Sodium hydroxide dissolves in water and is a **strong base** – it dissociates (ionises) completely into sodium ions and hydroxide ions:

$$NaOH(aq) \rightarrow Na^+(aq) + OH^-(aq)$$

Bases that dissolve in water, such as sodium hydroxide, are called **alkalis** (Fig. 5).

Fig. 5 Relationship between alkalis and bases

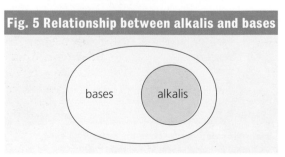

If you get oven cleaner on your skin, your skin will feel soapy. If the alkali is not removed quickly, your skin will dry out and be damaged, as the natural grease is removed. Alkali can be removed from the skin by washing with water, or it can be neutralised by reacting with an acid. Hydrochloric acid is a **strong acid** and in water it ionises completely, releasing hydrogen ions. Hydrochloric acid and sodium hydroxide react together in solution.

$$HCl(aq) \rightarrow H^+(aq) + Cl^-(aq)$$

$$HCl(aq) + NaOH(aq) \rightarrow NaCl(aq) + H_2O(l)$$

This equation does not show what happens to the ions in the solution. When we re-write it showing all the ions present, some ions appear on both sides of the equation:

$$Cl^-(aq) + H^+(aq) + Na^+(aq) + OH^-(aq) \rightarrow Na^+(aq) + Cl^-(aq) + H_2O(l)$$

The sodium ions and chloride ions do not take part in the reaction. So we can write this **neutralisation** reaction as:

$$H^+(aq) + OH^-(aq) \rightarrow H_2O(l)$$

Other strong acids and strong bases (Table 1) react similarly.

Table 1 Some common strong acids and strong bases	
Strong acids	Strong bases
hydrochloric acid HCl	sodium hydroxide NaOH
sulphuric acid H_2SO_4	potassium hydroxide KOH
nitric acid HNO_3	
phosphoric acid H_3PO_4	

 1 **Write full equations and ionic equations for the reactions between:**
 a **hydrochloric acid and potassium hydroxide solution**
 b **sulphuric acid and sodium hydroxide solution.**

All soluble acids release hydrogen ions (protons) when they dissolve in water. The Swedish chemist, Arrhenius, in 1884 described an **acid** as a substance which contains hydrogen and will release hydrogen ions when it dissolves in water. In reactions in water, a **base** is a substance which reacts with an acid to form a **salt** and water.

These definitions are limited to substances that dissolve in water. But some proton-transfer reactions do not involve water at all. For example, hydrogen chloride gas reacts with ammonia gas to form ammonium chloride:

$$HCl(g) \quad + \quad NH_3(g) \quad \rightarrow \quad NH_4Cl(s)$$
hydrogen   ammonia   ammonium
chloride   chloride

In this reaction, hydrogen chloride has donated a proton to ammonia to form the ammonium ion (Fig. 6).

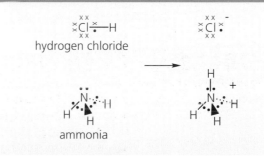

Fig. 6 Protonation of ammonia by hydrogen chloride

Student holding stoppers from ammonia and hydrochloric acid bottles near each other

In 1923 the Danish scientist Brønsted and the British chemist Lowry extended the theory of acid–base behaviour to non-aqueous reactions. They defined an acid as a **proton donor**. Not all compounds containing hydrogen are acids. In organic molecules, the hydrogen atoms attached directly to a carbon atom are not available for donation. Only a hydrogen atom that is attached to an electronegative atom such as oxygen, nitrogen or chlorine is acidic.

 2 Explain why methane does not act as a proton donor, but methanol (CH_3OH) and methanoic acid (HCOOH) do.

3 Write an equation to show how methanoic acid ionises in water.

Brønsted and Lowry also argued that if an acid donates protons, then something which accepts protons is the opposite of an acid. They defined a base as a **proton acceptor**. Brønsted–Lowry definitions apply to all reactions of acids, not just those that take place in aqueous solutions. When an acid reacts it gives hydrogen ions to a base:

$$CH_3COOH(l) + OH^-(aq) \rightarrow CH_3COO^-(aq) + H_2O(l)$$
ethanoic acid | base accepts | ethanoate ion
donates proton | proton

$$HCl(g) + NH_3(g) \rightarrow NH_4^+ Cl^-(s)$$
acid donates proton | base accepts proton

$$HCl(g) + H_2O(l) \rightarrow H_3O^+(aq) + Cl^-(aq)$$
acid donates proton | base accepts proton

$$H^+(aq) + OH^-(aq) \rightarrow H_2O(l)$$
proton acceptor

In the third of these equations $H_3O^+(aq)$ represents a hydrated proton, which is often written simply as $H^+(aq)$.

 4 Identify the acids and bases in the following reactions:
a $CuO(s) + H_2SO_4(aq) \rightarrow CuSO_4(aq) + H_2O(l)$
b $NH_4^+(aq) + OH^-(aq) \rightleftharpoons NH_3(aq) + H_2O(l)$
c $CH_3COO^-(aq) + H_3O^+(aq) \rightleftharpoons CH_3COOH(aq) + H_2O(l)$

Strong acids and alkalis are usually too harmful to body tissue to be used on hair and skin. We must look at some alternatives.

The strong base sodium hydroxide can completely remove the burnt-on grease that collects on ovens

Key ideas

- Acids are proton donors.
- Bases are proton acceptors.

- Acid–base reactions involve transfer of protons.

8.4 Soaps

Soaps have been used for a long time to remove grease and dirt from skin and clothes. Soaps are made when a strong alkali reacts with an organic fatty acid. The earliest soaps were made by boiling wood ash which contains some potassium carbonate, together with some animal fat.

Soaps make good cleansers because their molecules contain a long hydrocarbon chain which interacts with grease and oil, helping to **emulsify** the oil (Fig. 7).

The reaction that produces a soap is the same as the one between an acid and a base that produces a salt:

$$RCOOH + NaOH \xrightarrow{\text{H}^+ \text{ transfer}} RCOONa + H_2O$$

acid	base	salt	water
fatty acid	sodium hydroxide	soap	

where R represents the long hydrocarbon chain of a fatty acid.

Q5 Stearic acid, $CH_3(CH_2)_{16}COOH$, is often used to make soap. Write the equation for the reaction between stearic acid and sodium hydroxide.

Soaps can remove too much of the natural oil from the hair, as well as cleaning off the surface dirt. This can make the hair very dry. In hard water areas, soaps can leave scum in the hair.

Fig. 7 Soap action

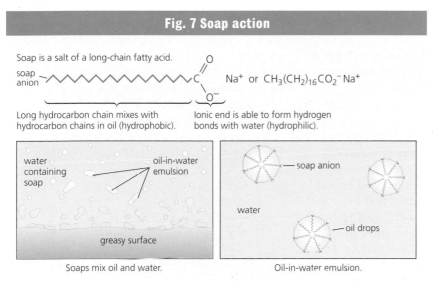

Soap is a salt of a long-chain fatty acid.

soap anion

$CH_3(CH_2)_{16}CO_2^- Na^+$

Long hydrocarbon chain mixes with hydrocarbon chains in oil (hydrophobic).

Ionic end is able to form hydrogen bonds with water (hydrophilic).

water containing soap

oil-in-water emulsion

greasy surface

Soaps mix oil and water.

soap anion

water

oil drops

Oil-in-water emulsion.

8.5 The pH scale

Put universal indicator on soap, and the colour will change from green to blue, showing that soap is alkaline. Shampoos, too, will change the colour of universal indicator – to orange, yellow or green depending on their formulation (Fig. 8). Universal indicator changes colour according to the concentration of hydrogen ions in the solution, i.e. how acidic or alkaline the solution is. Other indicators, such as methyl orange and phenolphthalein, also respond to changes in hydrogen ion concentration.

Fig. 8 Hair care products and the pH scale

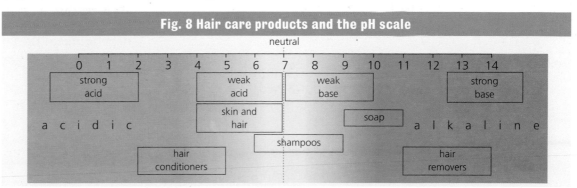

neutral

0 1 2 3 4 5 6 7 8 9 10 11 12 13 14

strong acid

weak acid

weak base

strong base

skin and hair

soap

acidic

alkaline

shampoos

hair conditioners

hair removers

Indicators give a rough measure of the **pH** of a solution. pH is used to express the acidity of a solution, an exact measure is given by a pH meter. We could use hydrogen ion concentration as a measure of acidity, but if we do, we find we have very small numbers to handle. The pH scale converts them into a less awkward form.

The pH of a solution is the negative of the log (to the base 10) of the hydrogen ion concentration in the solution.

$$pH = -\log_{10} [H^+]$$

Acids and pH

We can apply this definition to calculate the pH of a solution of hydrochloric acid – say a 0.1 mol dm^{-3} solution.

Hydrochloric acid is a strong acid. All the hydrogen chloride present is fully dissociated into hydrogen ions and chloride ions. So in 1 litre of 0.1 mol dm^{-3} hydrochloric acid there are 0.1 moles of H$^+$ ions and 0.1 moles of Cl$^-$ ions.

$$
\begin{aligned}
[H^+] &= 0.1 \\
\text{So, } pH &= -\log_{10} [H^+] \\
&= -\log_{10} 0.1 \\
&= -(-1) \\
&= 1
\end{aligned}
$$

It's a lot easier to talk about 'a pH of 1' than to say 'a hydrogen ion concentration of 0.1 mol dm^{-3}'.

 6 **Calculate the pH of 0.01 mol dm^{-3} hydrochloric acid.**

Moving up the pH scale by 1 unit means that the hydrogen ion concentration reduces tenfold.

 7 **Calculate the pH of**
   a 0.1 mol dm–3 nitric acid
   b 0.2 mol dm–3 hydrochloric acid
   c 5 mol dm–3 nitric acid.

pH of shampoos

The salt linkages that hold keratin molecules together are stable only within the pH range 4.5–6. Outside that pH range, they begin to break down and the hair may be permanently damaged. So it is important that the pH of a shampoo lies close to that range; it is usually between 5.5 and 8.5. Given a pH, we can calculate the hydrogen ion concentration in the solution. What is the hydrogen ion concentration in a shampoo of pH 6?

$$
\begin{aligned}
pH &= -\log_{10} [H^+] \\
6 &= -\log_{10} [H^+] \\
-6 &= \log_{10} [H^+] \\
\text{So, } [H^+] &= 1 \times 10^{-6}
\end{aligned}
$$

In a shampoo of pH 6 the hydrogen ion concentration is 1×10^{-6} mol dm^{-3}. The hydrogen ion concentration in 0.1 mol dm^{-3} hydrochloric acid is a million times greater than that in this shampoo.

 8 **What is the hydrogen ion concentration in:**
   a a hair conditioner of pH 3?
   b a shampoo of pH 5.5?

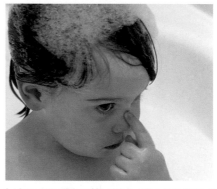

A shampoo with a pH of 6.5 will not irritate the eyes, which is a particular advantage in children's shampoos

pH of water

Water can act as an acid or a base depending on the conditions. It acts as a proton acceptor (base) when hydrogen chloride dissolves in it:

$$HCl(g) + H_2O(l) \rightarrow H_3O^+(aq) + Cl^-(aq)$$

It acts as an acid when ammonia dissolves in it:

$$NH_3(g) + H_2O(l) \rightleftharpoons NH_4^+(aq) + OH^-(aq)$$

Pure water is very weakly ionised:

$$H_2O(l) \rightleftharpoons H^+(aq) + OH^-(aq)$$

The equilibrium constant (see Chapter 7) for this process is:

$$K = \frac{[H^+][OH^-]}{[H_2O]}$$

The concentration of water molecules is enormous, because of the low degree of ionisation of water. We can consider it constant. This gives us a useful expression:

$$K_w = [H^+][OH^-]$$

where K_w is called the **ionic product of water**. At 25 °C, K_w is 10^{-14} mol^2 dm^{-6}.

We can calculate the pH of pure water, using the fact that it contains equal numbers of hydrogen ions and hydroxide ions:

$$[H^+] = [OH^-]$$

At 25 °C, from K_w:

$$[H^+]^2 = 10^{-14}$$
$$[H^+] = 10^{-7}$$

$$\begin{aligned} pH &= -\log_{10}[H^+] \\ &= -\log_{10} 10^{-7} \\ &= 7 \end{aligned}$$

The pH of pure water is thus 7 at 25 °C.

 9   **What is the concentration of hydroxide ions in pure water at 25 °C?**

Even though the pH of pure water is the same as that of a shampoo, it won't get your hair clean!

 10 **The ionic product of water increases slightly with increasing temperature.**
  a Is the ionisation of water exothermic or endothermic?
  b Will the pH of water at 60 °C be greater or less than 7?
Explain your answers.

Bases and pH

When bases dissolve in water they produce hydroxide ions. These hydroxide ions shift the equilibrium of the ionisation of water so that there are far fewer hydrogen ions. The ionic product of water remains constant.

$$H_2O(l) \rightleftharpoons H^+(aq) + OH^-(aq)$$

We can calculate the pH of a strong alkali. It is a little more complex than calculating the pH of a strong acid. Sodium hydroxide ionises fully in solution:

$$NaOH(aq) \rightarrow Na^+(aq) + OH^-(aq)$$

In 1 litre of 0.1 mol dm^{-3} sodium hydroxide solution, there are 0.1 moles of hydroxide ions. We use the water ionisation equilibrium to calculate the hydrogen ion concentration:

$$K_w = [H^+][OH^-]$$

At 25 °C, K_w is 10^{-14} mol^2 dm^{-6}.

So, $[OH^-] = 0.1$

$$\begin{aligned} [H^+] &= \frac{K_w}{[OH^-]} \\ &= \frac{10^{-14}}{0.1} \\ &= 10^{-13} \end{aligned}$$

$$\begin{aligned} pH &= -\log_{10}[H^+] \\ &= -\log_{10} 10^{-13} \\ &= -(-13) \\ &= 13 \end{aligned}$$

The pH of a 0.1 mol dm^{-3} solution of sodium hydroxide at 25 °C is 13.

11 Calculate the pH of
a 0.01 mol dm⁻³ sodium hydroxide solution
b 0.3 mol dm⁻³ potassium hydroxide solution.

a 0.01 mol dm^{-3} sodium hydroxide solution
b 0.3 mol dm^{-3} potassium hydroxide solution.

If hair is treated with a solution of very high pH, then the hydrogen bonds, the salt linkages and the disulphide links are all broken, and the hair structure collapses. Hair removers are creams or lotions with a high pH (Fig. 8, page 93) which actually destroy unwanted hair. Unless used with great care, they will also damage the skin.

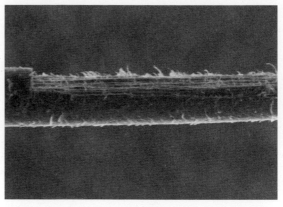

Photomicrograph of a hair disintergrating in high-pH conditions

Key ideas

- The pH of a solution is the negative of the log to the base 10 of the hydrogen ion concentration in the solution:
  $pH = -\log_{10} [H^+]$.

- Water is weakly ionised in an equilibrium reaction.

- The ionic product of water is the product of the concentrations of hydrogen ions and hydroxide ions in pure water:
  $K_w = [H^+(aq)] [OH^-(aq)]$.

- At 25 °C, $K_w = 1 \times 10^{-14}$ mol^2 dm^{-6}.

8.6 Controlling the pH of shampoos

If a shampoo is within the pH range 5.5–8.5, it may be either weakly acidic or weakly alkaline. How can this be achieved by the manufacturer?

One way to get a weakly acidic solution is to dissolve a weak acid in water. Acids like ethanoic acid, citric acid and lactic acid are weak acids. For example, ethanoic acid (CH₃COOH, the acid in vinegar) only releases

part of its available acidic hydrogen when it dissolves in water (Fig. 9). An equilibrium (see Chapter 7) is set up between the undissociated acid and the ethanoate ions in solution:

$$CH_3COOH(aq) + H_2O(l) \rightleftharpoons CH_3COO^-(aq) + H_3O^+(aq)$$
ethanoic acid   ethanoate ion

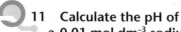

Fig. 9 Ionisation of strong and weak acids in solution

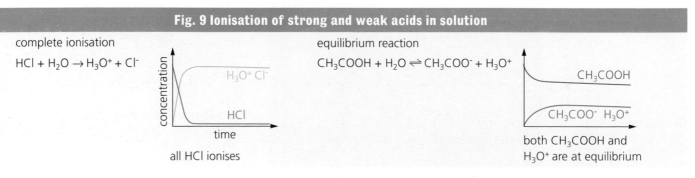

complete ionisation

$HCl + H_2O \rightarrow H_3O^+ + Cl^-$

all HCl ionises

equilibrium reaction

$CH_3COOH + H_2O \rightleftharpoons CH_3COO^- + H_3O^+$

both CH₃COOH and H₃O⁺ are at equilibrium

The extent of dissociation is given by the equilibrium constant for the process:

$$K_c = \frac{[CH_3COO^-(aq)]\,[H_3O^+(aq)]}{[CH_3COOH(aq)]\,[H_2O(l)]}$$

Because the ionic product of water is so low, water molecules are present in vast excess. So the concentration of water molecules hardly changes. We can rewrite the equilibrium expression as:

$$K_a = \frac{[CH_3COO^-(aq)]\,[H_3O^+(aq)]}{[CH_3COOH(aq)]}$$

where K_a is called the **acid dissociation constant** for the weak acid. For ethanoic acid, K_a is 1.7×10^{-5} mol dm^{-3}.

For the dissociation of any weak acid, general formula HA, K_a is given by:

$$K_a = \frac{[A^-]\,[H^+]}{[HA]}$$

where all concentrations are those at equilibrium.

 12 **Write an expression for the dissociation constant of butanoic acid, $CH_3(CH_2)_2COOH$.**

Shampoos could be made weakly alkaline by adding a weak alkali, such as ammonia solution. Weak alkalis, like weak acids, are only partly ionised in solution:

$$NH_3(aq) + H_2O(l) \rightleftharpoons NH_4^+(aq) + OH^-(aq)$$

In fact, a weakly acidic shampoo does not normally contain a weak organic acid. Its pH depends instead on the salts it contains. We might expect all salts to be neutral, but they are not (Table 2).

All soluble salts ionise completely in water. For example, when sodium ethanoate dissolves in water it ionises completely to form sodium ions and ethanoate ions:

$$CH_3COONa(s) \xrightarrow{\text{dissolves in water}} CH_3COO^-(aq) + Na^+(aq)$$

Ethanoic acid is a weak acid. The presence of ethanoate ions means that the equilibrium reaction involving ethanoic acid can be set up:

$$CH_3COO^-(aq) + H_3O^+(aq) \rightleftharpoons CH_3COOH(aq) + H_2O(l)$$

(This is the same equation as the ionisation of ethanoic acid, but written the other way round – remember, equilibria can be approached from either direction.) As this reaction reaches equilibrium, it removes some hydrogen ions from the solution to give undissociated acid. As the hydrogen ion concentration falls, more hydroxide ions are produced (because the ionic product of water remains constant). As a result, the pH of the solution increases, and it becomes slightly alkaline.

For similar reasons, ammonium chloride solutions are acidic:

$$NH_4Cl(s) \xrightarrow{\text{dissolves in water}} NH_4^+(aq) + Cl^-(aq)$$

When ammonia or ammonium ions are present in solution the following equilibrium is set up:

$$\underset{\text{acid}}{NH_4^+(aq)} + OH^-(aq) \rightleftharpoons \underset{\text{weak base}}{NH_3(aq)} + H_2O(l)$$

Table 2 pH of some salts in 0.1 mol dm^{-3} aqueous solution at 25 °C		
sodium chloride	7.0	salts of strong base + strong acid, neutral solutions
sodium nitrate	7.0	
potassium nitrate	7.0	
potassium sulphate	7.0	
sodium carbonate	9.7	salts of strong base + weak acid, alkaline solutions
sodium lactate	8.0	
potassium lactate	8.0	
sodium citrate	8.1	
sodium ethanoate	8.9	
ammonium chloride	5.1	salts of weak base + strong acid, acidic solutions
ammonium nitrate	5.1	
butylammonium chloride	5.9	
ammonium citrate	6.2	salts of weak base + weak acid, pH of solutions depends on relative strengths
ammonium ethanoate	7.0	

Some of the ammonium ions from ammonium chloride, and some of the hydroxide ions from water, are used up in the formation of undissociated ammonia. The net effect is a slight excess of hydrogen ions in solution – so the solution is acidic.

Key ideas

- Strong acids and bases are fully ionised or dissociated in aqueous solution.

- Weak acids and bases are partially dissociated in solution.

- The acid dissociation constant of a weak acid HA is given by the expression

$$K_a = \frac{[A^-(aq)] [H^+(aq)]}{[HA(aq)]}$$

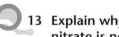 **13** Explain why a solution of sodium nitrate is neutral.

14 Explain why a 0.1 mol dm^{-3} potassium carbonate solution will have the same pH as 0.1 mol dm^{-3} sodium carbonate solution.

8.7 Composition of shampoos

Table 3 Some soapless anionic detergents	
sodium lauryl sulphate	white powder or paste
monoethanolamine lauryl sulphate	liquids varying
triethanolamine lauryl sulphate	from pale yellow
ammonium lauryl sulphate	to orange
sodium lauryl ether sulphate	colourless liquid
sodium alkylbenzenesulphate	powder or paste

The degreasing agents in modern shampoos are soapless detergents (Table 3). These soapless detergents are all salts. Like soap, their molecules contain both a long hydrocarbon chain and an ionic group (Fig. 9). Also like soap, they emulsify oil; in fact, they are better emulsifiers than soap. They do not form scum in hard water.

$$C_{12}H_{25}OSO_3Na(s) \xrightarrow{\text{dissolves in water}} C_{12}H_{25}OSO_3^-(aq) + Na^+(aq)$$
sodium lauryl sulphate   emulsifying anion

Detergents like this are called anionic detergents, because it is the anion that is the active emulsifier. They do not remove all the natural oils from hair, because they are less alkaline than soap.

Lauryl sulphonic acid is used to make some of these detergents. It is a much stronger acid than stearic acid. So sodium stearate (soap) is more strongly alkaline in solution than sodium lauryl sulphate (Fig. 10).

Fig. 10 Dissociation of some salts of fatty acids

$$StNa(s) + H_2O(l) \xrightarrow{100\%} St^-(aq) + Na^+(aq)$$
$$St^-(aq) + H_2O(l) \rightleftharpoons St\,H(aq) + OH^-(aq)$$

StH is a weak acid, many St$^-$ ions react

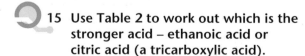

OH$^-$ StH
high [OH$^-$], alkaline
St$^-$

$$LSNa(s) + H_2O \xrightarrow{100\%} LS^-(aq) + Na^+(aq)$$
$$LS^-(aq) + H_2O \rightleftharpoons LSH(aq) + OH^-(aq)$$

LSH is a stronger acid, few LS$^-$ ions react

LS$^-$
lower [OH$^-$], less alkaline
OH$^-$ LSH

15 Use Table 2 to work out which is the stronger acid – ethanoic acid or citric acid (a tricarboxylic acid).

Manufacturers formulate different shampoos for different hair types (Table 4). Soapless detergents alone would give a runny shampoo, so sodium chloride or ammonium chloride is added as a thickener. Shampoos also contain preservatives, to stop the growth of bacteria and give the shampoo a longer shelf-life. Colour and perfume make the product attractive. The combination of the different components means that the pH of the shampoo is not dependent on the pH of the detergent alone. Components are often added to adjust the pH to an appropriate level.

Table 5 Formulations of shampoos/% by mass, based on triethanolamine lauryl sulphate			
	Dry hair	Normal hair	Greasy hair
triethanolamine lauryl sulphate	30	35	40
coconut diethanolamide	4	3	2
water	66	62	58
ammonium chloride – to thicken	a little		
perfume, colour, preservative	a little		

Q 16 Explain why the proportion of triethanolamine lauryl sulphate is different for shampoos intended for different hair types.

8.8 Hair conditioners

Washing hair, even with the gentlest of soapless detergents, can leave it dry and brittle, and chemical treatments like perming and bleaching can make matters worse. A conditioner can be used alongside a shampoo to counteract this effect.

The natural pH in the bulk of hair and on the surface of the skin is in the range 4–6, but that of hair conditioners is much lower, about 2–3. At first glance this may seem odd.

The reason lies in the balance of charges on the surface of the hair. This is affected by wind, weather and combing. Negative charges build up on the ends of the hair, so that the hairs become charged with 'static electricity' and repel each other. The pH on the hair surface rises, and its surface roughens as the cuticle scales no longer lie smoothly. In this condition it can become quite unmanageable.

Hair conditioners are designed to restore the balance of charges. At their low pH, they can supply positively charged ions (cations) which lower the pH of the hair surface to its more normal value. The cuticle surface regains its smoothness, and the hair becomes soft, silky and easy to keep in order again.

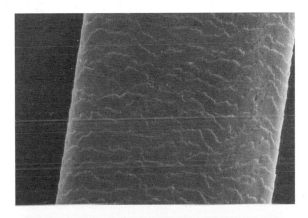

Top. Photomicrograph of a single hair, in good condition. Bottom. The same hair, after perming: the surface is roughened and needs special treatment to make it lie smooth again

8.9 Buffers

Human skin is weakly acidic, because its outermost layer contains a mixture of water-soluble acids and salts, which are secreted in sweat. But weak acids and alkalis do not alter the pH of the skin surface. This is because the skin secretions form a natural **buffer**.

A buffer is a system which resists changes in pH when acid or alkali is added to it. Many buffers contain either a weak acid and a corresponding salt, or a weak base and a corresponding salt. The buffering action of skin is mainly due to a mixture of lactic acid (2-hydroxypropanoic acid, $CH_3CH(OH)COOH$) and a lactate. Lactic acid, written here as LaH, is a weak acid:

$$LaH(aq) + H_2O(l) \rightleftharpoons La^-(aq) + H_3O^+(aq)$$

So we can write the acid dissociation constant:

$$K_a = \frac{[La^-(aq)]\,[H_3O^+(aq)]}{[LaH(aq)]}$$

If sodium lactate is added to lactic acid the concentrations of both La^- and LaH are high.

$$LaNa(aq) \xrightarrow{\text{dissolves in water}} La^-(aq) + Na^+(aq)$$

The presence of lactate ions pushes the lactic acid equilibrium towards undissociated acid.

A buffer normally contains relatively high concentrations of both undissociated acid and acid anions. If acid is added to the buffer, the equilibrium adjusts to give more

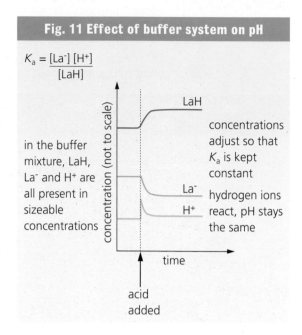

Fig. 11 Effect of buffer system on pH

$K_a = \dfrac{[La^-]\,[H^+]}{[LaH]}$

in the buffer mixture, LaH, La^- and H^+ are all present in sizeable concentrations

concentrations adjust so that K_a is kept constant

hydrogen ions react, pH stays the same

concentration (not to scale)

time

acid added

undissociated acid (Fig. 11). If alkali is added to the buffer, the equilibrium adjusts to give more acid anions. Except in the presence of large quantities of acid or alkali, the buffer maintains the equilibrium reaction and the pH remains steady. K_a remains constant throughout. So moderate amounts of acids or alkali have no effect on skin; only the strongest acids and alkalis cause serious burns.

Shampoos and conditioners, and indeed most other cosmetics, are often buffered to keep their pH constant. Some products even advertise their pH as matching that of skin. But when you see 'pH balanced' on a hair care product, remember that all products are formulated so that their pH is appropriate for their use.

Key ideas

- A buffer is a mixture which is resistant to changes in pH.

Colour from chemicals

'I design and make decorative ceramics, especially vases, teapots and mugs.

When I'm making a mug, I mould the damp clay into shape and brush it over with a liquid glaze. Then I put the mug into a kiln, where it is fired at a very high temperature. This dries out the clay and makes it hard and strong. The ingredients of the glaze melt together to form a glassy coating over the surface of the mug. That stops liquids like coffee or tea from soaking into it when it's being used.

Glazes give me the chance to decorate the ceramics imaginatively. I can choose from an enormous range of colours and create unique designs.'

Ceramic ware has been around for thousands of years. The ancient Egyptians, and later the Greeks and Romans, produced beautiful ceramic pieces, and like today's potters they glazed them for both decoration and protection. Look into any houseware shop in the high street, and you will see just a few of the huge number of coloured glazes that are available. What goes into these glazes? How do the potters produce so many different colours?

Modern china uses a stunning range of colourful glazes

9.1 Learning objectives

After working through this chapter, you should be able to:

- **describe** transition metals as elements with an incomplete d electron sub-shell in their atoms or ions;

- **describe** the characteristic properties of transition metals, including variable oxidation state, formation of complex ions, formation of coloured ions and catalytic activity;

- **explain** oxidation as electron loss and reduction as electron gain;

- **recall** that oxidation and reduction happen together in a redox reaction;

- **derive** the oxidation state of elements in compounds and ions;

- **explain** redox reactions in terms of changes in oxidation state;

- **describe** a complex transition metal ion as a central metal ion bonded to ligands;

- **describe** the coordination number of a transition metal in a complex ion.

9.2 Pigments for glazes

Glazes are based on oxides of silicon, aluminium, sodium, calcium and boron, finely powdered and suspended in water. The simplest glazes are colourless, but most glazes are coloured to provide decoration. Colours are produced by adding to the glaze a small amount of metal oxide – usually a transition metal oxide. In order to understand how transition metal compounds can be used to produce coloured glazes, we need to know something about the arrangement of electrons within the metal atoms.

Left. Applying the glaze

Top right. Pottery being loaded into a kiln

Bottom right. Pottery being taken out of a kiln after firing

Table 1 Some properties of Period 4 elements										
	Sc	Ti	V	Cr	Mn	Fe	Co	Ni	Cu	Zn
melting point/°C	1539	1675	1900	1890	1244	1535	1495	1453	1083	420
first ionisation energy/kJ mol^{-1}	633	659	650	653	717	762	759	736	745	906
outer electron configuration	$3d^1\,4s^2$	$3d^2\,4s^2$	$3d^3\,4s^2$	$3d^5\,4s^1$	$3d^5\,4s^2$	$3d^6\,4s^2$	$3d^7\,4s^2$	$3d^8\,4s^2$	$3d^{10}\,4s^1$	$3d^{10}\,4s^2$
atomic radius/nm	0.164	0.147	0.135	0.129	0.137	0.126	0.125	0.125	0.128	0.137

Transition metals

The transition metal elements can be found at the centre of the Periodic Table (see page 30). The first transition metals in the Periodic Table (in order of atomic number) are the elements from scandium to copper. These are situated in Period 4.

The transition metals in this period are quite similar in some of their properties (Table 1). These similarities can be explained by looking at how electrons fill electron shells or energy levels.

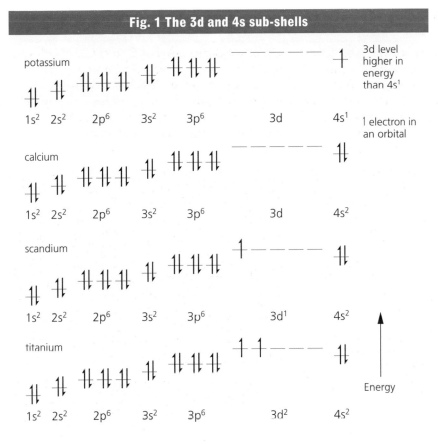

Fig. 1 The 3d and 4s sub-shells

potassium

$1s^2$ $2s^2$ $2p^6$ $3s^2$ $3p^6$ $3d$ $4s^1$

3d level higher in energy than $4s^1$

1 electron in an orbital

calcium

$1s^2$ $2s^2$ $2p^6$ $3s^2$ $3p^6$ $3d$ $4s^2$

scandium

$1s^2$ $2s^2$ $2p^6$ $3s^2$ $3p^6$ $3d^1$ $4s^2$

titanium

$1s^2$ $2s^2$ $2p^6$ $3s^2$ $3p^6$ $3d^2$ $4s^2$

Energy

The second electron shell or energy level in atoms has two sub-shells or sub-levels: s and p. The third shell has three sub-shells: s, p and d. The fourth shell has four sub-shells: s, p, d and f. You might expect these sub-shells to be filled in the order 2s, 2p, 3s, 3p, 3d, 4s, 4p, and so on. This is indeed the case up until the element argon, but the extra electron in potassium atoms does not go into the 3d sub-shell (Fig. 1). Instead, it goes into the 4s sub-shell. The 4s sub-shell is filled with a second electron to form calcium atoms. This is because in potassium and calcium atoms the 4s sub-shell is lower in energy than the 3d sub-shell. The 3d sub-shell gradually fills as the first row of transition metals is crossed (Fig. 1). You can see from Table 1 that the **atomic radii** of the transition metals are similar across Period 4, with a very slight decrease going from scandium to copper. The **first ionisation energies** are similar too. Compare this with the elements sodium to argon in Period 3, where the

atomic radius decreases markedly, and the first ionisation energy increases.

For the elements sodium to argon the 3s and 3p sub-shells are being filled as the period is crossed. The outermost 3s and 3p electrons do not shield each other from the increase in nuclear charge caused by the additional protons in the nucleus. This means that the electrons are held more tightly, so that the radius decreases and the first ionisation energy increases.

In transition metals the situation is different, because the outer 4s electrons remain the same across the row, while the inner 3d electron sub-shell is being filled. The increasing number of 3d electrons across the period shields the 4s electrons from the increase in nuclear charge. The addition of more electrons to the 3d sub-shell does not greatly affect this shielding, so that both the atomic radius and the ionisation energy remain similar.

The outer electron configuration of copper is not $3d^9 4s^2$ (Table 1). This is because a full 3d sub-shell with one 4s electron ($3d^{10} 4s^1$) is more stable than $3d^9 4s^2$.

1 Can you suggest a reason why the outer electron configuration of chromium is not $3d^4 4s^2$?

2 Suggest another property that might be similar for transition metals.

Zinc: an exception

Zinc has a much lower melting point than the other elements in Period 4, and a higher first ionisation energy. This is because in zinc the 3d and 4s sub-shells are full, and therefore more stable. Transition metals are often defined as those elements which have an incomplete d sub-shell in their atoms or ions. Therefore, zinc is not normally regarded as a transition metal. Scandium does not have an incomplete d sub-shell in its common ion scandium(III). The 3d sub-shell is empty. Scandium compounds do not show the properties of transition metal compounds.

9.3 Colours of glazes

Transition metals are characterised by the following properties:
- their **oxidation states** are variable;
- they form **complex ions**;
- their ions are coloured;
- they take part in catalytic activity.

It is the combination of the first three of these properties that makes transition metals so useful as colourants for glazes.

The Chinese used iron oxides and copper oxides in glazes as long ago as 200 BC . The potters of the time could produce glazes in a whole range of shades using just these compounds as colourants. How did they do it?

Iron and copper, like all transition metals, can form more than one oxide.

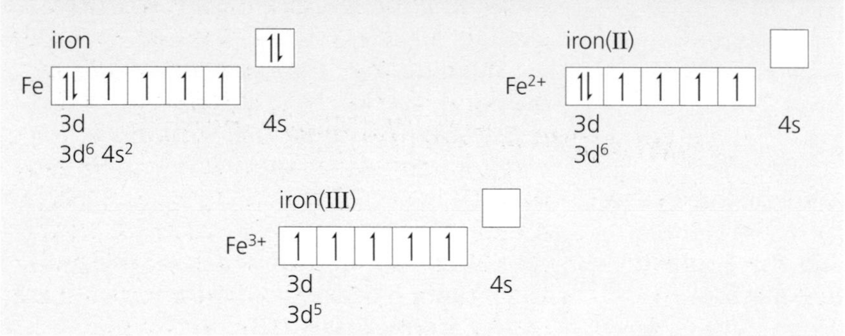

The stable oxides of iron include iron(II) oxide (FeO) and iron(III) oxide (Fe$_2$O$_3$). When a transition metal atom ionises, it loses its outermost 4s electrons first. In the case of iron an iron(II) ion forms. The outer electron configuration of the Fe^{2+} ion is thus 3d^6. The iron(II) ion can lose another electron to form an iron(III) ion with an outer electron configuration of 3d^5 (Fig. 2). In a similar manner, the oxides of copper are copper(I) oxide (Cu$_2$O) and copper(II) oxide (CuO). These four oxides each have a different colour (Table 2).

Fig. 2 Electron configuration of iron and its ions

iron

Fe | 3d | 4s
3d^6 4s^2

iron(II)

Fe^{2+} | 3d | 4s
3d^6

iron(III)

Fe^{3+} | 3d | 4s
3d^5

Table 2 Colours of iron and copper oxides

Compound	Colour
iron(II) oxide	green
iron(III) oxide	brown
copper(II) oxide	black
copper(I) oxide	red

3 What is the outer electron configuration for each of the following ions:
a Cu$^+$?
b Cu^{2+}?
c Mn^{2+}?
d Cr^{3+}?

9.4 Redox reactions in the kiln

The colour of a glazed product depends on the oxide used, and also on other factors. These include:
- whether there are **oxidising** or **reducing agents** present inside the kiln;
- how much pigment the glaze contains;
- what other chemicals are in the glaze, particularly acids or alkalis.

Iron(II) oxide is easily oxidised to iron(III) oxide on heating in air. If a potter is using iron oxide glazes and wants a brown colour, the iron must be present as iron(III) ions. For this to happen there must be oxidising conditions in the kiln. In the oxidation of iron(II) oxide to iron(III) oxide, an electron is lost from each Fe^{2+} ion. The oxide ion remains unchanged. We can show this process by a **half-equation**:

$$Fe^{2+} \rightarrow Fe^{3+} + e^-$$ (Equation 1)

The half equation shows exactly what is being oxidised. Notice that the charges on each side balance. **Oxidation** is a process of electron loss. For every species that is oxidised, another is reduced. If oxygen is the oxidising agent, then the oxygen itself will be reduced to form oxide ions.

We can show this by another half-equation:

$$O_2 + 4e^- \rightarrow 2O^{2-} \qquad \text{(Equation 2)}$$

This half-equation shows that the oxygen atoms gain electrons to form oxide ions. Again, the charges on each side balance. **Reduction** is a process of electron gain.

If you combine these two half-equations, you can find the full equation for the reaction. Start by looking at the numbers of electrons involved. The iron(II) ions give electrons to the oxygen atoms. In combining the two half-equations the number of electrons must cancel out, as they are transferred from the reducing agent to the oxidising agent. Half-equation 1 must be multiplied by 4 to make this happen:

$$4Fe^{2+} \rightarrow 4Fe^{3+} + 4e^-$$
$$O_2 + 4e^- \rightarrow 2O^{2-}$$

Combining these gives:

$$4Fe^{2+} + O_2 \rightarrow 4Fe^{3+} + 2O^{2-} \qquad \text{(Equation 3)}$$

The full equation, showing the iron oxides and oxygen instead of just the ions, is:

$$4FeO + O_2 \rightarrow 4Fe_2O_3$$

This describes the reaction correctly, but Equation 3 shows more clearly what is being oxidised and what is being reduced. Chemists call reactions involving oxidation and reduction **redox reactions**.

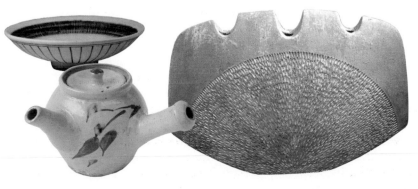

Glazes containing manganese produce different coloured glazes depending on the reducing or oxidising conditions in the kiln

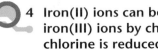 **4** Iron(II) ions can be oxidised to iron(III) ions by chlorine. The chlorine is reduced to chloride ions (Cl^-).
  a Write half-equations for the oxidation step and the reduction step.
  b Combine them to give a full redox equation.

More complex redox reactions

Redox reactions form the basis of a great deal of chemistry. As well as reactions between simple anions and cations, there are more complex redox reactions. For example, potassium manganate(VII) ($KMnO_4$) can oxidise iron(II) ions. In this reaction the manganese is reduced. It is useful to look at how we can explain this in terms of transferring electrons, and what the 'VII' means.

Manganese is a transition metal and has several valencies or **oxidation states**. It has an outer electron configuration of $3d^5\,4s^2$ in its ground state. Manganese can easily lose the two 4s electrons to form Mn^{2+} ions. It can also form compounds in which more than two outer electrons are involved in bonding. For example, in the oxide MnO_2, four electrons are involved in bonding. In the ion MnO_4^-, however, there is no simple Mn^{7+} ion. All seven outer electrons are involved in making covalent bonds with the oxygen atoms.

Manganese(IV) oxide (MnO_2) is brown. Adding manganese and iron oxides to a clear glaze gives it a brown transparent look, called 'Rockingham brown'. Manganate(VII) ions are purple. They too can be used as colourants; they can produce a pink or purple colour, depending on their concentration. In *oxidising* kiln conditions, manganese glazes will be purple; in *reducing* kiln conditions they will be brown. This is because the manganese can be either oxidised to MnO_4^- or reduced to MnO_2.

$$\overset{\text{oxidation}}{\underset{\text{reduction}}{MnO_2 \;\rightleftharpoons\; MnO_4^-}}$$

brown   purple

9.5 Oxidation states

Transition metals have many different oxidation states. Fortunately, there is a straightforward way of describing redox changes involving ions and elements.

In the MnO_4^- ion the manganese is described as being in oxidation state +7 or (VII). (This doesn't mean that there is a 7+ charge on the manganese.) In iron(II) oxide, the iron has an oxidation state of +2 or (II), and the oxygen is in oxidation state of –2. We can think of the oxidation state of an element in a compound or ion as the charge the element would have if it was entirely electrovalently bonded.

You can use the rules set out in Fig. 3 to work out the oxidation state of many elements. For example, in the SO_4^{2-} ion the oxygen has an oxidation state of –2, because it is in a compound. Four oxygen atoms give a total of –8. The ion also carries a 2– charge, which must be taken into account. Sulphur therefore has an oxidation state of +6 to balance the oxygen and leave a 2– charge on the ion. The ion is called the sulphate(VI) ion.

Fig. 3 Simple rules for assigning oxidation states

You can use these rules with most inorganic substances.

1 The oxidation state of an element in its elemental form is zero, e.g. O_2, Cl_2, Fe.

2 The oxidation state of an elemental cation or anion is the charge on the ion. For example:
Fe^{2+}: oxidation state +2
Na^+: oxidation state +1
Cl^-: oxidation state –1
S^{2-}: oxidation state –2.

3 The oxidation state of fluorine in an compound is always –1 as it is the most electronegative element.

4 The oxidation state of oxygen in a compound is always –2. (Except in peroxides, where it is –1.)

5 The oxidation state of chlorine in a compound is always –1. (Except when it is combined with oxygen.)

6 The oxidation state of hydrogen in a compound is always +1. (Except in alkali metal hydrides, such as NaH, where it is –1.)

 5 Does the sulphur in H_2SO_4 have the same oxidation state as the sulphur in SO_4^{2-}? (Use Fig. 3 to help you.)

6 Use the rules in Fig. 3 to check that the oxidation state of manganese in the manganate(VII) ion is +7.

7 a What is the oxidation state of manganese in MnO_2 and $MnCl_2$?
b Names the compounds.

Green glazes

If a potter using iron oxides as pigments wants a green glaze, the iron oxide has to be kept in the iron(II) state. So there must be reducing conditions in the kiln. In ancient China potters would allow woodsmoke to enter the kiln: particles of carbon in the smoke were then oxidised to carbon monoxide in the limited air supply. Carbon monoxide is a strong reducing agent. It will reduce any iron(III) oxide present in the kiln to iron(II) oxide:

$$Fe_2O_3 \quad + \quad CO \rightarrow 2FeO + CO_2$$

iron reduced;	carbon	
oxidation state	oxidised;	
reduced by 1	oxidation state	
	increased by 2	

The oxidation state of the carbon changes from +2 to +4. Oxidation can be described as an increase in oxidation state. The oxidation state of the iron changes from +3 to +2. Reduction can be described as a decrease in oxidation state. The oxidation state of the oxygen has not changed as it is combined with other elements throughout.

 8 Creating a reducing atmosphere in a kiln with woodsmoke can also ensure that copper(II) oxide is reduced to copper by carbon monoxide. Write the equation and oxidation state changes for this reaction.

9.6 How much pigment?

The amount of metal oxide in a glaze can affect the depth and shade of the colour. For example, cobalt(II) oxide is a powerful colourant. As little as 0.02% cobalt(II) oxide in a transparent glaze produces a noticeable tint when it is fired. At about 0.2% cobalt(II) oxide content, the glaze will have a definite blue colour. At 12% the colour is so intense it looks nearly black. The glass of the Portland vase, which was imitated in ceramics by Wedgwood, is coloured dark blue by cobalt.

A potter needs to know how much metal oxide a glaze contains. Quality control analysts can use redox titrations for determining the percentage of metal oxide.

Suppose that a glaze contained iron(II) oxide as the only reducing agent and the only metal oxide, and you needed to know how much iron(II) oxide was in the glaze and what colour the glaze would produce. You could weigh out 10 g of the glaze and warm it with dilute sulphuric acid to dissolve the iron(II) oxide. You would filter off the undissolved residue and make up the iron(II) sulphate solution to 250 cm^3 with dilute sulphuric acid. You could then titrate 25.0 cm^3 portions of the iron(II) sulphate solution against a solution of potassium manganate(VII) of a suitable concentration, say 0.005 mol dm^{-3}.

In acid solution, the manganate(VII) ion is reduced by iron(II) ions to manganese(II) ions (the oxidation states of hydrogen and oxygen do not change). The half-equation for this reduction is:

$$MnO_4^-(aq) + 8H^+(aq) + 5e^- \rightarrow Mn^{2+}(aq) + 4H_2O(l)$$

purple   pale pink

Combine this with the half-equation for the oxidation of iron(II) ions (Equation 1), which must this time be multiplied by 5:

$$MnO_4^-(aq) + 8H^+(aq) + 5Fe^{2+}(aq) \rightarrow Mn^{2+}(aq) + 4H_2O(l) + 5Fe^{3+}(aq)$$

Potassium manganate(VII) is useful for titrations because it acts as its own indicator. As you run the purple potassium

The glass of the Portland vase, which was imitated in ceramics by Wedgwood, is coloured dark blue by cobalt

manganate(VII) solution into the titration flask, it reacts rapidly. The manganese(II) ions form in such low concentrations that the solution seems colourless. As soon as all the iron(II) ions have reacted with the added manganate(VII) ions, a pink tinge of excess manganate(VII) appears in the flask.

Suppose you had to add 24.00 cm^3 of potassium manganate(VII) solution before the pink colour appears. You can work out how much iron(II) oxide the glaze contains as follows.

The number of moles of manganate(VII) ions used is given by number of moles
= (titre × concentration)/1000
= (24.00 × 0.005)/1000
= 1.2×10^{-4}

You know from the redox equation that each mole of manganate(VII) reacts with 5 moles of iron(II). In the 25.0 cm^3 sample of iron(II) solution taken from the volumetric flask there are therefore.
$5 \times 1.2 \times 10^{-4}$ moles = 6×10^{-4} moles of iron (II) ions
In the complete 250 cm^3 solution there are 10 times this number of moles, i.e.
6×10^{-3} moles of iron(II) ions

So in the original 10 g sample of glaze there are 6×10^{-3} moles of iron(II) ions. This is 6×10^{-3} moles of iron(II) oxide. Using atomic masses

1 mole of iron(II) oxide (FeO) = 56 + 16 g
$$= 72$$

so 6×10^{-3} moles has a mass of
$6 \times 10^{-3} \times 72$ g = 0.432 g
In 10 g of glaze there is therefore 0.432 g of iron(II) oxide, i.e. 4.32% of the glaze by mass is iron(II) oxide.

In a reducing kiln atmosphere, different proportions of iron(II) oxide in the initial glaze will give different colours:
0.5%–1%: pale blue-grey
2%–5%: green or blue
8%–10%: black.

So you could expect this glaze to give a green or blue colour when it is fired.

9.7 Colours and complex ions

The potters of ancient China did not understand the theory of redox chemistry, but they could use iron oxide glazes to obtain a range of colours – from green to dark brown – by adjusting the kiln conditions. Their copper oxide glazes gave them a different range of colours. Under reducing conditions, these glazes are coloured red-brown by elemental copper and the rather unstable copper(I) oxide. In oxidising conditions, their colours depend on the presence of acids and bases.

Copper(II) oxide is black. Glazes containing copper(II) oxide are blue or green when fired, depending on the balance of acidic and basic compounds present. Alkaline glazes containing copper(II) oxide give a blue colour. Acid glazes give green. This difference is due to the way in which the copper(II) ions are bonded in the fired glaze. This itself is related to the way in which transition metals, including copper, can form **complex ions**.

In a transition metal complex ion, a central transition metal ion is bonded via coordinate or dative bonds to atoms, groups of atoms or ions called **ligands**. This is possible because ligands have lone pairs of electrons, which form a bond with empty orbitals on the transition metal ion.

Copper(II) oxide is insoluble in water. It is a basic oxide, so it dissolves in hydrochloric acid. The colours of its solutions depend on the concentration of the different ions present. Each solution contains complex copper(II) ions. When there is a high concentration of chloride ions, the complex ion $CuCl_4^{2-}$ (tetrachlorocuprate(II)) forms. When this solution is diluted an equilibrium is set up between the $CuCl_4^{2-}$ ion and the hydrated copper(II) ion:

$CuCl_4^{2-}(aq) + 4H_2O(l) \rightleftharpoons$
$$Cu(H_2O)_6^{2+}(aq) + 4Cl^-(aq)$$
yellow   blue

This solution looks green because it contains yellow and blue complex ions.

If you add ammonia to the solution containing the hydrated copper(II) ion, pale blue insoluble copper(II) hydroxide forms. This dissolves when you add more ammonia solution. A deep blue colour develops, due to the tetraamminecopper(II) complex ion $(Cu(NH_3)_4^{2+})$.

The tetrachlorocuprate(II) ion is an anionic complex ion. It has an overall negative charge. The central copper(II) ion

Copper(II) ions in solution (from left to right): in concentrated hydrochloric acid, dilute hydrochloric acid, neutral solution, dilute ammonia solution, concentrated ammonia solution

is bonded with four chloride ions, using the lone pairs on the chloride ions (Fig. 4). The **coordination number** of the copper in this complex is four, as it is bonded to four ligands. The ion is tetrahedral in shape, as you would expect from an ion with four identical bonds.

Both the hydrated copper(II) ion and the tetraamminecopper(II) ion are cationic complexes. The copper(II) ion is bonded via the lone pairs of atoms in neutral molecules – oxygen in the water molecule, nitrogen in the ammonia (Fig. 5). You might expect these ions to be tetrahedral in shape too. They are not. Most transition metal complex ions are based on an octahedral structure. Although copper is bonded to only four ligands in these ions, two further water molecules are very loosely associated with the complexes. The shape of these complex ions is described as 'square planar'.

The octahedral structure is clearer in other complex ions. The hydrated cobalt(II) ion ($Co(H_2O)_6^{2+}$) is pink and is octahedral in shape (Fig. 6). The coordination number of cobalt in this complex ion is six. The cobalt ion is bonded to six ligands.

When chloride ion concentration is high, the blue tetrachlorocobalt(II) $CoCl_4^{2-}$ ion forms. This is tetrahedral.

You can use the different colours of these cobalt complexes to test for the presence of water. Cobalt chloride paper contains high levels of chloride ions and so the blue $CoCl_4^{2-}$ ion is present. If you moisten cobalt chloride paper it turns pink. Water molecules replace the chloride ligands and the hydrated cobalt(II) ion forms.

9 **What is the coordination number of cobalt in $CoCl_4^{2-}$?**

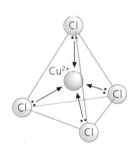

Fig. 4 Tetrachlorocuprate (II) ion

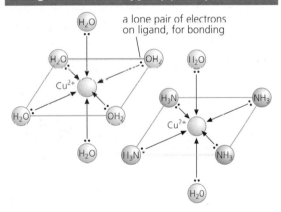

Fig. 5 Cationic copper(II) complex ions

a lone pair of electrons on ligand, for bonding

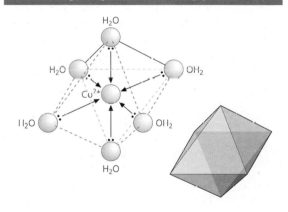

Fig. 6 Hydrated cobalt(II) ion

9.8 Glazes come in all colours!

The brilliant blue colour of this design is obtained using cobalt as an 'underglaze'

Ancient Chinese potters used cobalt and manganese oxides in glazes, as well as iron and copper oxides. The finely divided cobalt pigment was painted on to the vase or plate in the required design and a colourless glaze was added over it. The finest cobalt ore was obtained from Persia and was known as Mohammedan blue. It was used on the pottery of the Manchu dynasty. Today's cobalt glazes give a brighter, harsher blue colour; this is because the cobalt oxide used is purer. Mohammedan blue probably contained minute traces of manganese, iron and copper oxides in just the combinations needed to give a distinctive, glowing blue.

Metal oxide	% addition	Colour when fired in oxidising atmosphere	Colour when fired in reducing atmosphere
titanium(IV)		white	
vanadium(V)	6	yellow	
chromium(III)	2	yellowish green	emerald green
manganese(IV)	4	purple	brown
iron(III)	1		willow green
	2	tan	olive green
	4	brown	mottled green
	10	black–brown	red–brown
cobalt(II)	0.5	medium blue	medium blue
	1	strong blue	strong blue
nickel(II)		grey	grey–blue
copper(II)	0.5		copper red
	1	turquoise	deep red
	2	turquoise	red and black
	8	blue–green	black

Table 3 Transition metal oxides used in glazes

Nowadays all the first-row transition metals, except scandium, are used in glazes. They can give a wide range of colours, depending on the compounds used and the kiln conditions (Table 3).

10 a Manganese(IV) oxide is brown. Suggest what species gives the purple colour when manganese is used under oxidising conditions.

b Write a redox half-equation to show how this species is formed from manganese(IV) oxide.

11 What electron configuration in the cobalt ion would you expect to find in a cobalt glaze fired under reducing conditions?

Potters combine different oxides in the same glaze to get an even wider range of colours. This is related to the way in which transition metal compounds absorb visible light.

Hydrated copper(II) ions appear turquoise because they absorb the red part of the visible spectrum and reflect the blue and green parts (Fig. 7). Tetrachlorocuprate(II) ions appear yellow because they absorb the blue light of the spectrum.

This absorption of light of particular wavelengths is due to the way in which the d sub-shells (orbitals) are used in bonding in transition metal compounds. If you could look at a gaseous copper(II) ion, you would find all the d orbitals at the same energy. When transition metal ions combine with a ligand, these d orbitals split (Fig. 8). The overall energy of the levels remains the same. Electrons in the lower levels can absorb energy and be promoted to the higher levels. The size of this energy transition is equivalent to the wavelength of part of the visible spectrum. If the ligands are changed, the difference in energy between the higher and lower levels also changes. Different ligands attached to the same central transition metal ion give rise to different colours.

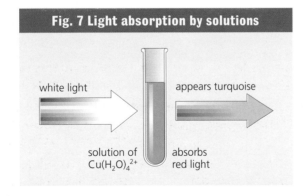

Fig. 7 Light absorption by solutions

white light → solution of $Cu(H_2O)_4{}^{2+}$ absorbs red light → appears turquoise

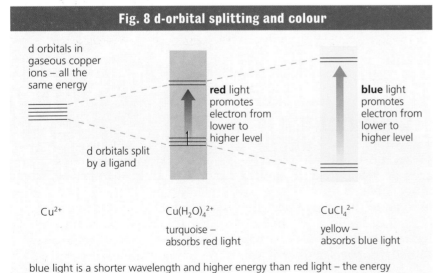

Fig. 8 d-orbital splitting and colour

d orbitals in gaseous copper ions – all the same energy

d orbitals split by a ligand

Cu^{2+}

$Cu(H_2O)_4{}^{2+}$
turquoise – absorbs red light

red light promotes electron from lower to higher level

$CuCl_4{}^{2-}$
yellow – absorbs blue light

blue light promotes electron from lower to higher level

blue light is a shorter wavelength and higher energy than red light – the energy transition is therefore slightly bigger

9.9 Transition metal catalysts

Many transition metals are useful industrial catalysts. For example, iron is used as a catalyst in the Haber process for the manufacture of ammonia (see Chapter 7), vanadium(V) oxide in the manufacture of sulphuric acid and nickel in the hydrogenation of oils (see Chapter 11).

Transition metals can change their oxidation state quite easily. Transition metal ions act as catalysts by changing their oxidation states during reactions on the catalyst surface. This creates an easier reaction path. There is more about the mechanism of catalysis in Chapter 16.

Rhodium–platinum wire, woven into a gauze, is used as the catalyst in the oxidation of ammonia to nitric acid

Key ideas

- Transition metals have incomplete d electron sub-shells in their atoms or ions.

- Oxidation states can be assigned using a set of rules.

- Oxidation is a process in which an element loses electrons and increases in oxidation state.

- Reduction is a process in which an element gains electrons and decreases in oxidation state.

- Oxidation and reduction always happen together.

- Transition metals can form complex ions in which the central transition metal ion is bonded to ligands.

- Different complexes have different shapes, depending on their coordination number.

- Transition metals form coloured compounds. The colour depends on the oxidation state and the nature of the bonding.

- Transition metals can act as catalysts.

10 Putting halogens to work

'*Swimming pool water is constantly recirculated and filtered. The filtration takes out some of the pool debris, but chemical treatment is needed to remove the bacteria introduced by people's bodies. Without chemical treatment, the bacteria would thrive at swimming-pool temperatures, typically around 25 °C.*'

On a hot, sticky day, it's great to plunge into the clear blue water of a swimming pool. You come out after your swim feeling really clean and fresh. So do all the other swimmers who have been sharing the water with you! How is the water kept so clean and clear? What chemicals are suitable, and under what conditions do they need to be used?

Clean water is essential in swimming pools for both comfort and safety

10.1 Learning objectives

After working through this chapter, you should be able to:

- **recall** the members of the halogen group of elements, and the similarities in their physical and chemical properties;

- **describe** trends in boiling point, electronegativity and reactivity down Group VII of the Periodic Table;

- **describe** the reactions of chlorine with water and with sodium hydroxide solution, and explain the importance of these reactions in maintaining safe water supplies;

- **describe** trends in the oxidising power of halogens and derive equations for displacement reactions;

- **explain** how to determine the concentration of chlorine in solution by redox titration;

- **explain** how to test for halide ions in solution and distinguish between them;

- **describe** trends in the reducing power of halide ions;

- **describe** the reactions of solid halides with concentrated sulphuric acid.

10.2 Disinfection of swimming pools

Bacteria introduced by swimmers into pools need to be killed. There are only a few chemicals that are efficient at killing bacteria and which are also safe and affordable. Chlorine and its compounds are the most widely used, but two other halogens, bromine and iodine, have also been used. To check the effectiveness of the chemicals, samples of pool water are smeared on to agar plates, which are kept in a warm place. Any faecal bacteria will show up as colonies under a microscope.

10.3 Living things and the halogens

The halogens – the elements fluorine, chlorine, bromine and iodine – all kill bacteria. They are toxic to humans too, even at quite low concentrations, so they have to be handled and used with great care. A recommended **threshold limit value** (TLV) has been set for each halogen (Table 1).

Table 1 Physical properties of the halogens			
Halogen	Boiling point/°C	Appearance at room temperature	Toxicity: recommended TLV in air by volume/ppm
fluorine	−187	pale yellow gas	1.0
chlorine	−35	dense green gas	1.0
bromine	59	red liquid	0.1
iodine	183	black solid	0.1

The unit parts per million (ppm) is often used to indicate extremely low concentrations.

In World War I the use of chlorine by both sides injured many soldiers

Freight containers used for transporting chlorine have notices warning that the contents are hazardous

113

TLV is the highest level to which workers can be safely exposed. Exposure to halogen levels above the TLV can be dangerous (Table 2).

 1 In a laboratory with a volume of 100 m³, how many cm³ of chlorine would need to be released to produce a dangerous concentration?

Table 2 Effects of chlorine dosage	
Effect of chlorine	Concentration in air by volume/ppm
smallest amount to produce slight effects after several hours exposure	1
smallest amount to produce a detectable smell	3.5
maximum amount inhaled for 1 hour without producing a serious disturbance	4
smallest amount to cause irritation of the throat	15.1
smallest amount to cause coughing	30.2
amount dangerous in 30–60 minutes	40–60
amount that kills most animals in a very short time	1000

Source: Kirk–Othmer

10.4 Chlorinating swimming pools

Chlorine in swimming pool water is present in more than one form. **Free available chlorine** is the form that kills bacteria. **Combined chlorine** is chlorine that is not available as a disinfectant. The total chlorine content is made up of the free available chlorine plus the combined chlorine.

The **bactericide** used in the disinfection of smaller pools is mainly chloric(I) acid (HOCl). This can be introduced into the water as a solution of its sodium salt (liquid bleach) or as the solid calcium salt. Chlorine gas is only suitable for use in large, very busy pools. Although chlorine itself is not expensive, it is hazardous to use and the equipment for handling it costs a lot to install.

Chlorine dissolves in water to form a mixture of chloric(I) acid and hydrochloric acid.

$$Cl_2(g) + H_2O(l) \rightarrow HOCl(aq) + H^+(aq) + Cl^-(aq) \quad \text{(Equation 1)}$$
chloric(I) acid

$$HOCl(aq) \rightleftharpoons H^+(aq) + ClO^-(aq) \quad \text{(Equation 2)}$$
chlorate(I) ion

Chloric(I) acid is a weak acid. Its dissociation depends on the pH of the water. At pH 5, almost 100% HOCl is present, but at pH 10 almost 100% ClO⁻ is present. (The dissociation and pH of weak acids are discussed in Chapter 8. Equilibria are discussed in Chapter 7)

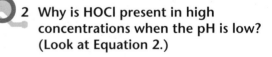 **2 Why is HOCl present in high concentrations when the pH is low? (Look at Equation 2.)**

Sodium chlorate(I) is widely used as a bleach and disinfectant. Sodium chlorate(I) solution is made on an industrial scale by the action of chlorine gas on cold, dilute sodium hydroxide solution. Chlorine reacts faster with alkali than it does with water:

$$Cl_2(g) + 2NaOH(aq) \rightarrow$$
$$NaCl(aq) + NaOCl(aq) + H_2O(l)$$
sodium   sodium
chloride   chlorate(I)

Sodium chlorate(I) dissociates fully in solution:

$$NaOCl(aq) \rightarrow Na^+(aq) + ClO^-(aq)$$

The chlorate(I) ion again sets up an equilibrium with chloric(I) acid:

$$HOCl(aq) \rightleftharpoons H^+(aq) + ClO^-(aq)$$

Controlling the pH of the swimming pool water allows the staff to control the level of chloric(I) acid. Chloric(I) acid is 80 times more effective than the chlorate(I) ion at killing disease-carrying bacteria.

Swimming pool managers regularly test the water – at least twice a day at busy pools. The water is tested for both free and combined chlorine, and for pH. The test kits have colour charts which show these levels. The level of free available chlorine has to be between 1.5 and 3.0 mg dm^{-3},

Testing the pH of swimming-pool water with a phenol red indicator kit

and the combined chlorine less than 1 mg dm^{-3}. To maintain these levels pool staff sometimes have to add more chlorinating agent.

 3 What swimming-pool water pH would seem to be the best for high disinfectant action?

The pool manager must keep the pool pH close to 7.5. Too low a pH (high hydrogen ion concentration) would irritate swimmers' eyes and corrode the metallic parts of the pool system; although it would give high levels of chloric(I) acid. Too high a pH would give a much weaker disinfectant action, and scale would form in the water from carbonate ions. A pH range of 7.2–7.6 offers the best compromise between disinfectant action and the comfort of swimmers.

The pool staff determine the pH of the water using phenol red indicator. Phenol red is useful because it gives clear colour indications in the pH range 6.8–8.4. The test is reliable as long as the free available chlorine level is below about 10 mg dm^{-3}. More free available chlorine than this bleaches the indicator, so that the pH reading looks too low.

The pH of the water can be controlled easily and cheaply by adding chemicals. Hydrochloric acid solution or sodium hydrogensulphate pellets are used to lower the pH, and sodium carbonate pellets are used to raise it.

10.5 Oxidising action – free and combined chlorine

If your eyes feel irritated when you go swimming, the pH of the pool water may be too low, or there may be little free available chlorine in the water.

Chlorine reacts with ammonia, urea and amino acids (which come from the swimmers' perspiration and urine) to produce **chloramines**. Chloramines, like ammonia, are irritants. They do have some disinfectant properties, but they tie up

chlorine which would be more effective in other forms. Chloric(I) acid is 280 times more effective than monochloramine (NH_2Cl) against faecal bacteria.

The kit that the pool manager uses to test for both free and combined chlorine makes use of a coloured indicator called DPD (short for N, N-diethyl-p-phenylenediamine). Chlorine reacts with DPD to give a red colour that can be matched with a reference colour to indicate the level of chlorine. It is a reliable test up to chlorine levels of about 4 mg dm^{-3}. The pool staff can then work out whether they need to add any chlorinating agent in order to keep the free available chlorine at the most efficient level, between 2.0 and 3.0 mg dm^{-3}.

 4 **Concentrations at low levels are often expressed in mg dm^{-3} or ppm. What is 3.0 mg dm^{-3} in ppm, assuming that 1 dm^{-3} of solution has a mass of 1000 g?**

5 **Chemists often express concentration in moles per dm^3 (litre). What is 3.0 mg dm^{-3} of chlorine atoms in mol dm^{-3}?**

The DPD test gives a quick measure of the level of low concentrations of chlorine. Higher concentrations, such as the level in domestic bleach, can be determined by **redox titration**. The method works because chlorine is a strong oxidising agent. It will easily oxidise bromide ions to bromine:

$$Cl_2(aq) + 2Br^-(aq) \rightarrow 2Cl^-(aq) + Br_2(aq)$$

This reaction is used in the production of bromine from sea water. Chlorine also easily oxidises iodide ions to iodine:

$$Cl_2(aq) + 2I^-(aq) \rightarrow 2Cl^-(aq) + I_2(aq)$$

In this reaction chlorine has gained electrons and been reduced; the iodide ions have lost electrons and been oxidised. Chlorine has moved from **oxidation state** 0 in the elemental state to –1 in chloride ions.

 6 **What is the oxidation state change for iodine in this reaction?**

7 **Bromine will oxidise iodide ions to iodine. Write the equation for this reaction.**

The oxidation of iodide ions by chlorine is used as the basis for the quantitative determination of free chlorine in bleach or sodium chlorate(I) solution. Adding bleach to a solution of potassium iodide turns the solution brown, because the free chlorine oxidises the potassium iodide to form iodine. The iodine can be titrated against sodium thiosulphate solution. When most of the iodine has reacted, the solution turns a straw colour. Adding a little freshly prepared starch solution turns the mixture blue. Starch indicator should not be added at the beginning of the titration; if it is, the iodine molecules get trapped in the starch molecules. This prevents starch from working efficiently as an indicator in high iodine concentrations. The blue colour and the traces of iodine disappear as a little more sodium thiosulphate solution is added. The end-point of the titration is when the blue colour just disappears.

This reaction is a redox reaction – the iodine oxidises the thiosulphate ion to the tetrathionate ion and is itself reduced to iodide ions:

$$I_2(aq) + 2S_2O_3^{2-}(aq) \rightarrow 2I^-(aq) + S_4O_6^{2-}(aq)$$
$$\text{thiosulphate ion} \qquad\qquad \text{tetrathionate ion}$$

The oxidising power of the halogens decreases down the group. Fluorine is the most strongly oxidising halogen and iodine the least. This is matched by the trend in **electronegativity** (Table 3). Fluorine is the most electronegative and reactive of all the elements.

Table 3 Electronegativities of the halogens	
Halogen	Electronegativity (Pauling index)
fluorine	4.0
chlorine	3.0
bromine	2.8
iodine	0.5

10.6 Superchlorination

If the combined chlorine concentration (total chlorine minus free chlorine) in the pool water rises above 1.0 mg dm^{-3}, the pool manager needs to superchlorinate the pool water. This makes sure that no irritating chloramines (combined chlorine) are present. In chlorinated water, monochloramine is formed rapidly from ammonia:

8 Look back at Equation 1 on page 114. Chlorine is the only species in this reaction which undergoes redox change. Part of the chlorine is oxidised and part is reduced. Work out the oxidation state changes of the chlorine.

$$NH_3(aq) \quad + \quad HOCl(aq) \quad \longrightarrow \quad NH_2Cl(aq) \quad + \quad H_2O(l)$$

nitrogen in oxidation state –3   chlorine in oxidation state +1   nitrogen been oxidised to – 1

chlorine has been reduced to –1

Increased dosage thus produces a linear increase in combined chlorine. Adding still more chlorinating agent gives unstable dichloramine, which then decomposes to form nitrogen:

$$NH_2Cl(aq) \quad + \quad HOCl(aq) \quad \longrightarrow \quad NHCl_2(aq) \quad + \quad H_2O(l)$$

monochloramine   dichloramine

$$2NHCl_2(aq) \quad + \quad H_2O(l) \quad \longrightarrow \quad N_2(g) \quad + \quad HOCl(aq) \quad + \quad 3HCl(aq)$$

These reactions reduce the free chlorine present and so reduce the disinfectant action. After the addition of still more chlorinating agent, the breakpoint is reached, and the free chlorine level starts to rise again (Fig. 1) and the water is said to be superchlorinated.

Chlorine can help to remove other impurities in swimming pool water besides bacteria. It can oxidise metal ions which can enter when the water is topped up or if metallic parts of the circulation system corrode. Some metal ions can discolour the water and cause staining of the pool area. Superchlorination treatment oxidises soluble iron(II) and manganese(II) salts to the insoluble solids iron(III) hydroxide and manganese(IV) oxide. These solids are removed when the recirculating water passes through the filters.

$$Cl_2(aq) + 6H_2O(l) + 2Fe^{2+}(aq) \rightarrow 2Cl^-(aq) + 2Fe(OH)_3(s) + 6H^+(aq)$$

$$Cl_2(aq) + 2H_2O(l) + Mn^{2+}(aq) \rightarrow 2Cl^-(aq) + MnO_2(s) + 4H^+(aq)$$

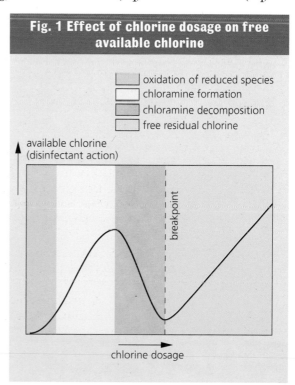

Fig. 1 Effect of chlorine dosage on free available chlorine

oxidation of reduced species
chloramine formation
chloramine decomposition
free residual chlorine

available chlorine (disinfectant action)

breakpoint

chlorine dosage

10.7 Chlorination of drinking water

A decision by Peruvian officials not to chlorinate much of the country's drinking water – based on studies by the US Environmental Protection Agency (EPA) showing that chlorine may create a slight cancer risk – is being blamed for the devastating cholera epidemic that is now sweeping Peru. More than 300 000 cases have been reported and 3516 people have died.

Officials believe that the bacteria first arrived with a Chinese freighter, which released contaminated bilge water into the harbour at Lima, Peru. The bacteria quickly made their way to the shellfish and fish, probably reaching humans in the form of *ceviche*, a

raw seafood dish popular in Peru. Once the disease appeared in humans, it soon moved into the water supply, infecting many people.

US and international health officials have blamed Peruvian water officials for a gross miscalculation in not chlorinating the entire water supply. Old pipes and open unchlorinated wells allowed the cholera bacteria to enter the water supply after filtration. Researchers are now asking whether the EPA should have given more emphasis to the disaster potential of not disinfecting water supplies.

Source: Adapted from Anderson, 1991

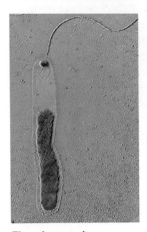

The microscopic bacterium *Vibrio cholerae* found in contaminated water can cause cholera in humans

Domestic water supplies must be fit to drink. That means that any harmful bacteria and viruses must be removed before the water reaches the people who will drink it. At the treatment works, chlorine is pumped into the water supply. The water is then stored for about two

hours – long enough for complete disinfection. Sufficient chlorine is added to ensure that the water remains bacteria-free until it reaches people's homes. As little chlorine as possible is used, ensuring that the water supply is safe without affecting the taste of the water.

Water has to be treated chemically to make it safe to drink

In Brazil, as in many other places in the world, some people do not have access to clean, piped water. They collect water where they can and it is often contaminated

Water treatment: the halogens compared

Chlorine is very widely used for water treatment. Why aren't bromine and iodine used too? One group of water analysts set out to compare the effects of these three halogens on amoebic cysts. These micro-organisms are sometimes found in sewage and in untreated water supplies in tropical countries. They cause amoebic dysentery, a serious illness. Amoebic cysts are resistant to disinfectants and can survive treatment that would kill most other organisms.

The team looked at the effects of chlorine, bromine and iodine on amoebic cysts in water (Fig. 2), in ammonium chloride solution and in sewage effluent, at different concentrations and at different pH.

 9 a Which halogen is the most effective at killing amoebic cysts in water at pH 8?
  b Which halogen is the most effective at killing amoebic cysts in water across the pH range 6–8?

The analysts found that bromine was the best killer of cysts in water, but that in sewage iodine was best. All the halogens performed better at low pH.

 10 Bromine reacts with water to form bromic(I) acid (HOBr) in the same way that chlorine reacts to form chloric(I) acid.
  a Write equations for the reactions of bromine with water.
  b Explain why bromine kills amoebic cysts more efficiently at low pH.

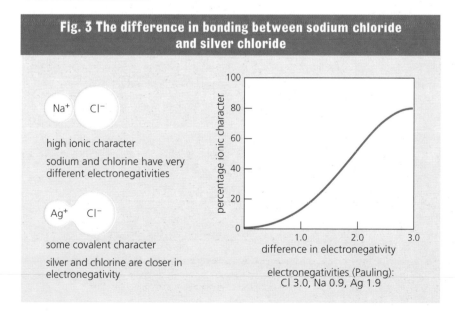

Fig. 2 Disinfectant action of halogens (2 mg dm⁻³ in water)

10.8 Halides in water sources

Fig. 3 The difference in bonding between sodium chloride and silver chloride

Na⁺ Cl⁻

high ionic character

sodium and chlorine have very different electronegativities

Ag⁺ Cl⁻

some covalent character

silver and chlorine are closer in electronegativity

electronegativities (Pauling):
Cl 3.0, Na 0.9, Ag 1.9

Halogens are not found in their elemental state in the Earth's crust, because they are so reactive. They are found naturally as a range of halide salts. Because halides can be washed out of rocks and soil by rain water, both sea water and tap water contain chloride ions, though in very different concentrations.

Chloride ions are easily detected in a solution by adding silver nitrate solution. Silver ions react readily with chloride ions to give a white precipitate of silver chloride. Silver chloride is insoluble in water because it has some covalent character in its bonds (Fig. 3).

$$Ag^+(aq) + Cl^-(aq) \rightarrow AgCl(s)$$

Silver ions also give precipitates with other anions such as carbonate ions. To make sure that these do not interfere with this test, dilute nitric acid is added with the silver nitrate solution. Silver carbonate and other insoluble silver salts react with nitric acid to produce soluble compounds.

Tap water often shows cloudiness with this test because it contains low levels of chloride ions. Bromide ions and iodide ions also form precipitates with silver nitrate solution.

$$Ag^+(aq) + Br^-(aq) \rightarrow AgBr(s)$$

11 Write down the equation for the reaction between iodide ions and silver ions.

The silver halides are slightly different colours, and you can tell which is which just by looking at them. In theory you might identify a halide by precipitating the silver salt. But this won't work if there are different halide concentrations in different samples, or if a mixture of halide ions is present. The silver halides have different solubilities in ammonia solution (Table 4). This can be used to distinguish between precipitates of the silver halides.

Silver chloride and silver bromide are affected by light. The silver halide decomposes into silver and the halogen:

$$2AgCl(s) \rightarrow 2Ag(s) + Cl_2(g)$$

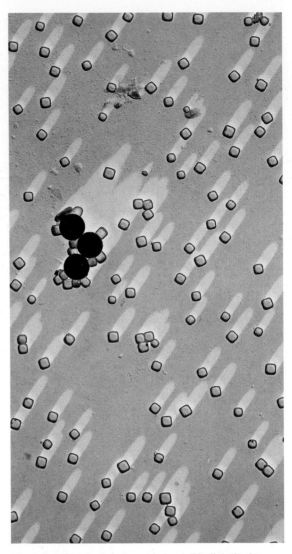

The instability of silver bromide in visible light is the basis of photographic film

Table 4 Reactions of halide ions in aqueous solution			
Reagent	Chloride	Bromide	Iodide
silver nitrate solution plus dilute nitric acid	white precipitate soluble in dilute ammonia solution	cream precipitate soluble in concentrated ammonia solution	yellow precipitate insoluble in concentrated ammonia solution
effect of light on silver halide	turns grey	turns yellow	no change

12 Explain why silver chloride turns grey when it is left to stand.

13 Silver chloride has more ionic character in its bond than silver iodide has. Suggest how trends in electronegativity down the halogens explain this.

Salts from the lake water have crystallised around the shores of this lake in China

A range of halide ions is found in sea water (Table 5). If sea water is evaporated, the most abundant salt in the residue is sodium chloride.

Table 5 Average composition of the dissolved salts in sea water	
Ion	% by mass of dissolved salts
anions	
chloride (Cl^-)	55.042
sulphate (SO_4^{2-})	7.682
hydrogencarbonate (HCO_3^-)	0.406
bromide (Br^-)	0.189
borate ($H_2BO_3^-$)	0.075
fluoride (F^-)	0.029
cations	
sodium (Na^+)	30.612
magnesium (Mg^{2+})	3.689
calcium (Ca^{2+})	1.160
potassium (K^+)	1.102
strontium (Sr^{2+})	0.038
Source: Open University	

10.9 Reactions of halides

Just as halogens are oxidising agents, halide ions can act as reducing agents. The reactions of sodium halides with concentrated sulphuric acid illustrate the trend in their reducing action (Table 6).

Concentrated sulphuric acid is an oxidising agent. If it is dripped on to solid sodium chloride, hydrogen chloride fumes form immediately. This is not a redox reaction. Concentrated sulphuric acid has a much higher boiling point (338 °C) than hydrogen chloride (–85 °C). This big difference in boiling points allows the reaction to happen.

$$H_2SO_4(l) + NaCl(s) \rightarrow HCl(g) + NaHSO_4(s)$$

hydrogen chloride, sodium hydrogen-sulphate

So why are the reactions of concentrated sulphuric acid with sodium bromide and sodium iodide different from those with sodium chloride? If concentrated sulphuric

Table 6 Reaction of solid halides with concentrated sulphuric acid		
Sodium chloride	Sodium bromide	Sodium iodide
fumes of hydrogen chloride	brown fumes of a mixture of bromine and hydrogen bromide	purple fumes of iodine

acid is warmed with solid sodium iodide, iodine – not hydrogen iodide – is formed. This is because any hydrogen iodide formed is quickly oxidised to iodine by the concentrated sulphuric acid. In this redox reaction, the concentrated sulphuric acid is reduced to a mixture of sulphur and hydrogen sulphide. The half-equations are as follows:

$$2I^-(s) \rightarrow I_2(g) + 2e^-$$

$$8H^+(aq) + SO_4^{2-}(aq) + 6e^- \rightarrow S(s) + 4H_2O(l)$$

 14 a **What is the oxidation state change of sulphur in this reduction?**
b **Use the two half-equations to write a full equation.**

 15 Sodium bromide is partially oxidised by concentrated sulphuric acid.
a **Write an equation to show how hydrogen bromide is formed in the reaction.**
b **Write an equation to show how bromide ions can be oxidised to bromine.**

An oxidising agent stronger than concentrated sulphuric acid is needed to oxidise chloride ions to chlorine. The reducing power (ease of oxidation) of the halide ions is in the order:
iodide > bromide > chloride.
The oxidising power (ease of reduction) is in the order:
chlorine > bromine > iodine.

10.10 Manufacturing chlorine

The electrolysis of sodium chloride solution, obtained from sea water or underground salt deposits, produces both chlorine and sodium hydroxide, the raw materials for the production of sodium chlorate(I).

The chlor-alkali industry currently produces 36 megatonnes (Mt) of chlorine and 39 Mt of sodium hydroxide per year. The chlorine produced is used to make a range of inorganic and organic chemicals, and also as a bleach for paper and textiles and in water treatment.

Key ideas

- Halogens are very reactive, electronegative elements. They are toxic.

- Halogens are oxidising agents. Halide ions are reducing agents.

- Halide ions can be detected by precipitating silver halides with silver nitrate solution.

- Chlorine reacts with water and with alkalis.

11 Saturated or unsaturated?

"Phew! After that game of squash, I need to grab a snack. Come on, I'll get us something in the café. I'm not buying you any chocolate biscuits though. You eat too many fat-laden chocolate bars as it is. We should be cutting our fat consumption, you know, so that it provides only provides 30% of our total energy requirements – not the current national average of 42%."

Mick seems to know what he is talking about. His friend is a typical example of someone who eats far too much fat. Food researchers know that such a diet can have a bad effect on health. However, many people still remain unconvinced or confused about the effects of fatty diets on their bodies. What exactly is healthy eating?

" Cutting cholesterol "

Fatty diet doubles heart disease risk

The risk of a heart attack could be cut by up to a half and tens of thousands of lives saved, if the average person in the UK ate less fat, according to studies in 17 different countries…

Reducing the amount of fat in the British diet by one sixth would cut blood cholesterol by 10 per cent, enough to prevent half of all heart attacks among men and women aged 40, and a fifth of attacks among those aged 70…

Professor Nicholas Wald, Professor of preventive medicine at St Bartholomew's [hospital], said "nearly everyone" in Britain and other Western countries had too high a blood cholesterol because they ate too much fat, especially saturated (animal) fat. "Eating less saturated fat would achieve substantial health benefits," he said.

Source: *The Times*, 1994

11.1 Learning objectives

After working through this chapter, you should be able to:

- **recall** that alkanes are a homologous series with the general formula C_nH_{2n+2};

- **describe** the molecular and structural formulae of the alkanes;

- **describe** the difference between molecular, structural and empirical formulae;

- **recall** that the alkenes are a homologous series with the general formula C_nH_{2n};

- **describe** the molecular and structural formulae of the alkenes;

- **describe** the nature of the bonding in alkanes and alkenes;

- **explain** the delocalisation of electrons in terms of σ and π electrons;

- **describe** *cis–trans* isomerism;

- **describe** the reaction mechanism for electrophilic addition;

- **describe** chemical tests to distinguish between alkanes and alkenes.

11.2 Too much fat?

We are what we eat? There is enormous variety in the amount and type of food that people eat. There is a huge variation in the food requirements of individuals too. How can people maintain a healthy diet?

In 1991, the UK Government published the results of what was probably the largest survey ever undertaken on diet. The report from the Department of Health's Committee on Medical Aspects of Food Policy (COMA) contained many detailed recommendations for national dietary goals, including some on fat intake (Table 1). Fatty acids are the long molecules that make up fat molecules.

Fat intake linked to disease

[The] imbalance [of fat intake] is one of the contributory causes of coronary heart disease in this country and is also linked to strokes, cancers, diabetes, gallstones, allergies and bowel disorders.

Source: Federation of Bakers

Fat intake linked to CHD

The major non-genetic determinant of serum cholesterol levels is diet, and death rates from CHD [coronary heart disease] in different countries are associated with national fat consumption.

Source: *COMA Report*, 1991

Table 1 Recommendations on fat intake	
Fatty acid	Contribution to total energy/%
saturated fatty acids	10
cis-polyunsaturated fatty acids	6
cis-monounsaturated fatty acids	12
trans fatty acids	2
total fatty acids	30

Source: *COMA Report*, 1991

1 Look at Table 1. Which foods supply the remaining 70% of our energy requirement?

2 What is the recommended ratio of saturated fats to unsaturated fats? (Include *trans* fatty acids with unsaturated fats.)

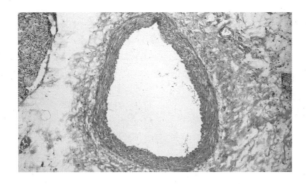

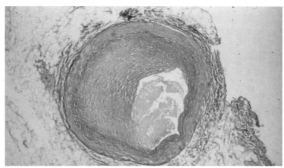

Right. The coronary artery supplies blood to the heart muscle, which keeps it working. In this cross section you can see the artery wall (in pink) and the space through which the blood flows, called the lumen (in white)

Far right. Fatty deposits cause the artery walls to constrict, producing a much narrower lumen. This condition is called *atheroma.* The later formation of a *thrombus*, or blood clot (in yellow), blocks the remaining lumen

Many researchers believe that high intakes of fat, especially saturated fat, are a prime cause of high cholesterol levels in the blood. Cholesterol is essential to the human body and is found in all body cells. Cholesterol is in the saturated fats we eat, and it is also manufactured in the liver. Cholesterol is not a fat: it is chemically related to bile acid, the sex hormones and vitamin D. About 93% of the body's cholesterol is found in the body cells. The remaining 7% circulates in the blood: it is this 7% which can cause problems.

Cholesterol is insoluble in water (and therefore in blood) and can become deposited in the arteries, particularly those of the heart. The cholesterol deposits then reduce the blood flow. If the coronary artery, which supplies blood to the heart muscle, becomes partly blocked, angina may occur. If the artery is completely blocked, part of the heart muscle is starved of oxygen and a heart attack occurs.

Although genetics plays a major role in determining an individual's risk of developing coronary heart disease, a reduction in intake of saturated fats can have a preventative effect. Some people are not able to absorb large amounts of cholesterol into their body cells, so they have more cholesterol than normal circulating in the blood. They too benefit by reducing their saturated fat intake. Mick's advice to his friend that he should cut down on fat intake seems sensible. But what do health experts mean when they talk about 'saturated' and 'unsaturated' fats? How do they differ?

11.3 The structure of saturated fats

During the process of digestion, fat molecules are broken down into fatty acids and glycerol. Fatty acids are long-chain molecules based on the element carbon. Carbon is unique among the elements in its ability to form strong covalent bonds with itself (Fig. 1).

The bond energy for C–C is 346 kJ mol^{-1}. This is a relatively strong bond. Silicon is in the same group as carbon in the periodic table and could be expected to form Si–Si bonds. However, the Si–Si bond energy is only 225 kJ mol^{-1}, which makes it a weak bond. Silicon does not form chains of covalently bonded atoms as readily as carbon.

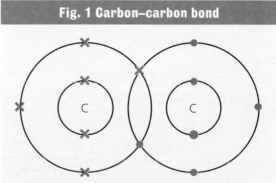

Fig. 1 Carbon–carbon bond

The C—C single bond. Dot-and-cross diagrams (see Chapter 4) show covalent bonds as electrons shared between atoms. The circles represent the electron energy level or shells.

Carbon chains can be of many lengths, and include branches and rings of carbon atoms. Chemists estimate that there are at least 2.5 million compounds containing carbon and hydrogen (hydrogen is the element most commonly bonded to carbon). This is more than all the known compounds involving other elements put together. The study of carbon compounds is called **organic chemistry**.

Hydrocarbons form families of compounds. All the compounds in one family have the same general molecular formula. These families are called **homologous series**. Fatty acids typically contain carbon chains of between 10 and 20 carbon atoms. The saturated fatty acid carbon chains are based on the homologous series of compounds called **alkanes**.

Alkanes

The simplest hydrocarbon is methane. Methane has the formula CH_4, and belongs to the alkanes (Table 2). The second column of Table 2 gives molecular formulae. A **molecular formula** tells you how many of each atom are present in one molecule. Compounds can also be represented by their **structural formulae**. A structural formula shows how the atoms are joined together in each molecule. A structural formula can be abbreviated by listing the groups of atoms in sequence (so long as the listing is not confusing) e.g. CH_3CH_3 for ethane. The **empirical formula** gives the ratio of carbon atoms to hydrogen atoms. It does not tell you how many atoms a molecule actually contains. The molecular formulae of the alkanes have the general form C_nH_{2n+2}.

Table 2 Chemical formulae of the first six alkanes			
Name	Molecular formula	Structural formula	Empirical formula
methane	CH_4		CH_4
ethane	C_2H_6		CH_3
propane	C_3H_8		C_3H_8
butane	C_4H_{10}		C_2H_5
pentane	C_5H_{12}		C_5H_{12}
hexane	C_6H_{14}		C_3H_7

Naming alkanes

The names of alkanes always end in '-ane'. This ending indicates that a compound is an alkane. The first part of the name refers to the number of carbon atoms, e.g.

$$\underset{\text{nine carbon atoms}}{\underbrace{\text{non}}}\underset{\text{alkane}}{\underbrace{\text{ane}}}$$

 3 Name the straight chained alkane containing eight carbon atoms.

4 Write down the molecular formula, structural formula and empirical formula of this alkane.

Fatty acids

Many organic compounds which are not alkanes contain alkyl groups (parts of alkane molecules). Their names denote the number of carbon atoms in the alkyl groups (Table 3). Some fatty acids contain large alkyl groups with a –COOH group at one end. The –COOH (**carboxylic**) group is known as an acid group, because the hydrogen atom can form a hydroxonium ion:

$$RCOOH(aq) + H_2O(l) \rightleftharpoons RCOO^-(aq) + H_3O^+(l)$$

The letter R is used to denote the rest of the molecule, i.e. the alkyl group. Lauric acid, found in coconut and palm kernel oil, is an example of a fatty acid. Its molecular formula is $C_{11}H_{23}COOH$, and its structural formula is

$$CH_3CH_2CH_2CH_2CH_2CH_2CH_2CH_2CH_2CH_2CH_2C{\overset{\displaystyle O}{\underset{\displaystyle OH}{<}}}$$

Table 3 Some alkyl groups	
Name	Formula
methyl	CH_3-
ethyl	C_2H_5-
propyl	C_3H_7-
butyl	C_4H_9-
pentyl	$C_5H_{11}-$
hexyl	$C_6H_{13}-$

Different fatty acids have different numbers of carbon atoms in their carbon chains. Myristic acid, found in nutmeg, has 13 carbon atoms, excluding the carbon atom in the –COOH group. Stearic acid, used to make soap, has 17 carbon atoms, excluding the carbon atom in the –COOH group.

 5 Write down the molecular and structural formulae for myristic acid and stearic acid.

These fatty acids are called saturated fatty acids, because each of the four electrons in the outer shell of every carbon atom forms a bond with one other atom. The saturated fatty acids we eat mainly come from animal sources such as milk, butter, cheese and meat. The acids are found in large quantities in foods such as sausages, cream cakes and biscuits.

Coconut oil is unusual. Most plant oils, such as olive oil and sunflower oil, contain unsaturated fatty acids. Coconut oil contains lauric acid, which is saturated

11.4　The structure of unsaturated fats

Alkenes

Unsaturated fats, like saturated fats, contain fatty acids with long carbon chains and a carboxylic acid group at one end. However, unsaturated fatty acids contain fewer hydrogen atoms than saturated fatty acids. The carbon electrons not used in bonding with hydrogen atoms form double bonds between the carbon atoms (Fig. 2). In the double bond, four electrons are shared and the bond is written as C=C. An area of high electron density exists between the two carbon atoms. Hydrocarbons containing double bonds are called **alkenes**. They too form an homologous series. The general formula for alkenes is C_nH_{2n} (Table 4). Alkenes are **unsaturated hydrocarbons**. Olive oil is derived from unsaturated fatty acids with the formula:

Fig. 2 Carbon–carbon double bond

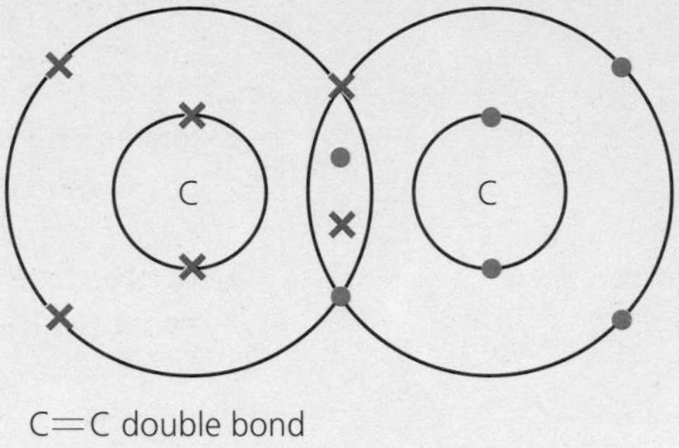

C=C double bond

$$CH_3CH_2CH_2CH_2CH_2CH_2CH_2CH_2CH_2CH = CHCH_2CH_2CH_2CH_2CH_2CH_2CH_2\ C\big(\!\!\begin{smallmatrix}O\\OH\end{smallmatrix}$$

Table 4 Chemical formulae of first five alkenes			
Name	Molecular formula	Structural formula	Empirical formula
ethene	C_2H_4	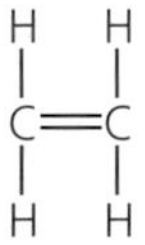	CH_2
propene	C_3H_6	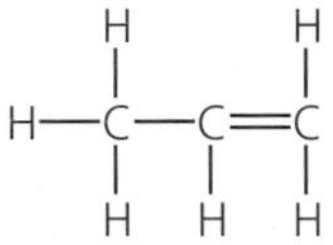	CH_2
but-1-ene	C_4H_8	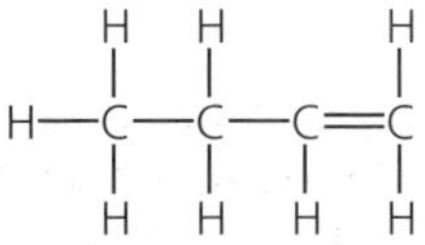	CH_2
pent-1-ene	C_5H_{10}	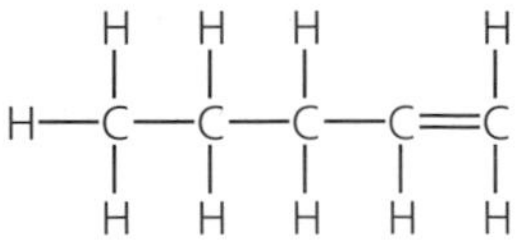	CH_2
hex-1-ene	C_6H_{12}	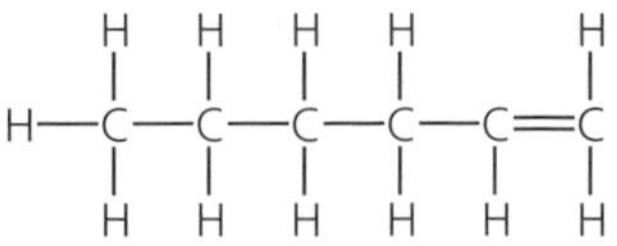	CH_2

Naming alkenes

The ending '-ene' signifies the presence of a double bond, and the first part of an alkene's name refers to the number of carbon atoms it has. A numeral denotes the position of a double bond, e.g. a '1' in the name would mean there is a double bond 'on the first carbon atom'. The carbon atoms are always counted to give the lowest number in the name. For example, $CH_3CH_2CH=CHCH_3$ is pent-2-ene, not pent-4-ene. When there is more than one double bond the numbers are separated by a comma.

pent-1,3-diene

number of carbon atoms | position of double bonds | two double bonds

  6 Draw the structural formula of hex-2,4-diene.

Monounsaturated fats have only one double bond in their carbon chain. Polyunsaturated fats have two or more double bonds in their carbon chain. Unsaturated oils are found chiefly in plants and fish, e.g. sunflower oil, corn oil and cod-liver oil.

We can find out more about the double bond and the nature of unsaturated fatty acids by looking at bond energies and bond lengths (Table 5). Bond energy is explained in Chapter 6. Bond length is the distance between the centres of the nuclei of two bonded atoms. It is usually measured in nanometres (nm).

Table 5 Comparison of single and double carbon bonds		
Bond	Bond energy/ kJ mol⁻¹	Bond length/nm
C–C	346	0.154
C=C	598	0.134

Although the double bond is stronger than the single bond, it is not by a factor of two. The reason for this is that a double bond is not the same as two single bonds put together. Instead, the double bond is thought to be composed of two different types of covalent bond, called a σ (sigma) bond and a π (pi) bond. The σ bond is formed between the two carbon atoms and is similar to a single covalent bond. The π bond is formed above and below the plane of the σ bond by the overlapping electron orbitals (Fig. 3).

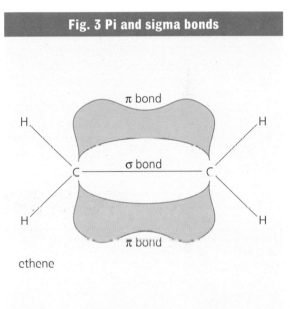

Fig. 3 Pi and sigma bonds

ethene

The 'bond areas' in figure 3 do not mean that the electrons are always in these positions. They indicate only where the electrons are most likely to be found. The electrons in the π bond are said to be **delocalised**.

  7 Suggest why the term 'delocalised' is used.

11.5 Unsaturated oils versus saturated fats

Mick's advice to eat less fat (page 123) did not distinguish between saturated and unsaturated fats. The *COMA Report*, however, recommends that over half of our fat intake should contain unsaturated fatty acids. Traditionally, countries such as the UK and the USA have relied on dairy products as one of their basic foods (Table 6). Dairy products are high in saturated fats. Foods high in unsaturated fats, such as soya products and vegetable oils, have only recently become popular in these countries.

Table 6 Saturated and unsaturated fatty acid content of some foods

Food	Saturated fatty acids/g per 100 g	Unsaturated fatty acids/g per 100g
bread	0.5	1.6
butter	49.0	28.3
cheddar cheese	20.0	11.6
chocolate	17.7	10.8
corn oil	16.4	78.6
eggs	3.4	5.4
lard	41.8	50.6
margarine (soft)	25.6	51.7
meusli	1.3	5.8
milk (full fat)	2.3	1.3
olive oil	14.0	80.9
peanut butter	10.6	40.7
sausage (grilled)	9.7	13.6

Source: *Family Guide to Alternative Medicine*, 1991

Dairy products such as milk, cream, butter and cheese, are big business in the UK and USA. These foods contain vitamins and minerals that are vital in a healthy diet. But they also contain a high proportion of saturated fats

Saturated and unsaturated fatty acids behave differently in the blood stream, because they have different physical properties. This difference is caused by the different shapes of the two molecules.

The presence or absence of a double bond in the carbon chain of a fatty acid affects the shape of the molecule, which in turn affects its physical properties. A carbon atom with four single covalent bonds, such as methane, has a tetrahedral arrangement of bonds. This is because the bonds are all areas of negative charge and therefore repel each other. This produces an angle of 109.5° for the H–C–H bonds in methane (Fig. 4).

Fig. 4 Bond angles in methane and ethene

methane
109.5°

ethene
117.3°

Two carbon atoms joined by a double bond, such as in ethene, have a flat or planar shape. This is because the π electrons positioned above and below the σ bond force the structure into a two-dimensional shape (Fig. 4). The H–C–H bonds in ethene have a bond angle of 117.3°.

Q8 If all three bonds were equally spaced around each carbon atom in ethene, each angle would be 360°÷3 or 120°. Why are the H–C–H bond angles in ethene less than 120°?

Saturated fatty acids have a zig-zag shaped carbon chain. When the fat is liquid, each carbon atom can rotate about the bond with its neighbouring atom (think about the tetrahedral bonding of each carbon atom). When the fat solidifies, the carbon atoms stop rotating and the chains lie closely side-by-side (Fig. 5). The loose but straight character of the carbon chain helps this solidification. This explains why saturated fats are usually solid at room temperature (e.g. butter, cheese, lard).

Fig. 5 Solidification of saturated fatty acid

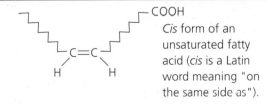

shape of molecules means that they can lie side-by-side, and solidify

Unsaturated fatty acids can have a bend in their carbon chains, caused by the double bond. The double bond is fixed in a planar shape, preventing the carbon atoms from rotating around the π bond. The double bond is therefore very inflexible.

Unsaturated fatty acid molecules can exist in two forms (Fig. 6). These two forms

Fig. 6 *Cis* and *trans* isomerism

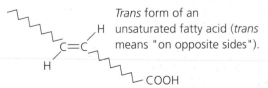

Cis form of an unsaturated fatty acid (*cis* is a Latin word meaning "on the same side as").

Trans form of an unsaturated fatty acid (*trans* means "on opposite sides").

share the same molecular formula but they have different structural formulae. The two types of molecule are called *cis* and *trans* isomers. They are examples of **geometric isomers**.

The *trans* isomer deviates little from a zig-zag chain. Molecules of fatty acids with the *cis* structure, however, cannot easily lie side-by-side to solidify (Fig. 7). They therefore tend to be liquid at lower temperatures, and have lower melting points than fatty acids containing the *trans* isomer. The *cis* isomer is the most common form of unsaturated fatty acids. The *trans* isomer only occurs in animal fats and in processed unsaturated fats such as margarine. Unsaturated fats are usually liquid (e.g. corn oil, sunflower oil, olive oil) at room temperature.

Fig. 7 Non-solidification of *cis*-unsaturated fatty acid

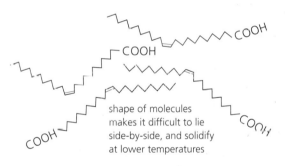

shape of molecules makes it difficult to lie side-by-side, and solidify at lower temperatures

Many doctors now think that eating large amounts of saturated or *trans*-unsaturated fatty acids increases the tendency for cholesterol to be deposited in the blood vessels. *Cis*-unsaturated fatty acids appear not to cause these deposits. In fact, there is evidence to suggest that they actually 'mop up' cholesterol deposits, and so reduce the chance of coronary heart disease. In Japan, where the national diet is traditionally low in saturated fat and high in unsaturated fat, the incidence of coronary heart disease is very low compared with the UK.

11.6 Margarines

The argument for eating less saturated fat is convincing, but it is not surprising that many people still consume large amounts of fat. For example, each year, thousands of tonnes of unsaturated fish and vegetable oils are converted to margarine, a more saturated product, in an attempt to imitate butter. In 1994, food companies spent around £555 million on advertising, whereas The Health Education Authority spent less than £1 million on conveying messages about healthy eating.

Margarines like this are made by hydrogenating unsaturated fish and plant oils

" Unhealthy subsidies "

Europe's Common Agricultural Policy is the other absurdity which may help to explain why Britons eat so much unhealthy food… We subsidise the production of excessive amounts of fat and sugar … dairy farmers receive the highest subsidies for producing full-fat milk, cheese and butter.

Source: A. Coghlan, 1991

The preference in Mediterranean countries for cooking with vegetable oils ensures a higher consumption of unsaturated fats. Butter and margarine consumption accounts for nearly 20% of the dietary fat in the average UK person's diet. Margarine is made by hydrogenating (adding hydrogen to) the double bonds in unsaturated fish and plant oils. The oils used in this process depend on the product. A manufacturer may use the cheapest oils available or a specific oil, such as sunflower oil, if sunflower margarine is being made. Hydrogenation is carried out using a nickel catalyst at a temperature of 180 °C, under a pressure of 10 atmospheres.

These margarines are made using a controlled degree of hydrogenation

This type of reaction is called an addition reaction. The degree of hydrogenation can be controlled to produce margarines of variable unsaturate content, and therefore variable 'softness'. The margarine produced is more saturated than its raw materials, and is therefore harder at room temperature, and has a higher melting point.

$$--CH=CH--+H_2 \xrightarrow[140\ °C]{Ni\ catalyst} --CH_2-CH_2--$$

 9 Explain why margarine has a higher melting point than the oils it is made from.

11.7 Detecting unsaturated oils

The degree of unsaturation of an oil can be found using bromine water. Bromine water is yellow and forms colourless compounds with alkenes by the addition of bromine atoms (Fig. 8) across double bonds. The reaction with ethene is as follows:

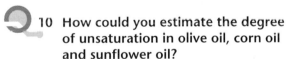

The product 1,2-dibromoethane is colourless. Its name is derived as follows:

1,2-	dibromo	ethane
bromine atoms on 1st and 2nd carbon atom	two bromine atoms	basic ethane structure

This reaction is called an **electrophilic addition reaction**. Such reactions can be used to distinguish between a saturated hydrocarbon, such as propane, and an unsaturated hydrocarbon, such as propene. Propane has no effect on the colour of bromine water.

10 How could you estimate the degree of unsaturation in olive oil, corn oil and sunflower oil?

11 Another example of electrophilic addition is the reaction between hydrogen bromide (HBr) and ethene. Bearing in mind that hydrogen bromide is polar, sketch out the reaction mechanism.

Fig. 8 Mechanism for electrophilic addition between bromine and alkenes

1 Ethene has a σ and a π bond between the two carbon atoms. This is an area of high negative charge density.

2 When bromine approaches the ethene molecule, the Br–Br bond is polarised by the area of high negative charge density.

3 The π electrons are attracted to the slightly positive bromine atom, forming a C–Br bond, and producing two ions. The positively charged **carbonium ion** is very unstable.

4 The carbonium ion quickly reacts with the bromine ion to produce 1,2-dibromoethane.

The reaction of bromine with ethene is called an electrophilic addition reaction. Bromine is described as an electrophile, because when its molecules are polarised they seek electrons. The reaction is an addition reaction, because bromine is being added to ethene.

11.8 The ideal diet

So what should we be eating? Ideally, we should include different amounts and types of foods in our diet (Fig. 9).

Most people in the UK eat too much animal fat and not enough grains or complex carbohydrates. Mick's advice about not eating chocolate bars was good (page 123). However, doctors, dieticians, food scientists, etc. are by no means convinced that this is the whole story. Arguments over saturated and unsaturated fats and cholesterol will continue as new scientific evidence comes to light.

Fig. 9 A healthy diet?

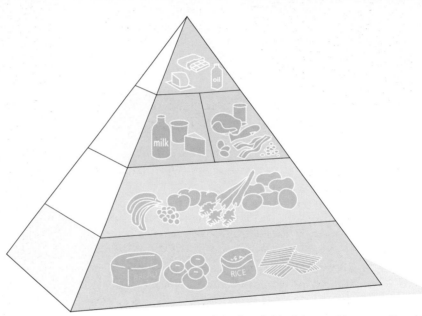

size of each block is roughly proportional to the amount of food recommended in diet

Mirror-image molecules

Bored with being kept indoors on a wintry afternoon, Alice held her kitten up to the looking-glass. 'How would you like to live in Looking-Glass House, Kitty? I wonder if they'd give you milk in there? Perhaps looking-glass milk isn't good to drink,' she speculated, as she set off on her journey of discovery through the looking-glass.

Drug manufacturers, in the light of recent experience, would certainly agree with Alice. They would not expect looking-glass milk to taste like ordinary milk. Neither would they expect the kitten to be able to digest the 'back-to-front' sugar and protein molecules in looking-glass milk.

Ricardo's mother took the drug thalidomide when she was pregnant, with no idea that it might harm her baby. But Ricardo was born with grave limb deformities. At that time, thalidomide was used extensively in Ricardo's country as a very effective treatment for leprosy. Why should this drug have disrupted Ricardo's development so badly? Surprisingly, there is a link between Alice's looking-glass milk and Ricardo's disability.

Ricardo Bezerra from Brazil is a thalidomide victim, born without arms

12.1 Learning objectives

After working through this chapter, you should be able to:

- **recall** the meaning of the term structural isomerism;

- **draw** structural isomers from molecular formulae;

- **recognise** simple asymmetric carbon atoms which give rise to optical isomers;

- **explain** the nature of plane polarised light;

- **describe** the effect of enantiomers on plane polarised light;

- **describe** the composition of a racemate.

12.2 Structural isomers

Chapter 11 looked at geometric isomerism in unsaturated compounds. In fact, there are several different kinds of isomerism. This chapter looks at two more kinds. We will start with the butane molecule, as an example. Butane has the molecular formula C_4H_{10} and the structural formula

$$
\begin{array}{cccccccc}
 & H & & H & & H & & H \\
 & | & & | & & | & & | \\
H- & C & - & C & - & C & - & C & -H \\
 & | & & | & & | & & | \\
 & H & & H & & H & & H
\end{array}
$$

This is not the only possible C_4H_{10} structure. The following structure also has the molecular formula C_4H_{10}.

$$
\begin{array}{ccccccc}
 & H & & H & & H \\
 & | & & | & & | \\
H- & C & - & C & - & C & -H \\
 & | & & | & & | \\
 & H & & H & & H \\
 & & & | & & \\
 & & H- & C & -H & & \\
 & & & | & & \\
 & & & H & &
\end{array}
$$

This second compound is called 2-methylpropane. The name is derived as follows:

2 - methylpropane

| position of methyl group on second carbon atom* | CH_3 (methyl) group | the longest chain has three carbon atoms |

*Count from the end that gives the lowest number.

We say that butane and 2-methylpropane are **structural isomers**. Structural isomers have the same molecular formula but different structural formulae.

 1 **Draw and name the structural isomers of C_5H_{12}.**

12.3 Optical isomers

Alice's kitten probably drank 'normal' lactic acid, if not the looking-glass variety. Lactic acid is the compound responsible for the sour taste in sour milk. The lactic acid molecule has two forms: one is a 'back-to-front' form, or mirror image, of the other. The two forms of lactic acid can be compared with your two hands. We say that lactic acid has two optical isomers (Fig. 1).

Fig. 1 Optical isomers of lactic acid

$$
\begin{array}{cc}
\text{OH} & \text{OH} \\
| & | \\
\text{HOOC}-\text{C}-\text{H} & \text{H}-\text{C}-\text{COOH} \\
| & | \\
\text{CH}_3 & \text{CH}_3
\end{array}
$$

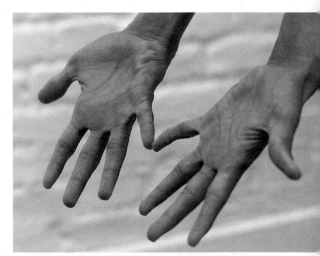

Your left hand is the mirror image of your right hand: both have the same structure, but one is the 'back-to-front' version of the other

Optical isomers are so called because they affect light in a particular way (see Section 12.6). In the early 1960s, a drug called thalidomide came on to the world market. It was marketed as a sedative and sleeping drug. Like lactic acid, the drug thalidomide has a formula that can be written in two ways, one being the back-to-front version of the other (Fig. 2).

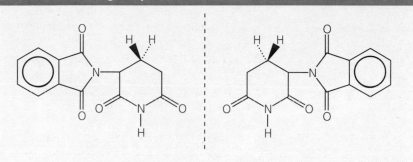

Fig. 2 Optical isomers of thalidomide

You will notice that the structural formulae in Figure 2 do not show every atom. The single lines represent single bonds and the double lines represent double bonds (see Chapter 11, pages 125 and 128). The hexagons containing circles represent rings of six carbon atoms. Unless otherwise shown, carbon atoms are located between the bonds, with sufficient hydrogen atoms bonded to them to satisfy the bonding requirements.

Before thalidomide was put on sale it was thoroughly tested. The tests included observing its effects on various animal species. All the tests indicated that it was a very safe and effective drug. Many doctors prescribed it for pregnant women who were suffering from anxiety, sleeplessness or sickness. However, the two optical isomers of thalidomide have very different effects on the human body. The thalidomide shown on the right-hand side in Figure 2 is a very effective sedative and sleeping drug. The thalidomide shown on the left-hand side causes dreadful deformities in the embryos of humans, and of some other species too. Drug manufacturers were not aware of this fact in the early 1960s, because the animal species on which thalidomide had been tested were all unaffected by the drug. The thalidomide that went on the market was actually a mixture of *both* forms of the drug: a 50:50 mixture of the two optical isomers, called a **racemate**.

Soon after the introduction of thalidomide the world was horrified by an 'epidemic' of babies born with misshapen or missing limbs, and often with other terrible deformities as well. Many of them died, and those who survived faced lifelong disabilities. It quickly became clear that the mothers of these children had taken thalidomide during the first few months of pregnancy. The drug was banned worldwide in 1962. In the short period during which it was available, it had affected 12 000 babies.

Optical isomerism is an example of **stereoisomerism**: in stereoisomers the atoms are connected together in the same way, but are arranged differently in space. Geometric (*cis/trans*) isomerism (see Chapter 11, page 131), is another example of stereoisomerism.

Key ideas

- Structural isomers have the same molecular formula but different structural formulae.

- Geometric and optical isomers are examples of stereoisomers.

- A racemate is a mixture of equal parts of two optical isomers.

12.4 Asymmetry and optical isomerism

Butane is a symmetrical molecule. It has an axis of symmetry, a plane of symmetry and a centre of symmetry (Fig. 3).

Symmetrical molecules, such as butane, cannot have optical isomers, because any two opposing halves of the molecule are the same. A molecule of butane and its mirror image are identical in every way. The lactic acid molecule is not symmetrical. It does not have an axis, a plane or a centre of symmetry. This lack of symmetry is what leads to the existence of optical isomers. Only molecules without symmetry – known as asymmetric molecules – have mirror images that are different from themselves.

Fig. 3 Symmetries of the molecule butane

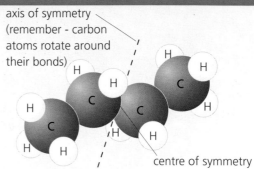

- axis of symmetry

centre of symmetry

axis of symmetry (remember - carbon atoms rotate around their bonds)

centre of symmetry

12.5 Compounds showing optical isomerism

Many organic compounds have optical isomers. Sometimes it is not easy to decide if a molecule has symmetry just by looking at the formula. You have to think about the three-dimensional structure of the molecule.

The carbon atom forms four bonds (see Chapter 4). If a carbon atom is bonded to four atoms (or groups) that are identical, as in methane, the molecule shows symmetry and has no optical isomers. If a carbon atom is bonded to four different atoms or groups (i.e. it is an asymmetric carbon atom), as in lactic acid, then the molecule itself will be asymmetric and will have optical isomers (Figs. 4 and 5).

The ability of molecules to form mirror images is called **chirality**. Molecules like this are said to be **chiral**. Both lactic acid and thalidomide are chiral. The two different optical isomers are called **enantiomers**.

2 **Which of these molecules would you expect to be chiral?**
a CH_2ClF
b butan-2-ol

H H OH H
| | | |
H—C—C—C—C—H
| | | |
H H H H

c alanine (an amino acid)

H
|
H_2N—C—COOH
|
CH_3

3 Look again at the structural formula for thalidomide (Fig. 2). Identify the asymmetric carbon atom in the thalidomide molecule.

Fig. 4 Structures of optical isomers

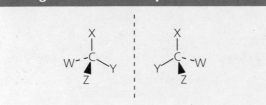

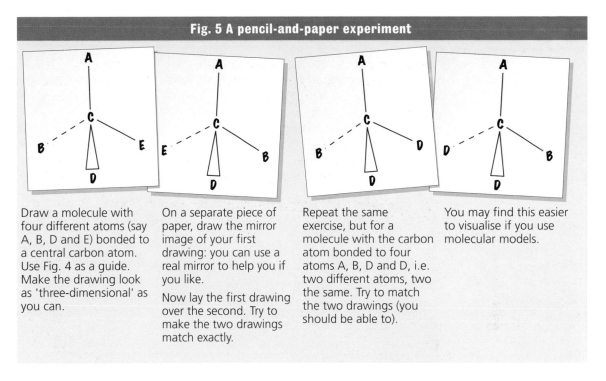

Fig. 5 A pencil-and-paper experiment

Draw a molecule with four different atoms (say A, B, D and E) bonded to a central carbon atom. Use Fig. 4 as a guide. Make the drawing look as 'three-dimensional' as you can.

On a separate piece of paper, draw the mirror image of your first drawing: you can use a real mirror to help you if you like.

Now lay the first drawing over the second. Try to make the two drawings match exactly.

Repeat the same exercise, but for a molecule with the carbon atom bonded to four atoms A, B, D and D, i.e. two different atoms, two the same. Try to match the two drawings (you should be able to).

You may find this easier to visualise if you use molecular models.

The chemical and physical properties of any pair of optical isomers are identical, with two exceptions. The isomers affect light differently, and they also react differently with other asymmetric molecules, particularly enzymes.

12.6 Optical activity

Optical isomers differ in their effects on **plane-polarised light**. Compounds with optical isomers, such as lactic acid and thalidomide, are called **optically active** substances.

A beam of sunlight, or light from a lamp, consists of waves that vibrate in all directions at right angles to the direction of the beam. Certain materials absorb all the waves except those that vibrate in one particular plane. The light that passes through these materials is said to be **plane-polarised** (Fig. 6).

Optically active substances are able to

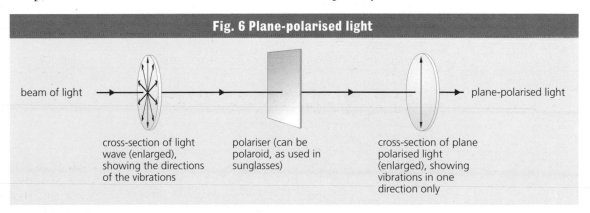

Fig. 6 Plane-polarised light

beam of light → cross-section of light wave (enlarged), showing the directions of the vibrations → polariser (can be polaroid, as used in sunglasses) → cross-section of plane polarised light (enlarged), showing vibrations in one direction only → plane-polarised light

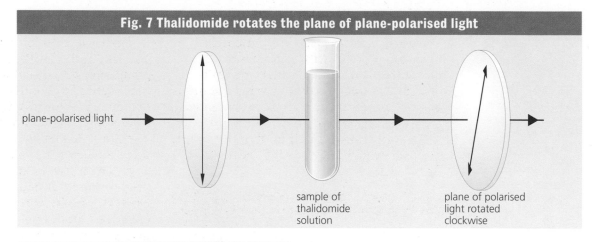

Fig. 7 Thalidomide rotates the plane of plane-polarised light

plane-polarised light →

sample of
thalidomide
solution

plane of polarised
light rotated
clockwise

The polarimeter is used to measure the direction and the angle of rotation of plane-polarised light; the reading is taken at the point at which the viewer can no longer see the division between the fields of view

rotate the plane of plane-polarised light. The two enantiomers rotate the plane by the same amount but in opposite directions. The enantiomer (–)-thalidomide, for example, rotates plane-polarised light to the left (anticlockwise) and is often called L-thalidomide, where 'L' stands for **laevorotatory**. (+)-thalidomide rotates plane-polarised light to the right (clockwise) and is called D-thalidomide, where 'D' stands for **dextrorotatory** (Fig. 7).

The isomer (+)-thalidomide is the sedative and sleeping drug. (–)-thalidomide is the compound that causes abnormalities in babies in the womb. Unfortunately thalidomide cannot be made safe just by purifying it so as to remove all the (–)-isomer. The (+)-isomer seems to be able to change into the (–)-isomer within the body.

Key ideas

- Asymmetric molecules form optical isomers.

- Enantiomers rotate plane-polarised light in opposite directions.

- Laevorotatory isomers rotate the plane of plane-polarised light anticlockwise.

- Dextrorotatory isomers rotate the plane of plane-polarised light clockwise.

12.7 Chirality in nature

The enzymes that digest milk and other foods are proteins with asymmetric molecules. During digestion of the milk protein, the enzyme molecule fits the milk protein molecule like two pieces of jigsaw puzzle fitting together (Fig. 8). An enzyme will fit only one of a pair of optical isomers, just as your right glove will fit only your right hand.

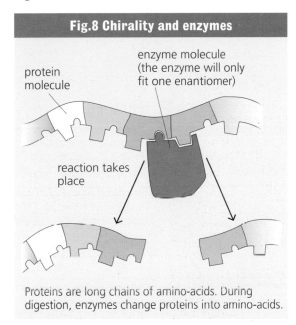

Fig.8 Chirality and enzymes

protein molecule

enzyme molecule (the enzyme will only fit one enantiomer)

reaction takes place

Proteins are long chains of amino-acids. During digestion, enzymes change proteins into amino-acids.

This is why the proteins in Alice's looking-glass milk could not be digested by the kitten's normal enzymes. The kitten's protein-digesting enzymes will only digest the (–)- forms. The cream in milk contains fat molecules, however, and these are symmetrical. They have no optical isomers, and the looking-glass fat molecules will fit the kitten's fat-digesting enzymes.

Living organisms contain, almost exclusively, (–)- enantiomers. This is probably the result of chance, in that the first proteins synthesised happened to be (–)- forms. Naturally produced drugs, like the penicillin made by the mould *Penicillium*, are pure (–)-forms. Synthetic processes produce drugs such as thalidomide as optically inactive mixtures (racemates).

Since the thalidomide disaster in the US and UK, in the 1960s, pharmaceutical companies have become very aware of the importance of chirality in drugs. For example, Parkinson's disease is a disorder of that part of the brain which controls voluntary movement. It can be treated using a chiral drug called L-dopa. In the early days of treatment, a racemate of the drug was used. It had serious side-effects. Doctors now know that L-dopa is an effective drug for treating Parkinson's disease, but that D-dopa is poisonous.

Manufacturers of chiral drugs therefore have to try to find synthetic methods that will produce one enantiomer only. One way that is being increasingly used is to copy biochemical methods, and to use enzymes.

Companies testing drugs in the US and Europe now have to provide information on the effects of both enantiomers and the racemate of any new chiral drug. Single-isomer drugs are increasing in importance. Table 1 shows the numbers of single-isomer and racemate drugs currently available, but these numbers are changing. One study predicts that single-isomer drugs will corner about 80% of the drug market by the year 2000, with racemates decreasing in importance. Racemates are likely to be both less effective and less specific. At best, half the mixture is inactive; at worst, it is a source of side-effects.

Table 1 Availability of chiral drugs

Number of drugs available	1675
Number of non-chiral drugs	726
Number sold as single isomer	519
Number sold as racemate	430

 4 **What is the major disadvantage to a pharmaceutical company of manufacturing chiral drugs as single isomers?**

L-Lactic acid is produced in this yoghurt by the bacterium *Lactobacillus*

Our senses also react differently to different enantiomers. For example, the amino acid tyrosine tastes sweet in the (+)-form and bitter in the naturally occurring (−)-form. Spearmint and caraway flavours are produced by the two enantiomers of the chemical carvone:

(−)-carvone (spearmint)

(+)-carvone (caraway)

Some people are convinced that yoghurt containing (−)-lactic acid is better for you than yoghurt containing the (+)-isomer. Manufacturers use this to give themselves a marketing advantage.

5 Suggest why the L-form of lactic acid might be better for you than the D-form.

The distinct flavours of spearmint (left) and caraway (right) are due to a pair of enantiomers, identical in every way except for the arrangement of their atoms in space

12.8 Ricardo and thalidomide

Ricardo Bezerra is one of an estimated 4000 thalidomide victims in his country (Brazil). Thalidomide is a very effective drug for treating the swollen sores of leprosy, and although it was withdrawn in 1962, it is being used again in certain countries where leprosy is common. Brazil has 240 000 lepers, 25 000 of whom are being treated with thalidomide. Many of them are illiterate through lack of education, and innocently may pass on their thalidomide pills in the belief that they may cure colds, fevers, skin rashes, stomach upsets or other ailments.

Many victims blame the Brazilian Government for not providing sufficient information. The Government have now banned the use of thalidomide by women between puberty and the menopause. A campaign to inform people about how dangerous the drug is, if used incorrectly, has been set up.

Key ideas

• Enantiomers have different effects on living organisms.

Problems with plastics

" Plasticiser migration "

We have been well aware of the possibility of plasticiser migration for five years. We introduced a low-migratory film wrap three years ago in response to ministry guidelines. On the strength of that there is no cause for alarm.

There are three main types of cling film or food wrap for sale in UK supermarkets. They are all made from a variety of chemicals and have different uses. Some contain chemicals called plasticisers, but as the newspaper article suggest, they are a potential threat to people's health. What are plasticisers and how do they affect your health? How do they escape from cling film into food? Are they as big a threat as the newspaper article suggests?

Cling film 'may endanger health'

Cling film may be a danger to health and should not be used to wrap food with a high fat content, such as cheese and cooked meats, Government scientists said yesterday. They called for more toxicological studies to be done on the chemicals used in food packaging. ...

The report was undertaken by the Steering Group on Food Surveillance, a committee of food department officials and independent scientists that advises the agriculture ministry on the chemical safety and nutritional value of food.

The Steering Group calls for more study of the plasticiser ATBC, which is widely used in cling film developed specially for use in microwave ovens. Use of plastic film in microwave and conventional ovens has previously raised fears that the leaking of chemicals into food could induce cancer.

Source: *The Times*, 1990

13.1 Learning objectives

After working through this chapter, you should be able to:

- **explain** that crude oil is a valuable source of alkane fuels and that it provides raw materials for the chemical industry;

- **describe** the fractional distillation of crude oil;

- **explain** the economic importance and the process of cracking long-chain alkanes to give shorter, more useful fuel molecules and alkenes;

- **describe** how ethene can be made from ethanol, and how ethanol can be made from ethene;

- **recall** that plastics can be made from alkenes by addition polymerisation;

- **describe** the structural and molecular formulae of the first six alcohols and carboxylic acids;

- **recall** how an ester is made from an alcohol and a carboxylic acid;

- **list** simple esters, alcohols and carboxylic acids.

13.2 Types of cling film

These three food wraps are all made from plastics and each package carries an important safety warning

One type of cling film is made from the plastic polythene (a common name for polyethylene, or poly(ethene)). It can be used to wrap foods to put in fridges, but manufacturers do not recommend putting polythene cling film in ovens.

Another type of cling film is made from the plastic PVC (poly(vinyl chloride) or poly(chloroethene)). PVC cling films contain **plasticisers** – chemicals added to make the cling film flexible and 'cling' better. They must not be used to wrap fatty foods such as cheese or cooked meat. Like polythene

films, PVC cling films can be used in fridges but not in ovens.

A third type of plastic film is specially made for use in microwave ovens. It is made from PVC that contains different plasticisers from those in ordinary PVC cling film.

This polythene film is suitable for wrapping cheese

13.3 The raw materials

The plastic molecules that make up cling film contain chains of carbon atoms, up to thousands of carbon atoms long.

Different plastics have different groups attached to the carbon atoms in the chains.

A polythene molecule has the structure:

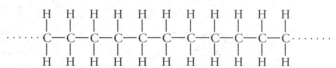

A PVC molecule has the structure:

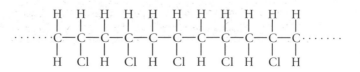

Crude oil

Polythene and PVC are both manufactured from **crude oil**. Crude oil is a mixture of about 150 different hydrocarbons, most of them straight-chain alkanes (see Chapter 11). Crude oil is difficult to ignite, and in itself it isn't very useful.

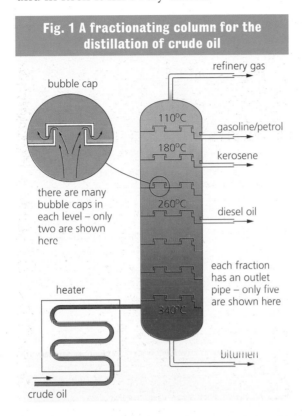

Fig. 1 A fractionating column for the distillation of crude oil

bubble cap

there are many bubble caps in each level – only two are shown here

heater

crude oil

refinery gas

110°C — gasoline/petrol

180°C — kerosene

260°C — diesel oil

each fraction has an outlet pipe – only five are shown here

340°C

bitumen

However, some of its components are very valuable, such as petrol, lubricating oils, heating oils and power station fuel. Crude oil is also the source of many raw materials, e.g. for making detergents, plastics, paints, antifreeze, synthetic rubber and medicines. Seventy per cent of organic chemicals are produced from crude oil. More than 3000 million tonnes of crude oil products are used worldwide every year.

The hydrocarbons in crude oil must be separated before they can be used. This is done by **fractional distillation** at an oil refinery (Fig. 1). The crude oil is heated until it vaporises. The gases pass into the fractionating column. The bottom of the column is at about 340 °C. The temperature falls further up the column and is coolest at the top. Any crude oil that is not in the gaseous state at 340 °C falls to the bottom, and is removed as residue. The other components rise up through the column. At the point where a particular component liquefies it is collected in trays. The products collected at the different points are called **fractions**. Each fraction contains a range of alkanes.

Boiling point trends

The alkanes in crude oil can be separated this way because of their different boiling points. The petrol fraction includes alkanes

In oil refineries across the world crude oil is separated into different fractions

Table 1 Crude oil fractions			
Fraction	Boiling point/°C	Length of carbon chain	Uses
refinery gas	up to 20	C_1—C_4	fuel
light petroleum	20–60	C_5—C_6	chemical feedstock
light naphtha	60–100	C_6—C_7	chemical feedstock
petrol	40–205	C_5—C_{11}	motor fuel
kerosene fuel	175–325	C_{12}—C_{18}	jet engine fuel, paraffin
diesel	275–400	C_{18}—C_{25}	diesel fuel
lubricating oil	non-volatile	C_{24}—C_{34}	lubricants
paraffin wax	non-volatile	C_{25}—C_{40}	polishes, Vaseline
bitumen	non-volatile	$C_{30}+$	road surfacing (tar)

with a carbon chain between five and eleven carbon atoms long (Table 1). The electronegativities (see Chapter 4) of the carbon and hydrogen atoms in an alkane are 2.5 and 2.1, respectively. Since these electronegativities are so close, the dipoles in alkane molecules are very weak. They are so weak in methane (CH_4), ethane (C_2H_6), propane (C_3H_8) and butane (C_4H_{10}) that these molecules are gases at ordinary temperature and pressure. The intermolecular forces are not strong enough to hold the molecules together in a liquid or solid pattern. In the longer-chain alkanes, however, van der Waals forces (see Chapter 5) can operate along the length of the molecule (Fig. 2). The longer the molecules, the greater are the forces between them and the greater the energy needed to change the alkane from a liquid to a gas. Therefore the boiling point increases as the chain length increases (Fig. 3).

The alkanes between C_5 and C_{17} are liquids at room temperature and pressure. Those with longer carbon chains are solids. In the liquids, viscosity increases with chain length. This is because longer chains tend to tangle more easily.

Fig. 2 Van der Waals forces in alkane molecules

van der Waals forces operate between carbon chains

long alkane molecules

Fig. 3 Relationship between boiling point and number of carbon atoms in alkanes

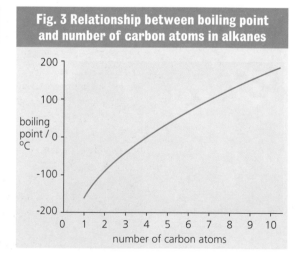

Cracking

Petrol is the component of crude oil that is in greatest demand. More and more vehicles are coming on to the roads each year, which means that the demand for petrol continues to rise. This demand far exceeds the amount available from current crude oil production. Scientists have discovered how to make the shorter-chain alkanes of petrol from the longer-chain, less useful alkanes in crude oil by a process called **cracking**. This is a free radical reaction in which a carbon–carbon bond is broken; for example:

$$CH_3(CH_2)_8CH_3(g) \xrightarrow[\text{Al}_2\text{O}_3/\text{SiO}_2 \text{ catalyst}]{400\text{-}500\ ^\circ\text{C}} CH_2{=}CH_2(g) + CH_3-\underset{\underset{CH_3}{|}}{CH}-(CH_2)_4-CH_3(l)$$

decane   ethene   2-methylheptane

Petrol burns most efficiently if the air–petrol vapour mixture in the cylinder is compressed before it is ignited. But this compression can lead to premature ignition ('auto-ignition'). The result is a sudden increase in pressure, which is heard as a 'knocking' or 'pinking' sound in the engine. Branched-chain alkanes produced by cracking cause less knocking than straight-chain alkanes.

As a measure of their knocking properties, fuels are given an 'octane number'. Heptane (a straight-chain alkane) causes a lot of knocking and has an octane number of 0. The branched alkane 2,2,4-trimethylpentane is a very good fuel; it has an octane number of 100. Most motor fuels have octane numbers approaching 100.

 1 What is the structural formula of 2,2,4-trimethylpentane?

Cracking is an economically efficient way of using longer-chain alkanes, for which there is otherwise less demand. Cracking also produces alkenes such as ethene and propene. Alkenes are far more reactive than alkanes, so they are excellent raw materials for the chemical industry. Cling film is made from ethene.

 2 Why does the cracking of alkanes always produce an alkene?

Sugar cane being processed at an alcohol-producing factory in Brazil

A substitute for oil?

The Earth's reserves of crude oil are finite. In the future we may need to find alternative sources of alkenes in order to manufacture plastics such as cling film. One possibility is to produce alkenes from alcohols. Ethanol can be produced from sugar by the **fermentation** process. The reaction is catalysed by the enzyme zymase, which is produced by yeast. This process is the basis of the brewing and wine-making industries:

$$C_6H_{12}O_6(aq) \xrightarrow{\text{yeast}} 2C_2H_5OH(aq) + 2CO_2(g)$$

glucose   ethanol   carbon dioxide

The ethanol produced by fermentation can be converted to ethene, by either
- using concentrated sulphuric acid as a catalyst;
- or passing ethanol vapour over a catalyst of heated aluminium oxide or heated pumice stone.

This reaction is known as an **elimination reaction**, or a dehydration, because a molecule of water is removed or eliminated from a molecule of ethanol (Fig. 4).

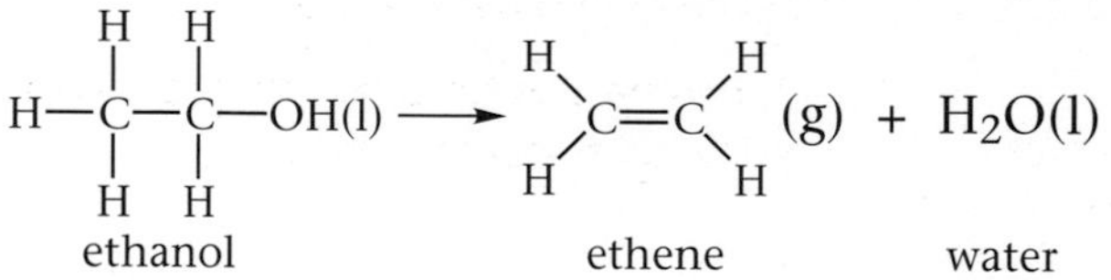

$$H-\underset{\underset{H}{|}}{\overset{\overset{H}{|}}{C}}-\underset{\underset{H}{|}}{\overset{\overset{H}{|}}{C}}-OH(l) \longrightarrow \underset{H}{\overset{H}{>}}C=C\underset{H}{\overset{H}{<}} \ (g) \ + \ H_2O(l)$$

ethanol   ethene   water

Fig. 4 Production of ethene from ethanol

1 The oxygen atom in ethanol attracts a proton (H^+) from the acid:

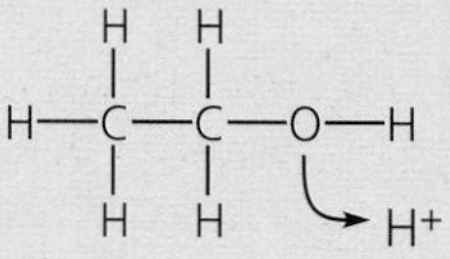

$$H-\underset{\underset{H}{|}}{\overset{\overset{H}{|}}{C}}-\underset{\underset{H}{|}}{\overset{\overset{H}{|}}{C}}-O-H$$
$$\curvearrowright H^+$$

2 Ethanol is **protonated**:

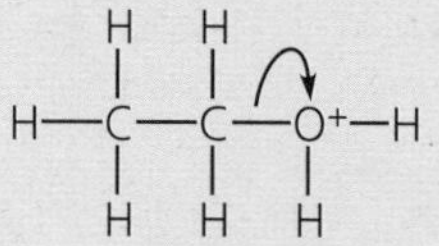

$$H-\underset{\underset{H}{|}}{\overset{\overset{H}{|}}{C}}-\underset{\underset{H}{|}}{\overset{\overset{H}{|}}{C}}-\overset{+}{O}-H$$

3 The protonated ethanol loses water to form a **carbonium ion**:

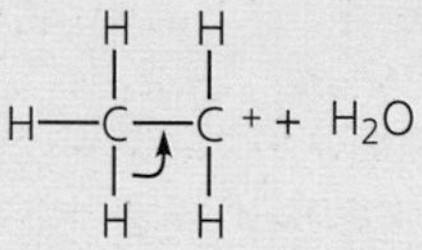

$$H-\underset{\underset{H}{|}}{\overset{\overset{H}{|}}{C}}-\overset{\overset{H}{|}}{C} + + \ H_2O$$

4 The carbonium ion loses a proton to form ethene. The proton remains as the acid catalyst. The acid catalyst (H^+) takes part in the reaction but remains unchanged at the end.

$$\underset{H}{\overset{H}{>}}C=C\underset{H}{\overset{H}{<}} + H^+$$

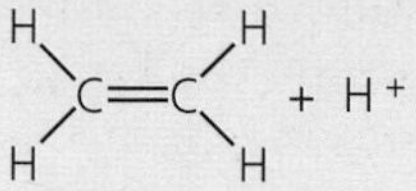

Ethanol is an important industrial solvent and raw material. Ethene can also be used to produce ethanol (Fig. 5). Where oil is available, it is now cheaper to produce ethanol from ethene than via the fermentation process.

You can see that both alcohols and alkenes are useful, and can be manufactured from one another depending on the demand for particular chemicals. Crude oil is a source of many valuable chemicals (Fig. 6). Other useful chemicals are made from plant products like sugar.

Fig. 5 Production of ethanol from ethene

Ethene can be converted to ethanol using concentrated sulphuric acid as a catalyst. When ethene is bubbled through concentrated sulphuric acid, ethyl hydrogen sulphate is formed:

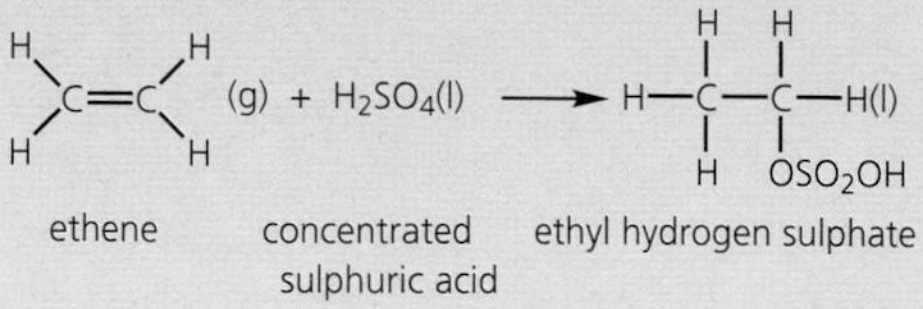

$$\underset{H}{\overset{H}{>}}C=C\underset{H}{\overset{H}{<}} \ (g) \ + \ H_2SO_4(l) \longrightarrow H-\underset{\underset{H}{|}}{\overset{\overset{H}{|}}{C}}-\underset{\underset{OSO_2OH}{|}}{\overset{\overset{H}{|}}{C}}-H(l)$$

ethene   concentrated   ethyl hydrogen sulphate
                sulphuric acid

Adding water hydrolyses these to form ethyl hydrogen sulphate, ethanol and sulphuric acid:

$$CH_3CH_2OSO_3H(l) + H_2O(l) \longrightarrow CH_3CH_2OH(l) + H_2SO_4(l)$$

ethyl hydrogen   water   ethanol   sulphuric
sulphate   acid

The sulphuric acid catalyst takes part in the reaction, but remains unchanged at the end. The overall result is the addition of water across the double bond. The process is carried out industrially using a catalyst of phosphoric acid.

$$CH_2CH_2(g) + H_2O(l) \xrightarrow[\text{H}_3\text{PO}_4 \text{ catalyst}]{300\ ^\circ\text{C, 60 atmospheres}} CH_3CH_2OH(l)$$

ethene   water   ethanol

Fig. 6 Many useful chemicals are made from crude oil;

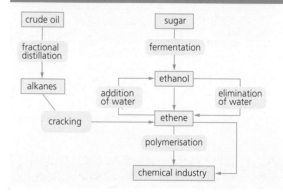

148

Key ideas

- Crude oil contains a mixture of alkanes. They can be separated by fractional distillation.

- Longer-chain alkane molecules can be converted into smaller fuel molecules and alkenes by cracking.

- Ethanol can be converted to ethene by the elimination of water.

- Ethene can be converted to ethanol by the addition of water.

13.4 Polythene

Where does cling film come from? Polythene cling film is made from ethene in a process called **polymerisation**. The term 'poly' refers to the many **monomers** that make up polythene. Ethene is the monomer and poly(e)thene is the **polymer**:

$$n\mathrm{CH_2}\!=\!\mathrm{CH_2}(g) \longrightarrow -(\mathrm{CH_2}\!-\!\mathrm{CH_2})_n-(s)$$

ethene   polyethene

The double bonds in ethene 'break open', enabling the ethene molecules to link together and form a chain. The chain can be up to 50 000 carbon atoms in length. This type of polymerisation is called **addition polymerisation**.

When ethene is polymerised at very high pressure (1000–2000 atmospheres) and at a temperature of 100–300 °C, the carbon chains in the polythene produced are branched. Because of the branching, the chains lie too far apart for van der Waals forces to operate. This type of polythene has a low melting point and low density. The polymer is quite flexible, because the polymer chains are free to slide over each other (Fig. 7).

When ethene is polymerised at a lower pressure (5–25 atmospheres) and at a temperature of 20–50 °C using a catalyst, most of the carbon chains in the resulting polythene are straight. Van der Waals forces can operate along the length of the polythene molecules. The polythene therefore has a higher melting point, a higher density and greater rigidity (Fig. 8).

Low-density polythene is used for making flexible items such as polythene bags and cling film. High-density polythene is suitable for making articles such as buckets, bowls and children's toys.

Fig. 7 Branched polymer chains in low-density polythene

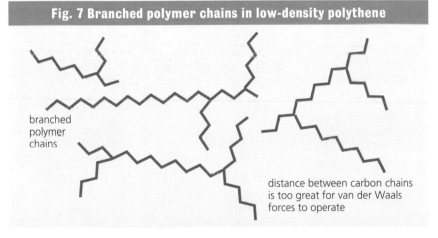

branched polymer chains

distance between carbon chains is too great for van der Waals forces to operate

Fig. 8 Straight polymer chains in high-density polythene

straight polymer chains – van der Waals forces can operate along length of chains

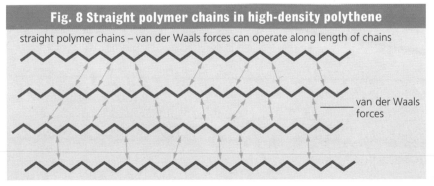

van der Waals forces

13.5 PVC

PVC is used to make cling films suitable for use in microwave ovens, as well as for making ordinary cling films. PVC is made from the monomer chloroethene by addition polymerisation:

$$n\mathrm{CH_2}{=}\mathrm{CHCl(g)} \longrightarrow {-}(\mathrm{CH_2}{-}\mathrm{CHCl})_n{-}(\mathrm{s})$$
$$\text{chloroethene} \qquad\qquad \text{poly(chloroethene) (PVC)}$$

 3 Other monomers produce different plastics. Write an equation showing the plastic produced from the monomer

$$\begin{array}{c} \mathrm{H} \qquad\qquad \mathrm{H} \\ \diagdown\qquad\diagup \\ \mathrm{C}{=}\mathrm{C} \\ \diagup\qquad\diagdown \\ \mathrm{H_3C} \qquad\qquad \mathrm{H} \end{array}$$

The PVC produced has long polymer chains. The carbon–chlorine bond is strongly polar and there is considerable intermolecular attraction between the polymer chains (Fig. 9). PVC is therefore a strong and rigid plastic, ideal for making items such as guttering and drainpipes. It is far too rigid to be used as cling film. PVC has to be specially treated to make it more flexible.

Fig. 9 Intermolecular forces in PVC

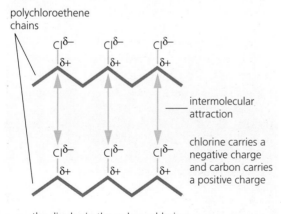

polychloroethene chains

intermolecular attraction

chlorine carries a negative charge and carbon carries a positive charge

the dipoles in the carbon–chlorine bonds attract adjacent polymer chains

Fig. 10

polychloroethene chains

plasticiser molecules

distance too great for intermolecular forces to be effective

PVC and plasticisers

PVC can be made more flexible by adding a chemical called a plasticiser. The plasticiser molecules penetrate the polymer and increase the distance between the polymer chains. The polar effects of the carbon–chlorine bond are weakened and the rigidity of the three-dimensional structure is reduced (Fig. 10). As a result, the polymer chains can slide over each other and the resultant plastic is soft and pliable, as cling film must be.

PVC that is used to make cling film normally contains up to 18% plasticiser by mass. The plasticisers used in cling film are compounds called **esters**. An ester is formed when an alcohol (Table 2) and a carboxylic acid (Table 3) react together in the presence of a concentrated acid (e.g. sulphuric acid). The equation for this type of reaction is:

$$\mathrm{R^1}{-}\overset{\displaystyle O}{\overset{\|}{\mathrm{C}}}\,{+}\,\mathrm{O}{-}\mathrm{R^2} \longrightarrow \mathrm{R^1}{-}\overset{\displaystyle O}{\overset{\|}{\mathrm{C}}}\, {+}\,\mathrm{H_2O}$$
$$\overset{\displaystyle \mathrm{O{-}H \quad H}}{}\qquad\qquad \overset{\displaystyle \mathrm{O{-}R^2}}{}$$

carboxylic acid   alcohol   ester   water

Esters have the general formula:

$$\mathrm{R^1}{-}\overset{\displaystyle O}{\overset{\|}{\mathrm{C}}}$$
$$\overset{\displaystyle \mathrm{O{-}R^2}}{}$$

Alcohols form a homologous series with the general formula ROH, where R is an alkyl group. The functional group is the –OH group.

Carboxylic acids form a homologous series containing the group

$$\mathrm{R}{-}\overset{\displaystyle O}{\overset{\|}{\mathrm{C}}}$$
$$\overset{\displaystyle \mathrm{O{-}H}}{}$$

where R is an alkyl group (or an aryl group – see Chapter 14). The functional group is the –COOH group. Carboxylic acids are weak acids, i.e. they are only slightly dissociated:

$$\mathrm{RCOOH(aq)} + \mathrm{H_2O(l)} \rightleftharpoons \mathrm{RCOO^-(aq)} + \mathrm{H_3O^+(aq)}$$

Table 2 First six alcohols

Name	Molecular formula	Structural formula
methanol	CH_3OH	
ethanol	C_2H_5OH	
propan-1-ol	C_3H_7OH	
butan-1-ol	C_4H_9OH	
pentan-1-ol	$C_5H_{11}OH$	
hexan-1-ol	$C_6H_{13}OH$	

Table 3 First six carboxylic acids

Name	Molecular formula	Structural formula
methanoic acid	$HCOOH$	
ethanoic acid	CH_3COOH	
propanoic acid	C_2H_5COOH	
butanoic acid	C_3H_7COOH	
pentanoic acid	C_4H_9COOH	
hexanoic acid	$C_6H_{13}COOH$	

Carboxylic acids are named as follows:

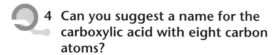

ethanoic acid

number of carbon atoms   acid group

 4 Can you suggest a name for the carboxylic acid with eight carbon atoms?

Esters are the 'smells and flavours' of chemistry. They are responsible for many flower scents and fruit flavours. Artificial fruit flavours (e.g. cherry, banana, pear) in some confectionery are made by mixing synthetic esters together. The flavour of peardrops is due to the ester ethyl ethanoate, which is made by the reaction of ethanoic acid with ethanol in the presence of concentrated sulphuric acid:

$$CH_3C\overset{O}{\underset{OH}{\diagup}} (l) + CH_3CH_2OH(l) \longrightarrow CH_3C\overset{O}{\underset{OC_2H_5}{\diagup}} (l) + H_2O(l)$$

ethanoic acid   ethanol   ethyl ethanoate   water

The name for this ester is derived as follows:

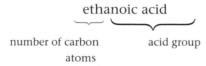

ethyl   ethanoate

alkyl radical   acid   indicates
from the   derivitive   ester
alcohol

The flavours of the sweets being sold in this Turkish shop are produced by esters introduced during their manufacture

 5 a Write an equation for the reaction between methanol and propanoic acid.
 b Name the ester produced.

The ester originally used as a plasticiser in cling film was di(2-ethylhexyl) adipate (commonly called DEHA). DEHA is an ester of 2-ethylhexan-1-ol and adipic acid (hexanedioic acid).

 6 a Draw the structural formula of 2-ethylhexan-1-ol.
 b Draw the structure of hexanedioic acid.
 c Write an equation for the formation of DEHA.

Unlike the acids and alcohols from which they are derived, esters have no –OH groups with which to form hydrogen bonds. They therefore have lower boiling points than their constituent acids and alcohols, and are more volatile. This accounts for their 'smelly' nature: volatile compounds can reach our noses more easily. The absence of any –OH group also means that they are not very soluble in water. The presence of carbon chains, however, makes them fat-soluble.

When esters are used as plasticisers in cling film, their volatility and solubility in fat poses problems. Plasticisers used in cling film have caused several health scares because esters can move from the film into food (Tables 4 and 5).

 7 Look at Table 4. Do you think there is a connection between the fat content of cheese and the amount of plasticiser that migrates?

8 Compare the plasticiser migration figures for cheese (Table 4), and fruit and vegetables (Table 5). What do you think is the major factor governing the amount of plasticiser that migrates?

Table 4 Migration of DEHA from PVC cling film into cheese

Type of cheese	Typical fat content/%	Migration/mg dm^{-2}	Calculated DEHA content of food/mg kg^{-1}
Edam	25.4	15.7	157
Wensleydale	31.5	16.3	163
Cheddar	33.5	15.1	151
Red Leicester	33.7	17.0	170
Cheddar (vegetarian)	35.8	17.3	173
Stilton	36.0	22.0	220
soft cheese (full fat)	36.8	5.2	52
French Roulé	55.0	22.5	225

(all foods were in direct contact with the film and were stored at 5 °C for 5 days)

Table 5 Migration of DEHA from PVC cling film into fruit and vegetables

Type of food	Storage conditions	Migration/mg dm^{-2}	Calculated DEHA content of food/mg kg^{-1}
avocado	5 days, 5 °C	11.1	53
grapefruit	5 days, 5 °C	3.0	3.0
stewed apple	7 days, −18 °C	0.2	2.6
cucumber	7 days, −18 °C	0.1	0.5
cabbage	7 days, −18 °C	0.3	4.8

(all foods were in direct contact with the film)

Adapted from MAFF, 1987

In 1986, a Department of Health Committee recommended that dietary intakes of DEHA should be reduced. They estimated that the maximum safe intake of DEHA per person per day was 16 mg, and in 1993 they revised this figure downwards to a maximum of 8.2 mg and an average of 2.4 mg per person per day. Their concern arose because American scientists had shown that DEHA caused liver tumours when fed in high doses to mice. Although no one is sure if the results of the studies on mice can be applied to humans, in 1986 the use of DEHA started to be phased out.

Since 1986, new PVC cling films have been produced for general use, as well as for use in microwave ovens. The new types of cling film contain either a mixture of two plasticisers – a polymeric plasticiser (typically 1–11%) and DEHA (typically 10–13%) – or a polymeric plasticiser only. The polymeric plasticiser contains long molecules of polymerised esters which cannot diffuse very easily, because of their high relative molecular masses.

Most PVC cling films are now labelled with instructions such as 'Do not use for wrapping fatty foods, e.g. cheese and cooked meats'. Many of the PVC films developed specifically for use in microwave ovens contain the plasticiser acetyl tributyl citrate (ATBC). ATBC is an ester of citric acid and the amount present in the cling film is typically around 4%. ATBC is also the plasticiser used in the plastic wrapping for vacuum-packed meats and cheeses. The migration rates for ATBC-plasticised film are lower (Table 6).

Table 6 Migration of ATBC plasticisers from film				
Food	Exposure	Migration/ mg dm^{-2}	Percentage loss from film	ATBC concentration in food/mg kg^{-1}
cheese	wrapped in film for 5 days at 5 °C	0.6	6.0	6.1
cake	wrapped in film for 5 days at 5 °C	0.2	2.0	3.2
stewed apple	container lined with film, initial hot contact, 1 day, 5 °C	0.1	1.0	0.9
roast beef meal	covered with film, reheated in microwave oven for 3 minutes on medium power	0.6	6.0	0.8
pizza	covered with film, reheated in microwave oven for 3 minutes on high power	4.9	49.0	35.0

 9 What is the effect of microwaving on the migration of ATBC plasticiser?

" ATBC plasticisers "

Safety advice sought

The increased use of ATBC has prompted MAFF to ask for better labelling on [products that contain] it, offering consumer advice on how to use the previously labelled "microwave-safe" films which, it suggests, are safe for "covering containers or reheating meals on plates", but not "for lining dishes or wrapping food while cooking in a microwave oven". .

Source: *The Times*, 1990

Publication of the migration figures on ATBC in 1990 prompted the newspaper article at the beginning of this chapter. One day later the Ministry of Agriculture, Fisheries and Food (MAFF) issued a statement (left).

The packaging on most cling film intended for use in microwave ovens now carries clear instructions. The instructions point out that the film should not be used in direct contact with food in a microwave, or to wrap fatty foods such as cheese. Cling film has been in general use since the early 1960s. Further tests may prove that DEHA and ATBC are completely safe. In the meantime, the Government and cling film manufacturers are being cautious and using low-migratory plasticisers.

Key ideas

- Alkenes undergo addition polymerisation to form polymers.

- The reaction between an alcohol and a carboxylic acid produces an ester.

Benzene rings

'I was taught in college that diamond and graphite were the only carbon allotropes. It's not true any more! They've found another allotrope, with a totally new structure. And that structure may have applications we never dreamed could be part of carbon chemistry: from electrical superconductors to revolutionary ways of giving drugs, perhaps stopping viruses from reproducing – maybe even HIV.'

This chapter is about a discovery that surprised even people who'd forgotten most of their chemistry. Excited science journalists and television reporters sent the story round the world. University professors and young students in Sussex, Germany and the United States – far too many to list individually in this book – collaborated to answer the novel and fascinating questions that it raised. But within ten years, the substance that so astonished its discoverers was being isolated by school students in their own laboratories.

> ## " New carbon allotropes "
>
> ## Carbon footballs
>
> During experiments aimed at understanding the mechanisms by which long-chain carbon molecules are formed in interstellar space and circumstellar shells, graphite has been vaporised by laser irradiation, producing a remarkably stable cluster consisting of 60 carbon atoms. Concerning the question of what kind of 60-carbon atom structure might give rise to a superstable species, we suggest a truncated icosahedron, a polygon with 60 vertices and 32 faces, 12 of which are pentagonal and 20 hexagonal. This object is commonly encountered as the football ...
>
> Source: Kroto *et al.*, 1985

The structure of the newly discovered allotrope of carbon is the same shape as a football

14.1 Learning objectives

After working through this chapter, you should be able to:

- **describe** the bonding in the benzene molecule and explain it in terms of shape and bond length;

- **explain** the stability of benzene's structure in terms of the delocalisation of its electrons, and understand the evidence for it;

- **describe** the substitution reaction of benzene with the electrophilic group NO_2^+;

- **recall** that certain bonds in organic molecules absorb certain frequencies of infrared radiation, and that this enables the molecules to be identified by infrared spectroscopy;

- **recall** that nuclear magnetic resonance spectroscopy can be used to identify the positions of hydrogen and carbon atoms in a molecule.

14.2 The new allotrope

In 1985 Harry Kroto, a professor at the University of Sussex, was interested in the molecules that are found in space. He had shown that some contained long chains of carbon atoms, and he wanted to prepare some of these substances himself. He arranged with two scientists at Rice University in Texas, Smalley and Curl, to use special apparatus there, in which he could vaporise graphite using a laser beam and monitor the products by mass spectrometry (see Chapter 1).

The 'football' team: O'Brien, Smalley, Curly, Kroto, and Heath

Together with some students, he began his experiments. Within a day or two, they were getting some unexpected mass spectra, with a very large peak at 720 and a smaller one at 840 (Fig. 1). The relative atomic mass (A_r) of carbon is 12, so the first peak must be due to a molecule of 60 carbon atoms, C_{60}, and the second to a molecule of 70 carbon atoms, C_{70}.

This suggested that the new clusters were new **allotropes** of carbon. Allotropes are different forms of the same element. They are made of identical atoms, bonded together in different ways, so that their physical properties, and often their chemical properties too are different.

The team began to wonder what the new molecules would be like. How did they differ from the allotropes everyone knew, graphite and diamond?

Diamond and graphite

A carbon atom has four outer electrons that it can share with other atoms. When two neighbouring carbon atoms share a pair of electrons, the electrons form a simple covalent bond (see Chapter 4).

Fig. 1 Mass spectrum of new allotrope

720

840

relative abundance

650   700   750   800   850   900
relative molecular mass

Diamond crystals sitting on a bed of graphite

Fig. 2 Structure of diamond

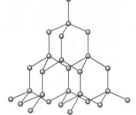

every carbon atom bonds to four other carbon atoms

Fig. 3 Structure of graphite

flat sheets of carbon atoms bonded into hexagons

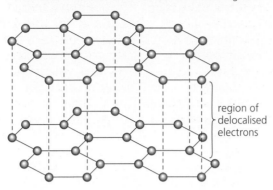

region of delocalised electrons

Top right. The glass dome at Expo '67, in Montreal, Canada, was designed by Richard Buckminster Fuller

If a carbon atom is linked by four identical bonds to four other carbon atoms, the bonds will repel each other to form a tetrahedral structure. In a diamond, this tetrahedral structure extends right through the crystal: all the carbon atoms are linked into a single enormous molecule (Fig. 2).

Graphite is different. In graphite, each carbon atom bonds to three other carbon atoms, making up flat sheets of carbon atoms, arranged in hexagons (Fig. 3). The unpaired electron on each atom lies in an orbit of a different shape from the others, at right angles to the sheet. These orbits overlap, so that all these electrons are shared by all the atoms in the sheet. Chemists call these **delocalised electrons**. You can imagine these shared electrons as being a kind of large 'super-bond' (see Chapter 4).

Both diamond and graphite have **atomic structures** – the molecule extends right through the particle of diamond or flake of graphite. But chemists in Sussex and Texas were faced with the problem that there are thousands, probably millions, of ways of fitting together 60 carbon atoms into a single structure. Which one was right?

Looking for a structure

The team wondered whether the new molecule might be a cage made of hexagons of carbon atoms – like chicken wire. Smalley thought it might include pentagons. Kroto remembered seeing an unusual dome made up of both hexagons and pentagons (see photograph above). At home, with his family, he had once modelled a three-dimensional map of the sky – a 'stardome' – with sticky tape and card, also with hexagons and pentagons. Using 20 hexagons and 12 pentagons cut from paper, with only a little distortion, Smalley made a structure with the same shape. It had a total of 60 points on its surface – perfect for the carbon atoms of a C_{60} molecule (Fig. 4). 'It was so pretty,' Kroto recalled later, 'it had to be right.'

Kroto nicknamed the C_{60} molecule buckminster fullerene, after the architect who designed the dome, R Buckminster Fuller. 'Fullerenes' is now the accepted name for this family of molecules.

Lots of unanswered questions remained. The team needed to know exactly how the carbon atoms were bonded together in the new allotrope. Were the bonds the same kind as those in diamond? Or like those in graphite?

Fig. 4 Soccer-ball structure of C_{60}

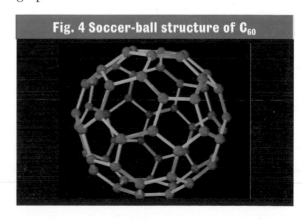

14.3 Benzene: the surprising hydrocarbon

For well over a century, chemists have been familiar with organic compounds containing hexagonal rings of carbon atoms. Benzene (C_6H_6) consists of six carbon atoms joined in a hexagon.

Fig. 5

 1 Does the structure in Fig. 5 satisfy the bonding requirements of carbon and hydrogen?

Benzene is a colourless liquid at room temperature, with a characteristic aromatic smell. For many years its structure was a mystery. Some chemists suggested alkene structures like $CH_2=C=CHCH=C=CH_2$. But benzene doesn't behave like an alkene – it is much less reactive.

An Austrian chemist called Joseph Loschmidt was the first to suggest that there could be a ring of carbon atoms in the benzene molecule. Several years later, in 1865, August Kekulé also put forward a ring structure. He added the idea that the ring could be made up of alternating single and double bonds:

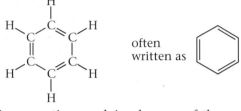

often written as

His suggestion explained many of the properties of benzene, but not all.

For example, benzene didn't behave according to the pattern followed by other hydrocarbons with six-carbon rings in their molecules. One of these has no double bonds in its molecule. Another has one double bond, and a third has two (Fig. 6).

A double bond can be changed into a single bond by adding hydrogen, in a reaction called **hydrogenation**.

As you would expect, the **enthalpy change of hydrogenating** the two double bonds in cyclohexadiene is about twice that of hydrogenating the one double bond in cyclohexene (Fig. 7).

Fig. 6 Six-carbon hydrocarbons with ring-shaped molecules

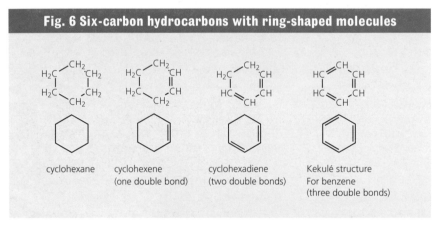

cyclohexane

cyclohexene (one double bond)

cyclohexadiene (two double bonds)

Kekulé structure For benzene (three double bonds)

Fig. 7 Enthalpies of hydrogenation for carbon rings

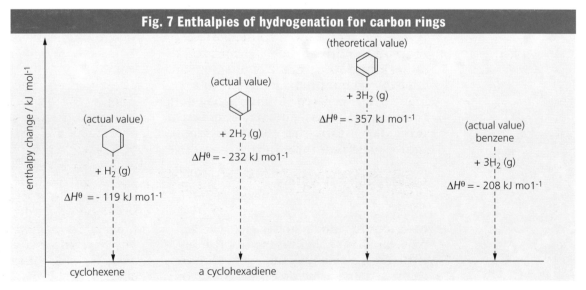

enthalpy change / kJ mol⁻¹

(actual value)

+ H₂ (g)

ΔH^θ = - 119 kJ mo1⁻¹

(actual value)

+ 2H₂ (g)

ΔH^θ = - 232 kJ mo1⁻¹

(theoretical value)

+ 3H₂ (g)

ΔH^θ = - 357 kJ mo1⁻¹

(actual value) benzene

+ 3H₂ (g)

ΔH^θ = - 208 kJ mo1⁻¹

cyclohexene   a cyclohexadiene

If benzene had a similar structure, but with three double bonds in the ring, the enthalpy change of hydrogenation of benzene should be three times as much (around 350 kJ mol^{-1}). But it's about 140 kJ mol^{-1} less than this. This difference means that benzene must be more stable than we might have expected.

 2 **If the actual enthalpy of hydrogenation of benzene was close to the theoretical value for a ring molecule containing three double bonds, what would this suggest for the reactivity of C_{60}?**

Fig. 8 Electron density map of benzene

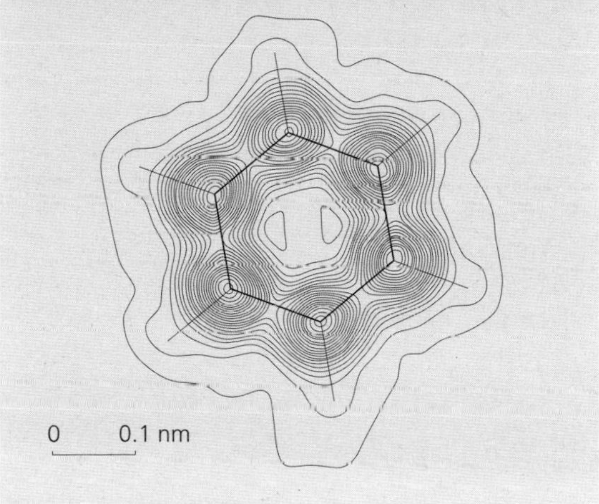

0   0.1 nm

Many years later, X-ray diffraction studies finally revealed the exact nature of the benzene structure (Fig. 8).

This technique was used to measure the C–C bond lengths in benzene molecules. All six of the bonds in benzene were found to be the same length – shorter than a single bond but longer than a double bond (Table 1). If Kekulé had been right, short and long bonds would have alternated around the benzene ring.

Table 1 Carbon–carbon bond lengths

Bond	Length/nm
carbon–carbon bond in alkanes	0.154
carbon–carbon bond in alkenes	0.133
carbon–carbon bond in benzene	0.139

 3 **Why do you think that the double bond in alkenes is shorter than the single bond in alkanes?**

Chemists now believe that some of the electrons in benzene are delocalised, rather like the electrons in graphite. Each carbon atom uses three of its four outer electrons in making either C–H or C–C bonds. The fourth electron lies in an orbit perpendicular to the hexagonal structure (Fig. 9).

Fig. 9 Electronic structure of benzene

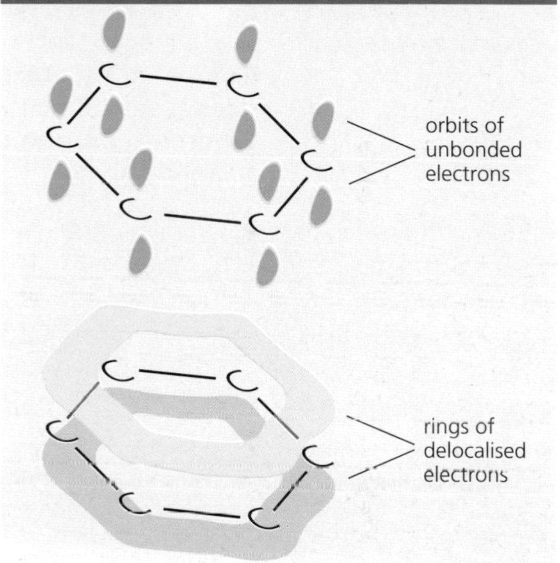

orbits of unbonded electrons

rings of delocalised electrons

In formulae, benzene is usually written as

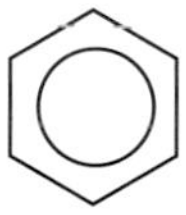

where the circle denotes the ring of delocalised electrons.

Chemists soon realised that the buckminster fullerene structure proposed by Kroto and his colleagues was full of six-carbon rings and that these could carry delocalised electrons, just as benzene does. Some thought that with the sheer number of carbon rings the C_{60} molecule contained, it would have 'a sea of electrons swarming over the surface'. But would the reactions of such a molecule be like those of benzene?

• Benzene, C_6H_6, has a ring structure of carbon atoms lying between two systems of delocalised electrons.

• The carbon–carbon bond lengths in benzene are shorter than single carbon–carbon bonds but longer than double carbon–carbon bonds.

• The structural formula of benzene is written as

14.4 A look at benzene chemistry

Compounds that contain six-carbon rings like the one in benzene are known as **aromatic compounds** (the early chemists thought that all these compounds had strong characteristic smells, or aromas). Benzene itself is an aromatic hydrocarbon, or **arene.**

Benzene is unsaturated, so you might expect it to undergo **addition reactions** readily. But any addition reaction would mean breaking up the ring of delocalised electrons, as follows:

This requires a good deal more energy than addition across a double bond. Benzene tends to keep its ring of delocalised electrons intact. Instead, most of its reactions are **substitution reactions**. One example is the reaction of benzene with the nitryl group (NO_2^+) to produce nitrobenzene (Fig. 10), which is used in the manufacture of dyes.

Nitrobenzene can be used to make a range of dyes, which produce a variety of colours suitable for fabrics and clothes

Fig. 10 Mechanism for electrophilic substitution reaction

The mechanism for the reaction is as follows:

1 A mixture of concentrated sulphuric acid and nitric acid contains the NO_2^+ (nitryl) ion.

2 The nitryl ion is attracted to the negatively charged ring of delocalised electrons.

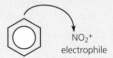

NO_2^+
electrophile

3 The ion adds to the benzene ring to form an intermediate, which contains both the nitryl ion and the original hydrogen atom. This disrupts the electron ring.

intermediate

4 The intermediate loses a proton, restoring the ring of delocalised electrons.

$+ H^+$

The overall reaction is

$+ HNO_3(l) \xrightarrow[50\ °C]{H_2SO_4}$ nitrobenzene $+ H_2O(l)$

Key ideas

- Benzene reacts with the nitryl group (NO_2^+) to produce nitrobenzene.

- The NO_2^+ group is an electrophile (an 'electron-seeking' group).

- Benzene reacts with the nitryl group by an electrophilic substitution reaction.

14.5 The power of spectroscopy

The next step in the investigation of buckminster fullerene was to use spectroscopic analysis to identify the groups of atoms in the molecule.

In spectroscopy, electromagnetic radiation (Fig. 11) is allowed to pass through the substance being studied in a **spectrometer**. The substance will absorb radiation of certain wavelengths. Spectroscopists measure the amount of radiation absorbed at particular wavelengths, and match the absorption patterns to the structure of the substance.

Fig. 11 The electromagnetic spectrum

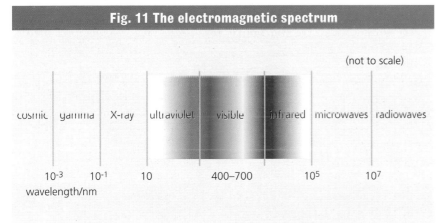

(not to scale)

cosmic | gamma | X-ray | ultraviolet | visible | infrared | microwaves | radiowaves

10^{-3} 10^{-1} 10   400–700 10^5 10^7
wavelength/nm

4 Wavelengths are usually measured in nanometres (nm); 1 nm is 10^{-9} m. What is the length of the smallest radiowave in centimetres?

NMR spectroscopy

Nuclear magnetic resonance (NMR) spectroscopy depends on the effect of a magnetic field on the nuclei of atoms.

If we can measure the wavelengths of radiowaves that are absorbed by a substance placed in a strong magnetic field, we can learn a lot about its molecular structure. For example, the wavelengths absorbed by hydrogen atoms depends on the position of the atoms in a molecule; in ethanol, for example, on whether they are part of an OH group, the CH_2 group or the CH_3 group. Each different wavelength absorbed produces a line on the NMR spectrum of the substance (Fig. 12). The technique provides a means of identifying the groups of atoms present in a substance. From this information it is often possible to identify the whole molecule.

Fig. 12 Proton NMR spectrum of ethanol

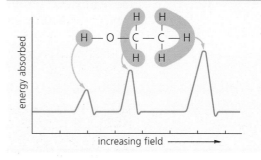

energy absorbed

increasing field ⟶

The proton or hydrogen-1 NMR spectrum is the most common type of NMR spectrum and relies on the spin of the nucleus in the hydrogen-1 atom.

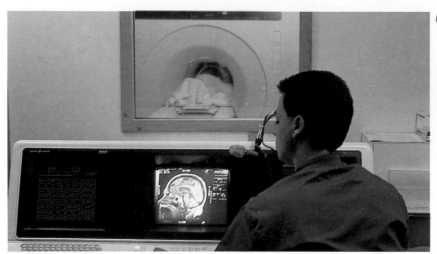

The patient is having a magnetic resonance imaging brain scan (MRI). The screen displays the grey and white matter of the brain, and relies on the spin of atoms in the patient being affected by the magnetic field of the scanner

Buckminster fullerene contains no hydrogen. So a different technique had to be used. Fortunately, in NMR spectroscopy the carbon-13 atom behaves similarly to the hydrogen-1 atom. An NMR spectrum that detects carbon-13 atoms is called a carbon-13 NMR spectrum.

In the proposed football structure for C_{60}, all the carbon atoms are positioned in the same way relative to the other carbon atoms. Kroto and his colleagues knew that the carbon-13 NMR spectrum of this structure would therefore have only one peak. It took them five years to prepare and purify enough C_{60} for the measurements. But in the end, that is what they found (Fig. 13).

They had been able to separate C_{70} from their C_{60} solution by chromatography. By now they had enough to measure its carbon-13 NMR spectrum as well (Fig. 13).

Q 5 Look at the carbon-13 NMR spectrum of C_{70}. What does it suggest?

The five peaks in the spectrum show that in this molecule there are five different planes on which the carbon atoms can be sited (Fig. 14).

These NMR spectra gave Professor Kroto and his colleagues some of the evidence they were looking for.

> **" Evidence for fullerenes "**
>
> 'We've been looking for this peak for five years,' says Kroto. 'I can't describe the feeling of exhilaration when we finally saw it. We are all extremely excited by these new results. They give strong evidence for a whole new family of fullerenes. A vast new area of carbon chemistry is on the verge of being opened up.'
>
> Source: Baggot, 1990

Fig. 14 Rugby-ball shape C_{70}

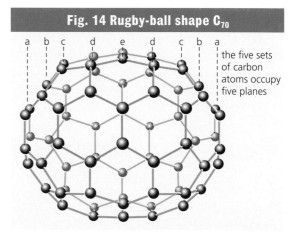

a b c d e d c b a

the five sets of carbon atoms occupy five planes

Fig. 13 Carbon-13 NMR spectrum of C_{60} and C_{70}

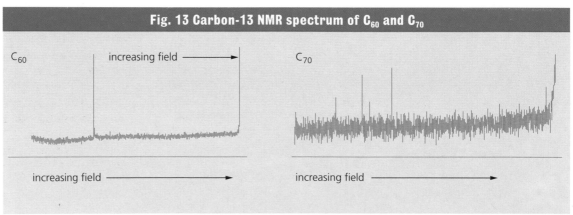

C_{60} increasing field →

C_{70}

increasing field →

increasing field →

IR spectroscopy

More evidence for the structure of the new allotrope was provided by another type of spectroscopy, infrared (IR) spectroscopy.

All organic compounds absorb IR radiation. The absorbed energy makes the bonds in the molecules vibrate more strongly. There are two types of vibration: stretching and bending (Fig. 15).

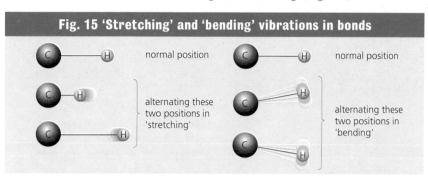

Fig. 15 'Stretching' and 'bending' vibrations in bonds

normal position

alternating these two positions in 'stretching'

normal position

alternating these two positions in 'bending'

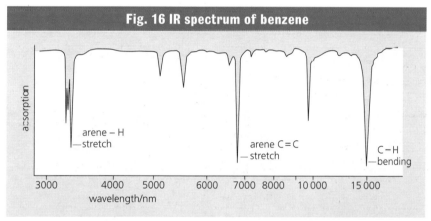

Fig. 16 IR spectrum of benzene

arene – H stretch

arene C=C stretch

C–H bending

absorption

3000 4000 5000 6000 7000 8000 10 000 15 000

wavelength/nm

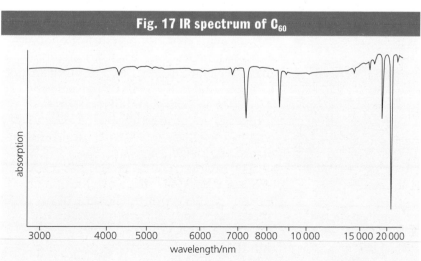

Fig. 17 IR spectrum of C_{60}

absorption

3000 4000 5000 6000 7000 8000 10 000 15 000 20 000

wavelength/nm

Each group of bonded atoms in a molecule absorbs radiation of certain wavelengths. For example, the C–H bond in an alkane absorbs radiation between 2960 nm and 3500 nm; this makes the 'stretching' vibrations more vigorous. The same bond absorbs radiation between 6800 and 7500 nm; this increases 'bending' vibrations.

Data books of IR spectra are available to identify unknown compounds. A few examples are given in Table 2.

Table 2 Vibrations of some functional groups, and wavelengths of radiation absorbed

Group	Vibration	Wavelength/nm
C–C	stretch	800–1500
C=O	stretch	5600–6100
C=C (arene)	stretch	6250–6900
O–H	stretch	2700–3000
C–H (arene)	bend	11 400–14 300
C–H (arene)	stretch	3300

6 Predict the wavelengths of IR radiation at which C_{60} should absorb.

An IR spectrometer records the absorptions on a printout. The IR spectrum shows the peaks (maximum absorption) drawn from top to bottom (Figs. 16 and 17).

The IR spectrum of C_{60} was first measured by chemists from Heidelberg in Germany and Tucson in Arizona. It shows four strong bands (Fig. 18). These were those expected for a football-shaped molecule. The bands can be used as the IR 'fingerprint' from which the C_{60} group can be identified in other samples.

Together, NMR and IR spectroscopy provided sufficient evidence to convince scientists worldwide that the C_{60} allotrope of carbon does exist, and that its molecule had the same structure as the familiar football.

- Spectroscopists study the wavelengths of electromagnetic radiation that are absorbed by the substances being studied.

- Spectroscopy provides information about the structures of molecules.

- NMR spectroscopy provides information about the positions of hydrogen (or carbon) atoms in a molecule.

- The bonds in an organic compound absorb IR radiation of certain definite wavelengths. Compounds may be identified from their IR spectra.

14.6 The new family of fullerenes

Buckminster fullerene is a mustard-coloured solid. It is stable in the dark, but in ultra violet radiation it decomposes. By 1990, the teams in Arizona and Heidelberg had developed a method of mass-producing buckminster fullerene, by the vaporisation of graphite electrodes in helium at low pressure (in order to prevent reaction with air). The soot thus formed contains 10% fullerene, the rest being graphite. C_{60} can be separated out by dissolving it in benzene; the insoluble graphite is left behind.

Students synthesising fullerene in the lab

Several fullerenes have been predicted, from C_{20} to C_{58}, as well as giant fullerenes with up to 700 carbon atoms! It seems that a whole family of fullerenes may exist.

Chemists originally thought that, like benzene, the fullerenes would have a delocalised electron structure and would be quite unreactive. They did not expect fullerenes to take part in addition reactions, because so much energy would be needed to disrupt the delocalised electron system.

The carbon rings in fullerenes are, however, slightly distorted in order to fit the football structure. As a result, overlap of the unbonded electrons is not as good as it is in benzene. The C=C bonds in C_{60} therefore behave more like those of alkenes than like those of benzene, and several fullerene derivatives have been prepared via addition reactions across these bonds. Hydrogen and halogens can be added to C_{60}, as well as alkyl groups.

Will these strange new allotropes of carbon ever be of any practical use? Some people think so, for instance, fullerenes may, like graphite, make good lubricants. It is hoped that $C_{60}F_{60}$ may be particularly good. Some alkali metal derivatives of fullerenes are promising superconductors – that is, they have no electrical resistance at all at very low temperatures.

The discovery of fullerenes has made Kroto and his co-workers internationally famous. He has confirmed some of his ideas about long-chain carbon molecules in space, but there are difficult experiments still to be done before these molecules are fully understood.

15 Detecting alcohol

'In the traffic police, we spend a lot of time trying to stop people from driving when they have had too much to drink. Almost all the drivers we stop are sure they are fit to drive.

At one time the police had to judge whether drivers were sober or not by deciding if they could talk clearly, or walk in a straight line. Since the first 'breathalyser' was invented in 1960, we've been able to measure the amount of alcohol in a driver's breath, rather than using crude measures like these. The electronic breathalysers we use today are more accurate, and easier to use too.'

A policeman routinely qestioning a motorist. This man was not under the influence of alcohol

The breathalyser is an important piece of equipment in helping police to detect drink-driving offenders. The first breathalysers relied on the reaction between the alcohol ethanol, found in alcoholic drinks, and an oxidising agent. What type of chemical reactions does this involve, and how could it be used to detect alcohol on people's breaths?

15.1 Learning objectives

After working through this chapter, you should be able to:

- **describe** the general and structural formulae of primary, secondary and tertiary alcohols;

- **describe** the general and structural formulae of simple aldehydes and ketones;

- **use** a chemical test to distinguish between aldehydes and ketones;

- **explain** the oxidation reactions of primary alcohols to aldehydes and carboxylic acids, and of secondary alcohols to ketones;

- **explain** why tertiary alcohols are not easily oxidised;

- **describe** how carboxylic acids can be reduced to aldehydes and primary alcohols, and how ketones can be reduced to secondary alcohols;

- **describe** the mechanism of nucleophilic addition, with reference to the reaction between the cyanide ion and carbonyl compounds.

15.2 Types of alcohol

When people use the word 'alcohol' they are usually talking about drinks made by the fermentation process (Chapter 6) – wine, beer, spirits and so on. More particularly, they mean the component of the drink that makes it 'intoxicating'. The alcohol in alcoholic drinks is ethanol, C_2H_5OH (Table 1). Ethanol is by far the most useful alcohol. To the chemist, an 'alcohol' is a chemical compound with the general formula ROH, where R represents an alkyl group and –OH is a functional group.

Table 1 Ethanol content of some alcoholic drinks

Drink	% ethanol by volume
beer, lager, cider	3.0–4.0
strong ale, ciders	4.1–6.0
table wine	9.0–14.0
sherry and fortified wine	16.0
spirits (gin, whisky, etc.)	40.0

Alcoholic drinks are made by **fermentation**. Grape juice, for example, is fermented to make wine. Grape juice contains the sugar glucose. Yeast is a tiny living fungus which metabolises (breaks down) glucose to release energy for its own needs; the reaction is catalysed by the enzyme zymase in the yeast. Ethanol and carbon dioxide are produced during this reaction.

$$C_6H_{12}O_6(aq) \rightarrow 2C_2H_5OH(aq) + 2CO_2(g)$$
glucose   ethanol

In wine making, the yeast dies when the level of ethanol reaches about 12%.

There are three classes of alcohols: **primary alcohols**, **secondary alcohols** and **tertiary alcohols** (Fig. 1). Ethanol is a primary alcohol.

All the alcohols, except the simplest, have several **isomers** (see Chapter 12). For example, there are three alcohols with the formula C_4H_9OH (Fig. 2)

Fig. 1 The different classes of alcohols

Primary alcohols have one alkyl group attached to the carbon atom linked to the –OH group:

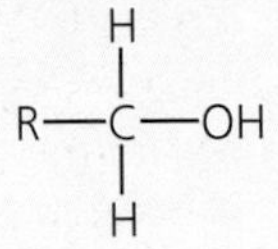

Secondary alcohols have two alkyl groups on the carbon atom linked to the –OH group:

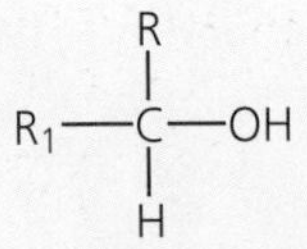

Tertiary alcohols have three alkyl groups on the carbon atom linked to the –OH group:

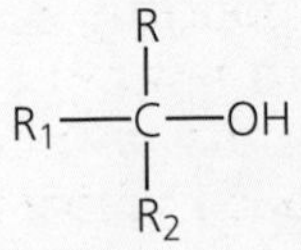

Fig. 2 Isomeric alcohols

a primary alcohol   butan-1-ol

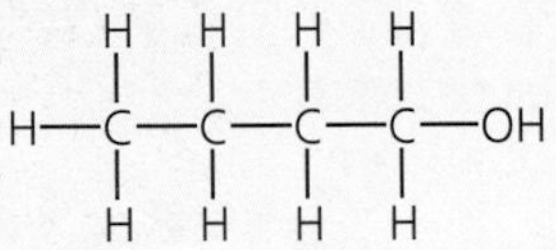

a secondary alcohol   butan-2-ol

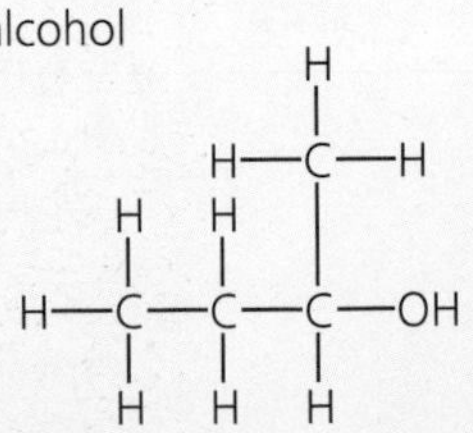

and a tertiary alcohol   2-methylpropan-2-ol

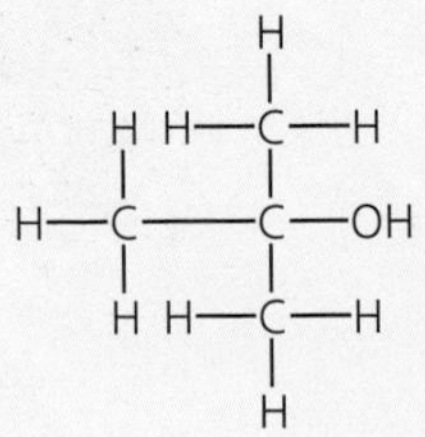

Alcohols are named as follows:

butan-1-ol

number of carbon atoms | denotes alcohol group

alcohol group is on the first carbon atom

butan-2-ol

number of carbon atoms | denotes alcohol group

alcohol group is on the second carbon atom

The longest chain in the molecule of 2-methylpropan-2-ol (Fig. 2) is the propane chain. This gives the molecule the last part of its name. The second carbon atom of the chain has both a methyl group and an –OH group attached to it.

 1 Draw all the structural formulae for pentanol and name them. Say whether each one is a primary, secondary or tertiary alcohol.

Key ideas

- Alcohols have the general formula ROH, where R is an alkyl group.

- There are three classes of alcohol: primary, secondary and tertiary alcohols.

15.3 Alcohol and the law

Look her in the eye. Then say a quick drink never hurt anybody.

DRINKING AND DRIVING WRECKS LIVES.

" Drink-driving offence "

(1) If a person –
   (a) drives or attempts to drive a motor vehicle on a road or other public place, or
   (b) is in charge of a motor vehicle on a road or other public place, after consuming so much alcohol that the proportion of it in his breath, blood or urine exceeds the prescribed limit he is guilty of an offence.

Source: *Road Traffic Act*, HMSO, 1988

The police woman in the introduction to this chapter enforces the 1988 Road Traffic Act. The Act makes it illegal to drive a motor vehicle if the proportion of alcohol in the driver's breath, blood or urine exceeds certain limits. Breath testing is quick, and is the method the police use at the roadside. However, the result of a breath test must be confirmed later, if necessary, by a blood or urine test. It is an offence to drive if you have more than

80 mg of ethanol per 100 millilitres (cm³) of your blood, or 35 micrograms (µg) of ethanol in 100 cm³ of breath.

Suppose a driver's breath contains 35 µg of ethanol per 100 cm³. That means that he or she has probably drunk the equivalent of three to five glasses of wine, or one or two pints of beer or cider.

Everyone reacts differently to alcohol, and to be more precise than this factors such as gender, age, and whether the driver had just eaten would need to be taken into consideration. Uniformed police officers can stop any driver they think may be 'over the limit' and carry out a roadside breathalyser test.

15.4 The original breathalyser

The police use two different types of breathalyser. Both have been approved by the government. The 'blow in the bag' chemical breathalyser depends on a chemical reaction that brings about a colour change. The driver blows through a glass phial packed with orange crystals of an oxidising agent, acidified potassium dichromate(VI). It is the ethanol that makes the crystals turn green. The police officer checks how much of the orange

packing has changed to green (Fig. 3). The extent of the change is related to the amount of ethanol in the driver's breath.

What happens inside the breathalyser? How can the colour of a few crystals provide evidence on which people may be fined, or lose their driving licence? We need to look more closely at the reactions of alcohols, and in particular about what happens when they are oxidised.

'Blow in the bag please!' One of the first trials of the original breathalyser

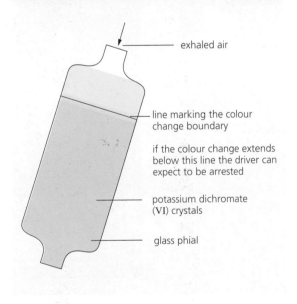

Fig. 3 Potassium dichromate(VI) crystals in the original breathalyser

exhaled air

line marking the colour change boundary

if the colour change extends below this line the driver can expect to be arrested

potassium dichromate (VI) crystals

glass phial

Oxidation of primary alcohols

Primary alcohols such as ethanol can be oxidised as follows:

$$H-\overset{\overset{\displaystyle H}{|}}{\underset{\underset{\displaystyle H}{|}}{C}}-\overset{\overset{\displaystyle H}{|}}{\underset{\underset{\displaystyle H}{|}}{C}}-OH(l) \xrightarrow[\text{acidified potassium dichromate(VI)}]{(-2H)} H-\overset{\overset{\displaystyle H}{|}}{\underset{\underset{\displaystyle H}{|}}{C}}-\overset{\displaystyle C}{\underset{\displaystyle}{}}\overset{\displaystyle O}{\underset{\displaystyle H}{}} (l)$$

ethanol   ethanal (an aldehyde)

The ethanal produced can be oxidised further to form a carboxylic acid:

ethanal $\xrightarrow[\text{acidified potassium dichromate(VI)}]{(+O)}$ ethanoic acid (a carboxylic acid)

The overall reaction is:

ethanol $\xrightarrow{(-2H)}$ ethanal $\xrightarrow{(+O)}$ ethanoic acid

Carboxylic acids form a series of compounds with the general formula RCOOH. Their structures and names are described later in this chapter. Ethanal is a **carbonyl** compound. That is, its molecule contains the carbonyl group.

There are two kinds of carbonyl compound: **aldehydes** and **ketones**. Aldehydes, including ethanal (Table 2), have the general formula RCHO.

Q2 Look at Table 2. Draw the structural formulae for the next three aldehydes in the series.

Aldehydes are named in a similar way to alcohols:

ethanal

number of carbon atoms including the carbon of the aldehyde group   denotes aldehyde group

Table 2 Three aldehydes		
Name	Molecular formula	Structural formula
methanal	HCHO	
ethanal	CH_3CHO	
propanal	C_2H_5CHO	

Slugs and snails are serious pests of crops but can be killed using metaldehyde bait, produced from ethanal

A bakelite radio. Bakelite, one of the first successful plastics, was made from methanol

Table 3 Three ketones		
Name	Molecular formula	Structural formula
propanone	CH_3COCH_3	H-C-C-C-H structure
butanone	$CH_3COCH_2CH_3$	H-C-C-C-C-H structure
phenylethanone	$C_6H_5COCH_3$	

Ketones have the general formula R_1COR_2 where R_1 and R_2 are alkyl or aryl (aromatic) groups (Table 3).

$$R_1—\underset{O}{\overset{\|}{C}}—R_2$$

Ketones are named as follows:

propanone

number of carbon atoms including the carbon of the ketone group — denotes ketone group

Oxidation of tertiary alcohols

Tertiary alcohols are not easily oxidised, because there is no hydrogen atom to be removed from the carbon to which the –OH group is attached.

Propanone is used to make Perspex, a hard, clear plastic with many uses including incubators for sick babies

In the chemical breathalyser, potassium dichromate(VI) oxidises the ethanol in the driver's breath to ethanal. It then oxidises the ethanal, to form ethanoic acid:

ethanol $\xrightarrow{(-2H)}$ ethanal $\xrightarrow{(+O)}$ ethanoic acid

The dichromate anion, $Cr_2O_7^{2-}$, is reduced to the Cr^{3+} cation:

$$Cr_2O_7^{2-}(aq) + 14H^+(aq) + 6e^- \rightarrow 2Cr^{3+}(aq) + 7H_2O(l)$$
orange   green

3 What is the change in the oxidation number of chromium in this reaction?

4 Write an equation to show the oxidation of propan-1-ol by potassium dichromate(VI).

Oxidation of secondary alcohols

Secondary alcohols are also oxidised to form carbonyl compounds – but instead of forming aldehydes they produce ketones:

propan-2-ol $\xrightarrow{\text{acidified potassium dichromate(VI)}}$ propanone (a ketone) $+ 2H^+ + 2e$

15.5 Reactions of aldehydes and ketones

Reacting similarly: nucleophilic addition

Both aldehydes and ketones have a carbonyl group in their molecules. So you would expect their reactions to be similar – and some of them are. They react similarly with hydrogen cyanide (HCN). Hydrogen cyanide is one of the most poisonous gases known (it often turns up in crime stories, sometimes under its old name of 'prussic acid'). It ionises in solution to produce hydrogen ions (H⁺) and cyanide ions (CN⁻). The cyanide ion is a **nucleophile** (it seeks positive charges). When hydrogen cyanide reacts with a carbonyl compound in solution, it attacks the double bond (Fig. 4). It does this because the carbonyl group is **polar**:

$$\overset{\delta+\ \ \ \delta-}{>\!C\!=\!O}$$

The overall reaction is:

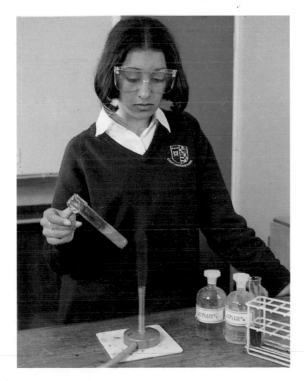

Fig. 4 Nucleophilic addition of cyanide

The reaction happens in stages.

1 The nucleophile attacks the partial positive charge on the carbon atom of the carbonyl group:

$$\underset{R^1}{\overset{R}{>}}\overset{\delta+\ \ \delta-}{C\!=\!O}$$
$$CN^- + H^+$$

2 The electrons of the C=O double bond are repelled by the approaching nucleophile towards the oxygen atom.

3 A reactive intermediate forms, with the oxygen atom carrying a negative charge. This reacts with a hydrogen ion from the hydrogen cyanide solution.

$$\underset{R^1}{\overset{R}{>}}\overset{O^-}{\underset{CN}{C}} + H^+$$

4 A hydroxynitrile forms.

$$\underset{R^1}{\overset{R}{>}}\overset{OH}{\underset{CN}{C}}$$

In the presence of aldehydes, Tollens reagent is reduced to metallic silver

171

Reacting differently: oxidation

Unlike aldehydes, ketones are not easily **oxidised** to form carboxylic acids. This is because there is no hydrogen atom attached to the carbon atom of the carbonyl group. Ketones can be oxidised only by very strong **oxidising agents**. This gives us a good way of telling aldehydes and ketones apart: we can test them with a very gentle oxidising agent. Fehling's solution can be used. Fehling's solution is blue and contains complex copper(II) ions. When the solution is warmed with an aldehyde, the aldehyde is oxidised to a ketone and the copper(II) is reduced to copper(I). Tollens reagent, a solution of silver nitrate containing ammonia, can be used instead of Fehling's solution.

5 a **Draw the structural formula for the ketone produced when butan-2-ol is oxidised.**
  b **Name the ketone.**

Recycling breathalysers?

Could the police save money by recycling breathalysers? It sounds like a good idea. But the breathalyser phials (tubes) that contain potassium dichromate(VI) crystals have to be replaced each time they are used. Though it is possible to reverse the oxidation process, it isn't a practical proposition. It is true that ethanoic acid can be **reduced** to form ethanol. But a strong **reducing agent** such as lithium tetrahydridoaluminate (LiAlH$_4$) has to be used:

Ethanal is more easily reduced than ethanoic acid. The reducing agent sodium tetrahydridoborate (NaBH$_4$) can be used. This has the advantage that it can be used in aqueous solution:

Ketones can also be reduced using sodium tetrahydridoborate. The reaction produces secondary alcohols:

$$H_3C-\underset{\underset{O}{\|}}{C}-CH_3(l) \xrightarrow[NaBH_4]{(+2H)} H_3C-\underset{\underset{OH}{|}}{CH}-CH_3(l)$$

6 a **Draw the structural formula for the alcohol produced when butanone is reduced.**
  b **Name the alcohol.**

Key ideas

- Primary alcohols can be oxidised to aldehydes and carboxylic acids.

- Secondary alcohols can be oxidised to ketones.

- Tertiary alcohols are not easily oxidised.

- Aldehydes can be reduced to primary alcohols.

- Ketones can be reduced to secondary alcohols.

- Aldehydes and ketones undergo nucleophilic addition reactions.

15.6 Electronic breathalyser

Apart from the cost and inconvenience of replacing the potassium dichromate(VI) phials each time, traditional breathalysers can be awkward to use because the yellow-to-green colour change is not always easy to see, especially at night. The police now prefer to use the modern electronic breathalyser – it's cheaper than the 'blow in the bag' device, too.

The electronic breathalyser is about the size of a pocket calculator. The driver is asked to blow into the plastic tube. Coloured lights indicate the level of ethanol in the breath. This can be converted into blood alcohol levels (Table 4).

This driver is being breathalysed using an electronic breathalyser

Table 4 Electronic breathalyser results

Colour of light	µg of ethanol per 100 cm^3 of blood	A typical police response
green	0–5	none
amber	6–69	a serious warning
red-amber	70–79	a stern warning
red	80+	arrested

The intoximeter

If the breathalyser light turns red the driver is arrested. At the police station the amount of ethanol in the driver's breath is measured again, using a machine called an intoximeter. The intoximeter is more accurate than a roadside breathalyser. The police check the intoximeter daily, and again after each time it is used: they have to be sure that evidence that will be produced in court is absolutely accurate. The intoximeter measures the ethanol content of the breath and provides a digital read-out of the level in µg per 100 cm^3 of breath.

The intoximeter works by measuring the amount of infrared (IR) radiation that the ethanol molecules absorb at different wavelengths (Fig. 5).

An intoximeter in use at a police station

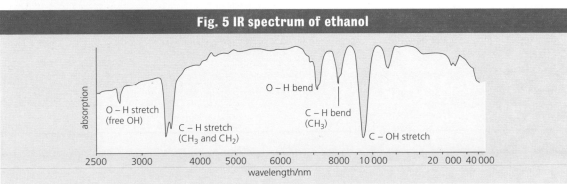

Fig. 5 IR spectrum of ethanol

absorption

O – H stretch (free OH)

C – H stretch (CH₃ and CH₂)

O – H bend

C – H bend (CH₃)

C – OH stretch

wavelength/nm

2500 3000 4000 5000 6000 8000 10 000 20 000 40 000

The absorbed energy makes certain bonds in the molecule vibrate more vigorously, either by stretching or bending (Fig. 6). The amount of IR radiation absorbed is proportional to the amount of ethanol present – that is, the higher the ethanol level, the larger the 'peaks'. (Remember that in a printout of an IR spectrum the peaks run from top to bottom!)

Propanone absorbs IR radiation at a wavelength close to that of one of the ethanol peaks, which has been something of a problem. Some diabetics have propanone in their breath because of their body chemistry, and this can affect their intoximeter results. Luckily, it was soon realised that this might produce falsely high read-outs. The intoximeter was adapted to compensate automatically for any propanone detected.

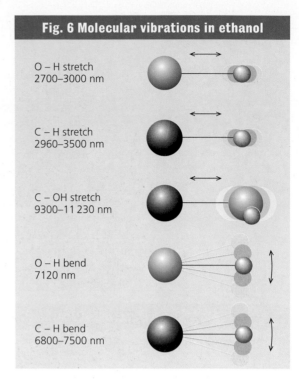

Fig. 6 Molecular vibrations in ethanol

O – H stretch
2700–3000 nm

C – H stretch
2960–3500 nm

C – OH stretch
9300–11 230 nm

O – H bend
7120 nm

C – H bend
6800–7500 nm

Key idea

- IR spectrometry (or spectroscopy) is an accurate method for measuring low concentrations of chemicals.

Reaction rates

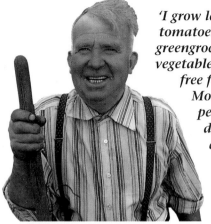

'I grow lettuces and tomatoes for sale to greengrocers. Salad vegetables need to be free from pests. Most of the pests and diseases that affect my crops come through the soil.

So I always sterilise the soil before I plant out young seedlings. The method I prefer is to cover the soil with polythene sheeting and pass bromomethane gas underneath it. Bromomethane is a good soil sterilant, because it quickly reaches and kills a wide range of pests. I'm careful to control how much bromomethane I use. It's toxic, and it isn't cheap; besides, it can escape into the atmosphere, where it may damage the ozone layer. I could use steam to sterilise the soil, but the costs are too high.*

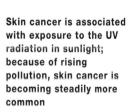

Skin cancer is associated with exposure to the UV radiation in sunlight; because of rising pollution, skin cancer is becoming steadily more common

As Chris Price says, pesticides like bromomethane are important in food production, yet they can damage the environment. Environmental pollution has even meant that enjoying the sun can be a health risk. How can we balance the good and the harmful effects of chemical reactions in the environment? How can we protect ourselves and our planet? We can begin by understanding how the risks arise.

16.1 Learning objectives

After working through this chapter, you should be able to:

- **describe** the mechanism of nucleophilic substitution in primary haloalkanes;

- **explain** how changes in temperature and concentration may affect the rate of a reaction;

- **use** diagrams that show the distribution of energies of molecules in a gas;

- **explain** how reactions only take place when colliding particles have sufficient energy;

- **explain** the term activation energy;

- **derive** a rate equation for a reaction, given data about initial rates;

- **explain** how changes in temperature may affect the rate constant of a reaction;

- **explain** how the presence of a catalyst may affect the rate of a reaction;

- **explain** the difference between a heterogeneous catalyst and a homogeneous catalyst.

16.2 Bromoalkanes

Using bromomethane to sterilise soil

Table 1 Boiling points of the first six primary bromoalkanes		
Bromoalkane	Formula	Boiling point/°C
bromomethane	CH_3Br	4
bromoethane	C_2H_5Br	39
1-bromopropane	C_3H_7Br	71
1-bromobutane	C_4H_9Br	102
1-bromopentane	$C_5H_{11}Br$	129
1-bromohexane	$C_6H_{13}Br$	156

Bromomethane (CH_3Br) is a gas at room temperature and is widely used in Europe as a soil sterilant. It is the simplest member of the family of bromoalkanes (Table 1). The term 'primary bromoalkane' means that the bromine atom is on the carbon atom at the end of the molecule.

 1 a Draw the structural formulae of the bromoalkanes from bromoethane to 1-bromohexane.
b Predict the boiling point of 1-bromoheptane.

Reactions of bromoalkanes

The carbon–bromine bond in bromoalkanes is polar (Fig. 1). This means that electrons in the bond are pulled towards the bromine atom. This leaves a small positive charge on its carbon atom, which means that bromomethane reacts easily with molecules that have a lone pair of electrons available for bonding. These often carry a negative charge, and are called **nucleophiles**. The hydroxide ion (OH^-) is a strong nucleophile. It readily attacks the carbon atom that carries the bromine. The hydroxyl (–OH) group is substituted for the bromine atom, and the bromine atom leaves as a bromide ion. The bromomethane is converted to an alcohol. Reactions like these are called **nucleophilic substitution reactions** (Fig. 2).

 2 a Draw the structural changes for the reaction between 1-bromopropane and hydroxide ions.
b Write the equation for the reaction.

Fig. 1 Bonding in bromomethane

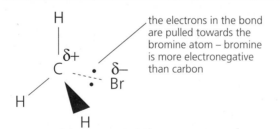

the electrons in the bond are pulled towards the bromine atom – bromine is more electronegative than carbon

Fig. 2 Mechanism of nucleophilic substitution reaction

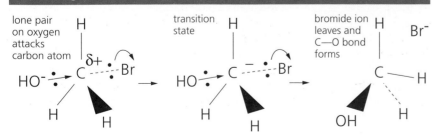

lone pair on oxygen attacks carbon atom

transition state

bromide ion leaves and C—O bond forms

Many other nucleophiles react with bromoalkanes (Fig. 3). These nucleophilic substitution reactions are important for all haloalkanes. They can be used to convert haloalkanes into other useful organic chemicals.

3 Write the equation for the formation of propanenitrile from 1-bromopropane.

Fig. 3 Nucleophilic substitution reactions of bromoalkanes

Alkalis react with bromoalkanes on heating to form alcohols (R indicates an alkyl group, e.g. CH_3, C_2H_5):

RBr	+	OH^-	→	ROH	+	Br^-
bromoalkane		hydroxide ion		alcohol		bromide ion

Cyanide ions react with bromoalkanes to form nitriles (an aqueous solution of potassium cyanide is **refluxed** with the bromoalkane dissolved in ethanol):

RBr	+	CN^-	→	RCN	+	Br^-
bromoalkane		cyanide ion		alkanenitrile		bromide ion

Ammonia reacts with bromoalkanes, on heating in a sealed tube, to form amines:

RBr	+	NH_3	→	RNH_2	+	HBr
bromoalkane		ammonia		alkylamine		hydrogen bromide

Understanding nucleophilic substitution reactions is useful when tracking bromoalkanes that are leached through soil. Soil contains a range of nucleophiles, so bromoalkanes can react in various ways. Some products may be harmless; others may be more toxic than the unreacted bromoalkanes.

Bromoalkanes can react with water in the soil to form alcohols, in a similar reaction to that with hydroxide ions. The reaction is much slower because water is a weaker nucleophile than the hydroxide ion. The lone pair of electrons on the oxygen atom in water is less readily available for bonding than the pair in the hydroxide ion.

16.3 Reaction rates

The type of nucleophile is not the only factor which affects the rate at which bromoalkanes react. Other factors are important, including:
- the temperature of the reaction mixture;
- the concentration of the reactants.

Temperature effects
Chris Price won't try to sterilise the soil with bromomethane on a frosty morning. Apart from the fact that below 4 °C bromomethane is a liquid, below about 10 °C its reactions are so slow that it is not an effective soil sterilant. Increasing the temperature increases the rate of its reactions. This is easier to

understand if we look at the energy of reacting molecules.

All molecules in a gas are in constant random motion, and are constantly colliding with each other. The energy involved in a collision determines whether or not the molecules will react. If the temperature is raised, the average energy of the molecules will be increased. So the average energy of the molecules in bromomethane gas will be higher at 15 °C than at 6 °C.

Not every molecule of bromomethane gas has the same energy at a particular temperature: the kinetic energy is shared across the molecules in such a way that a

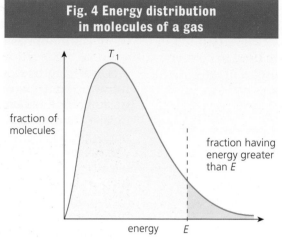

Fig. 4 Energy distribution in molecules of a gas

fraction of molecules

T_1

fraction having energy greater than E

energy E

very few have low energies and a very few have high energies (Fig. 4). This is called the **Maxwell–Boltzmann distribution**, after the two scientists who developed the theory.

When the temperature is raised, the energy distribution changes (Fig. 5). The average kinetic energy of the molecules increases. The fraction of molecules with low energies decreases and the fraction with high energies increases.

We can think of reactions in solution in a similar way. If bromomethane is bubbled into warm alkali, bromomethane molecules and hydroxide ions will collide. They will not react unless the kinetic energy of their collision is more than a certain threshold value. This threshold value is called the **activation energy**. The activation energy is

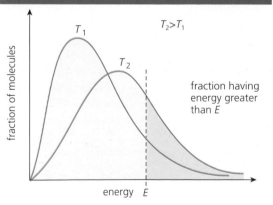

Fig. 5 Effect of increasing temperature on energy distribution

fraction of molecules

T_1

T_2

$T_2>T_1$

fraction having energy greater than E

energy E

different for different reactions (Table 2). At the same temperature, a reaction with a low activation energy is faster than one with a high activation energy.

Table 2 Activation energies for reactions of bromomethane at 298 K

Reactants	Activation energy (E_A)/kJ mol^{-1}
$CH_3Br + OH^-$	96.6
$CH_3Br + H_2O$	109.0
$CH_3Br + CN^-$	86.9

 4 Which of the reactions in Table 2 will be fastest? Explain your decision.

Table 2 can be used to draw an energy profile of the reaction between bromomethane and alkali (Fig. 6). The mechanism of the reaction is linked to its activation energy.

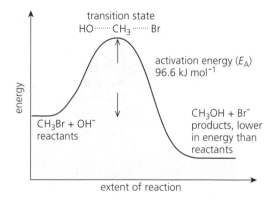

Fig. 6 Reaction profile for bromomethane and alkali

transition state
HO ┈┈ CH_3 ┈┈ Br

activation energy (E_A)
96.6 kJ mol^{-1}

energy

$CH_3Br + OH^-$ reactants

$CH_3OH + Br^-$ products, lower in energy than reactants

extent of reaction

Concentration effects

Chemists define the rate of a reaction as the rate at which a product is formed, or the rate at which a reactant is used up. Rate is therefore measured as a change in concentration over time. The units of rate for liquid-phase reactions are mol dm^{-3} s^{-1} (i.e. change in concentration per second).

A primary bromoalkane reacts with a hydroxide ion in a one-step reaction (look back at Fig. 2). Such a reaction is also known as an S_N2 reaction:

substitution — S_N2 — two molecules in
| rate-determining step
nucleophilic

At any particular temperature, the rate of the reaction is proportional to the concentration of the primary bromoalkane and the concentration of the hydroxide ions. A more useful mathematical description is

$$\text{rate} = k \ [RBr] \ [OH^-]$$
measured in mol dm^{-3} s^{-1} \qquad mol dm^{-3} \ mol dm^{-3}

where RBr stands for any primary bromoalkane and k is the **rate constant**. In this reaction, the units of k are mol^{-1} dm^3 s^{-1}. A general **rate equation** for the reaction

$$A + B \rightarrow \text{products}$$

can be written as

reaction rate $= k \ [A]^m \ [B]^n$

where m and n are usually 0, 1 or 2, depending on the reaction. For the reaction of primary bromoalkanes with hydroxide ions, for example,

rate $= k \ [RBr] \ [OH^-]$

A variable like m or n is known as the **order of reaction** with respect to the particular reactant. Both m and n are 1 for the reaction between primary bromoalkanes and hydroxide ions; the reaction is therefore first order with respect to the bromoalkane and first order with respect to hydroxide ions.

Pesticide sprays and soil sterilants can save a crop from devastation; these cabbages were destroyed by caterpillars because they were unprotected

Key ideas

- Haloalkanes contain polar carbon–halogen bonds. These bonds are attacked by nucleophiles.

- Molecules in a gas have a range of energies at a particular temperature. Increasing the temperature increases the average energy of the molecules.

- Molecules will not react when they collide unless the collision energy is greater than the activation energy of the reaction.

- A general rate equation for the reaction
  $A + B \rightarrow$ products
  can be written as rate $= k \ [A]^m \ [B]^n$

16.4 Bromoalkanes in the environment

Chris Price uses bromomethane because it is toxic enough to destroy pests at very low concentrations. He is careful to limit his use of bromomethane, so as to minimise seepage from the soil into the groundwater – this is water which is trapped in the permeable rocks underground and from which mains water supplies are drawn. Problems can occur, however, if large quantities of bromoalkanes leach into the groundwater. This happened at a disused chemical plant in Switzerland.

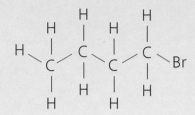

Fig. 7 Primary and tertiary bromoalkanes

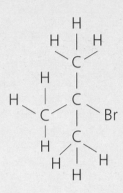

C_4H_9Br (1-bromobutane)

$(CH_3)_3CBr$ (2-bromo-2-methylpropane)

" Report on groundwater pollution "

We were surprised by the condition of the water. It had a bad-egg smell, contained no oxygen and was slightly alkaline. The bad smell was due to a low concentration of hydrogen sulphide. We used gas chromatography and mass spectroscopy to discover exactly which organic chemicals were present in the water. We found a range of alcohols, produced by reaction of the bromoalkanes with water over a long time. We also found many sulphur-containing compounds, which could be related to the bromoalkanes manufactured by the plant. These sulphur-containing compounds are very unpleasant chemicals and are slow to break down in the ground. We were interested in finding out how these compounds could have formed, so we tried some experiments to see if we could simulate the conditions. We were then able to suggest what reactions had produced the sulphur compounds.

Source: Schwarzenbach, 1985

Workers in safety wear taking samples for toxic analysis

The Swiss chemical plant manufactured several bromoalkanes. When it closed, the groundwater was found to be heavily polluted. Investigators realised that one of the plant's waste water tanks had been leaking for years, and that bromoalkanes had been seeping into the ground.

After a clean-up operation lasting seven years, a team of environmental chemists was brought in to find out whether the groundwater in the area was still contaminated. Part of their report is shown above.

The Swiss chemical plant had manufactured both primary and secondary bromoalkanes. The term 'secondary bromoalkane' means that there are two alkyl groups on the carbon attached to the bromine atom. Tertiary bromoalkanes have three alkyl groups on the carbon attached to the bromine atom. 1-Bromo-butane (primary bromoalkane) and 2-bromo-2-methylpropane (tertiary bromo-alkane) are **structural isomers** (Fig. 7)

 5 **Draw the structure of 2-bromobutane, the secondary bromoalkane that is isomeric with the bromoalkanes in Fig. 7.**

Tertiary bromoalkanes, like primary bromoalkanes, react with hydroxide ions to give alcohols. The equation for the reaction between 2-bromo-2-methylpropane and hydroxide ions is

$$(CH_3)_3CBr \quad + \quad OH^- \quad \longrightarrow \quad (CH_3)_3COH \quad + \quad Br^-$$

2-bromo-   hydroxide   2-methyl   bromide
2-methylpropane   ion   propan-2-ol   ion

You might expect the rate equation for this reaction to be

$$\text{reaction rate} = k\,[(CH_3)_3CBr]\,[OH^-]$$

as for the primary bromoalkane, but it is not. The Swiss investigators knew this when they were looking at the waste water problem. They knew that you cannot deduce the rate equation from the chemical equation – you have to determine the rate equation by following the reaction itself. This can be done by carrying out kinetics experiments to measure the rate under different conditions.

16.5 Reaction mechanisms

Fig. 8 Mechanism of nucleophilic substitution of tertiary bromoalkanes

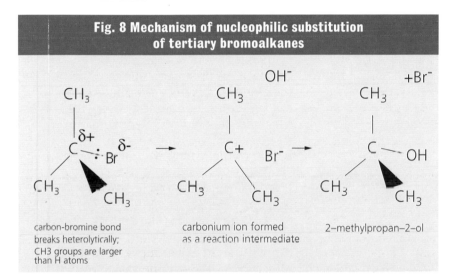

carbon-bromine bond breaks heterolytically; CH3 groups are larger than H atoms

carbonium ion formed as a reaction intermediate

2–methylpropan–2–ol

Fig. 9 Reaction profiles for S$_N$2 and S$_N$1 reactions

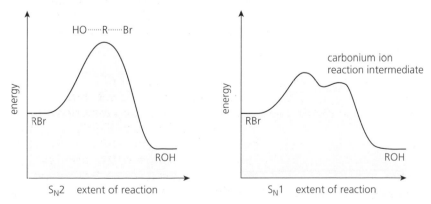

In a reaction between a tertiary bromoalkane and hydroxide ions, changing the concentration of the hydroxide ions doesn't alter the reaction rate. This means the reaction is zero order with respect to hydroxide ions. This is because the hydroxide ions take no part in the slowest step, the **rate-determining step**, of the reaction. The rate equation is

$$\underset{\text{measured in mol dm}^{-3}\,\text{s}^{-1}}{\text{reaction rate}} = \underset{\text{mol dm}^{-3}}{k\,[(CH_3)_3CBr]}$$

and the units for the rate constant k are s^{-1}.

The mechanism of this reaction is different from that of the reaction of bromomethane with hydroxide ions (Fig. 8). This is sometimes called an S$_N$1 reaction:

substitution   S$_N$1 —— one molecule in
nucleophilic   rate-determining step

Secondary bromoalkanes often undergo reactions which are intermediate between S$_N$1 and S$_N$2 mechanisms. You can see the difference between the reactions of primary and tertiary bromoalkanes if you look at the energy profiles of the reactions (Fig. 9).

 6 Which will be the fastest step in the two reactions?

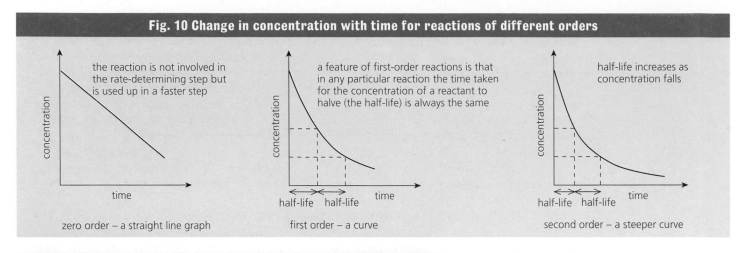

Fig. 10 Change in concentration with time for reactions of different orders

the reaction is not involved in the rate-determining step but is used up in a faster step

zero order – a straight line graph

a feature of first-order reactions is that in any particular reaction the time taken for the concentration of a reactant to halve (the half-life) is always the same

first order – a curve

half-life increases as concentration falls

second order – a steeper curve

Table 3 Initial rate data for the reaction of a primary bromoalkane with hydrogensulphide ions

$[C_4H_9Br]$ /mol dm^{-3}	$[HS^-]$ /mol dm^{-3}	Initial rate /mol dm^{-3} s^{-1}
0.1	0.1	1.11×10^{-5}
0.2	0.1	2.22×10^{-5}
0.3	0.1	3.33×10^{-5}
0.1	0.2	2.22×10^{-5}
0.1	0.3	3.33×10^{-5}

Table 4 Initial rate data (estimated) for the reaction of a secondary bromoalkane with hydrogensulphide ions

$[(CH_3)_3CBr]$ /mol dm^{-3}	$[HS^-]$ /mol dm^{-3}	Initial rate /mol dm^{-3} s^{-1}
0.1	0.1	1.5×10^{-2}
0.2	0.1	3.0×10^{-2}
0.3	0.1	4.5×10^{-2}
0.1	0.2	1.5×10^{-2}
0.1	0.3	1.5×10^{-2}

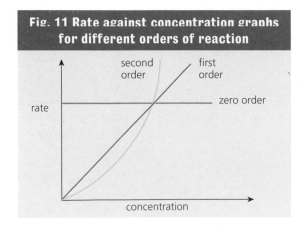

Fig. 11 Rate against concentration graphs for different orders of reaction

The Swiss chemists thought that a nucleophilic substitution reaction might be happening between bromoalkanes and hydrogensulphide ions (HS^-) present in the water. Working from experimental data and computer simulations, they were able to describe the chain of reactions that had led to the sulphur-containing compounds they had found. Simplified data allow us to follow how they deduced the nature of the reactions (Tables 3 and 4).

To work out a mechanism for a reaction, you first need to find the order of the reaction with respect to each of the reactants. To do this, experiments can be carried out using different initial concentrations of reactants. The initial rates found in the different experiments can be used to find the orders of the reaction (Fig.10). Conveniently, at the beginning of all three types of reaction the graphs approximate to straight lines.

In both series of experiments, the initial concentration of one reactant is kept constant while the initial concentration of the other is changed. If we look at the effect this has on the initial rates we can deduce the orders with respect to the reactants. We can do this either mathematically or graphically. If we have a lot of data, we can plot the initial rates against the initial concentrations of individual reactants (Fig. 11).

The data in Tables 3 and 4 allow us to derive the rate equations for the two reactions. We can then deduce the mechanisms of the reactions of bromoalkanes in the groundwater.

Look first at Table 3. If the initial concentration of the primary bromoalkane is increased, the initial rate increases proportionately. This means that the rate of the reaction is first order with respect to the primary bromoalkane. If the initial concentration of hydrogensulphide ions is increased, the initial rate also increases proportionately. The rate of reaction is therefore also first order with respect to hydrogensulphide ions. The rate equation can be written as

rate = k [C_4H_9Br] [HS^-]

So in the reaction of primary bromoalkanes, both the bromoalkane and hydrogensulphide ions are involved in the rate-determining step.

Now look at Table 4. The pattern of this data is slightly different from that in Table 3. Changing the concentration of the tertiary bromoalkane has a similar effect on the rate, so this reaction is also first order with respect to the bromoalkane. The difference shows up when the concentration of hydrogensulphide ions is changed: in this reaction, the rate stays the same. So this reaction is zero order with respect to hydrogensulphide ions. So we can write the rate equation as

rate = k [$(CH_3)_3CBr$]

The Swiss investigators suggested that the mechanisms for the reactions of bromoalkanes with hydrogensulphide ions are the same as for the reactions of bromoalkanes with hydroxide ions – S_N2 for primary bromoalkanes and S_N1 for tertiary bromoalkanes. Bromoalkanes react with hydrogensulphide ions to form thiols. For example:

$$C_4H_9Br \quad + \quad HS^- \quad \longrightarrow \quad C_4H_9SH \quad + \quad Br^-$$
$$\text{butane-1-thiol}$$

 7 Draw the reaction mechanism for each of the two reactions in Tables 3 and 4.

16.6 Competing reactions

The Swiss scientists were also able to explain why they had found the particular range of products in the water. They did this by comparing the rate constants for some reactions. The size of a rate constant indicates how fast a reaction is: a fast reaction has a large rate constant. Tables 3 and 4 show that the reaction of tertiary bromoalkanes is faster than the reaction of primary bromoalkanes – this can be seen from the initial rates. The data also allow the rate constant for each reaction to be calculated.

For the reaction of the primary bromoalkane with hydrogensulphide ions,

rate = k [C_4H_9Br] [HS]

Substituting the first row of values from Table 3 gives

$$1.11 \times 10^{-5} \quad = \quad k \times 0.1 \quad \times \quad 0.1$$
$$\text{mol dm}^{-3} \text{ s}^{-1} \qquad \text{mol dm}^{-3} \qquad \text{mol dm}^{-3}$$

and rearranging gives

$$k = 1.11 \times 10^{-3} \text{ mol}^{-1} \text{ dm}^3 \text{ s}^{-1}$$

 8 Check that you agree with this figure by working out the rate constant using the second row of values from Table 3.

For the reaction of the tertiary bromoalkane with hydrogensulphide ions

rate = k [(CH$_3$)$_3$CBr]

Substituting the first row of values from Table 4 gives

$$\underset{\text{mol dm}^{-3}\,\text{s}^{-1}}{1.5 \times 10^{-2}} = k \times \underset{\text{mol dm}^{-3}}{0.1}$$

and rearranging gives

$k = 0.15$ s^{-1}

This reaction has the higher rate constant.

 9 Why are the units of the two rate constants different?

Table 5 Rate constants for some reactions of bromoalkanes

Reactants	Rate constant/mol^{-1}dm^{3}s^{-1}
1-bromopropane (primary) + water	3.05×10^{-7}
2-bromopropane (secondary) + water	3.89×10^{-6}
1-bromohexane (primary) + water	1.94×10^{-7}
3-bromohexane (secondary) + water	1.67×10^{-5}
1-bromohexane (primary) + hydrogensulphide ions	1.11×10^{-3}

The investigating team used rate constant data like those in Table 5 to explain how the products they found had been formed. From Table 5 we can see that secondary bromoalkanes react much more quickly with water than primary bromoalkanes do. The team explained that the secondary bromoalkanes reacted only with water, whereas the primary bromoalkanes reacted with both water and hydrogensulphide ions. The concentration of hydrogensulphide ions was much lower than that of water molecules, but the rate constant for the reaction with hydrogensulphide is much higher than the rate constant for the reaction with water. Under these particular environmental conditions, the two reactions were competing with each other.

The rate constants in Table 5 were determined at 298 K (25 °C). The temperature underground would have been less than this and the reactions would be slower, because the molecules would have less kinetic energy. The rate constant would also be lower. If the temperature is increased, the rate constant will increase.

Key ideas

- The rate equation for a reaction cannot be deduced from the chemical equation; it must be determined experimentally.

- The mechanism of a reaction can often be deduced from the rate equation.

- The rate constant of a reaction is increased by increasing the temperature.

16.7 Ozone in the upper atmosphere

Chris uses as little bromomethane as possible when fumigating the soil. Even so, small amounts may escape into the air. Bromomethane gas has been found in the exhaust gas of cars burning leaded fuel. There is concern that bromomethane may reduce the concentration of ozone in the upper atmosphere.

The highest levels of atmospheric ozone are found in a sparse layer at a height that varies between 20 and 50 km above the Earth's surface. This 'ozone layer' prevents about 99% of the ultraviolet radiation reaching the Earth from the Sun. High-energy ultraviolet (UV) radiation damages plant and animal cells, and leads to an

Fig. 12 Structure of the Earth's atmosphere

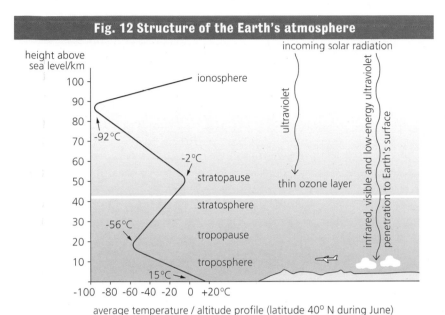

height above sea level/km

incoming solar radiation

average temperature / altitude profile (latitude 40° N during June)

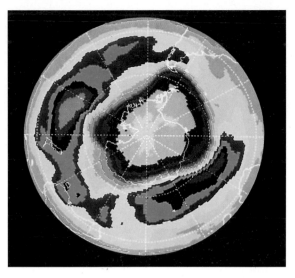

This false-colour satellite image shows a huge 'hole' (grey area) in the ozone layer over Antarctica; the hole reappears each spring

Fig. 13 Effect of UV radiation on chlorine molecules

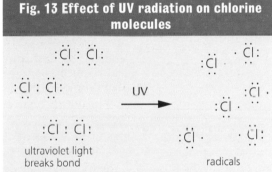

ultraviolet light breaks bond

radicals

increased risk of skin cancer. The concentration of ozone in some parts of the ozone layer has decreased in the last few years. More UV radiation can then penetrate the Earth's atmosphere (Fig. 12).

The United Nations Environment Programme set up the Montreal Protocol Committee to identify the compounds that damage the ozone layer and recommend limits for the production, sale and distribution of these chemicals ('ozone depletors'). By 1990, schedules had been drawn up for phasing out the production of some known ozone depletors by the years 2000–2005. These compounds include compounds of carbon with halogens, such as chlorofluorocarbons (CFCs), tetrachloromethane and 1,1,1-trichloroethane. Most countries

recognise the Montreal Protocol and are aiming to keep to the targets for the reduction of CFCs.

In 1992 bromomethane was added to the list of ozone depletors. The evidence for adding it to the list was not very clear, as it is difficult to obtain reliable data about all the competing reactions in the upper atmosphere. Chemists agree that bromomethane reacts with ozone, but more information is needed to establish the extent to which it depletes atmospheric ozone. Bromoalkanes react more rapidly with both nucleophiles and other reactants than chloroalkanes do; this means that the bromine compounds are far more efficient at destroying ozone. However, the less reactive chlorine compounds persist in the environment for longer. Judging which chemicals contribute most to ozone depletion is very difficult!

The chemistry of the ozone layer is complex, but it is based on the reactions of free atoms or **radicals**. Radicals are reactive species which have an odd (unpaired) electron available for bonding. They are formed when bonds in some molecules, such as chlorine, are broken **homolytically** by UV radiation (Fig. 13). The bond splits evenly to create chlorine atoms, which are radicals.

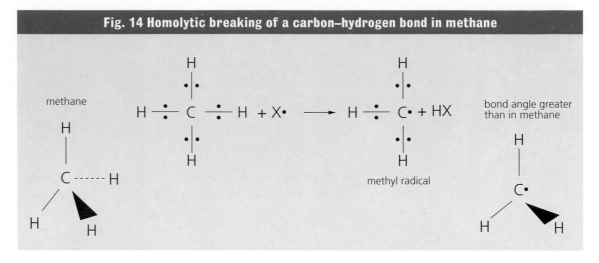

Fig. 14 Homolytic breaking of a carbon–hydrogen bond in methane

methane

methyl radical

bond angle greater than in methane

Bonds in larger molecules can be broken in the same way, especially when themselves attacked by radicals (X• in Fig. 14).

Ozone is formed in the upper atmosphere by the effect of UV radiation on oxygen, in a two-step reaction:

$$\underset{\text{ultraviolet light}}{O_2 \rightarrow O\cdot + O\cdot}$$

free oxygen atoms

$$O\cdot + O_2 + M \rightarrow O_3 + M$$

ozone   (M = inert particle)

Ozone is destroyed by a combination of two reactions, also initiated by UV radiation:

$$\underset{\text{ultraviolet light}}{O_3 \rightarrow O_2 + O\cdot}$$
$$O\cdot + O_3 \rightarrow O_2 + O_2$$

The ozone layer would be kept in balance by these processes of formation and destruction if there were no other radicals in the upper atmosphere. But chemicals such as CFCs released at ground level eventually reach the upper atmosphere, where they break down into radicals. Free chlorine radicals destroy ozone. During the process they are recycled:

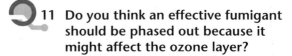

$$Cl\cdot + O_3 \rightarrow ClO\cdot + O_2$$
$$ClO\cdot + O\cdot \rightarrow Cl\cdot + O_2$$
net effect $\overline{O\cdot + O_3 \rightarrow O_2 + O_2}$

So a few chlorine atoms can destroy a great many ozone molecules.

Q10 Hydroxyl radicals (·OH) can also be found in the upper atmosphere. Write equations to show how they can destroy ozone.

It is difficult to predict how the ozone layer will change in the future, and how this change will affect life on Earth, because:

• scientists do not agree about which theoretical model is the best to use for their predictions;

• it is difficult and expensive to collect evidence from the upper atmosphere;

• it is difficult to separate the effects of all the competing processes going on in the atmosphere;

• it is difficult to conduct controlled trials of the effects of increased UV radiation on plants and animals.

Q11 Do you think an effective fumigant should be phased out because it might affect the ozone layer?

16.8 Radical substitution in methane

Radicals are involved in reactions to generate haloalkanes. Chlorine can react with methane in UV radiation to replace the hydrogen with chlorine. This is an example of a **radical substitution** reaction:

initiation step $\quad Cl_2 \xrightarrow{\text{ultraviolet light}} Cl\cdot + Cl\cdot$

propagation step $\quad Cl\cdot + CH_4 \rightarrow CH_3\cdot + HCl$

termination step $\quad Cl\cdot + CH_3\cdot \rightarrow CH_3Cl$
$$\text{chloromethane}$$

The propagation step is given this name because one radical is produced for every radical that reacts. Other propagation steps occur as the carbon–hydrogen bonds are attacked by further chlorine atoms:

propagation $\quad Cl\cdot + CH_3Cl \rightarrow CH_2Cl\cdot + HCl$

A range of chloroalkanes is formed, e.g.

termination $\quad CH_2Cl\cdot + Cl\cdot \rightarrow CH_2Cl_2$
$$\text{dichloromethane}$$

12a Show how trichloromethane (CHCl₃) and tetrachloromethane (CCl₄) can be formed from propagation and termination steps.

b Suggest why this is not a good reaction for producing only chloromethane.

16.9 Ozone at ground level

Ozone is also present in the lower atmosphere, close to the ground. Here, however, it is harmful to human health and plant growth. Some of this ozone is produced by the action of strong sunlight on nitrogen oxides.

Nitrogen oxides – together with unburnt hydrocarbons and carbon monoxide – are present in car exhaust fumes. Catalytic converters fitted to cars help to reduce the emission of these gases.

Cyclists can be protected from visible particles in car exhaust fumes

Catalysts like those in converters change the rate of a chemical reaction, while themselves remaining unchanged chemically at the end of the reaction. They do this by providing a reaction pathway with a lower activation energy (Fig. 15). As the activation energy is lowered, the temperature at which the molecules will have enough kinetic energy to react is also lowered.

Fig. 15 Reaction profile showing the effect of a catalyst

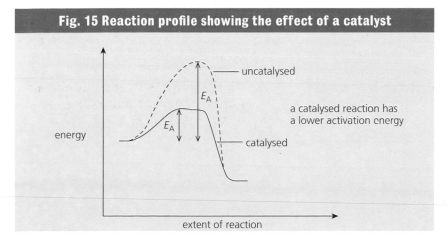

energy

E_A — uncatalysed

a catalysed reaction has a lower activation energy

E_A — catalysed

extent of reaction

Most catalytic converters are 'three-way': they are designed so that the nitrogen oxides oxidise carbon monoxide to carbon dioxide, and are themselves reduced to nitrogen. Unburnt hydrocarbons are also oxidised to carbon dioxide and water. The catalyst used is a mixture of platinum, rhodium and palladium – second- or third-row transition metals. Transition metals can have several different oxidation states, and this makes them good catalysts (see Chapter 9).

$$2CO(g) + 2NO(g) \xrightarrow{Pt/Rh/Pd} 2CO_2(g) + N_2(g)$$

The catalyst is spread in a very thin layer over the surface of a metal honeycomb which has a large surface area.

Nothing can live in the acid waters of this Norwegian lake; even the surrounding trees are dead or dying

Q13 Why is it important that the catalyst has a large surface area?

Cars fitted with catalytic converters should only use unleaded fuel: lead poisons the surface of the catalyst. Catalytic converters are examples of **heterogeneous catalysis**, i.e. the catalyst and the reactants are in different phases. In this case the catalyst is in the solid phase and the reactants are in the gas phase.

In **homogeneous catalysis**, both the catalyst and the reactants are in the same phase. Liquid-phase catalysis is involved in an important step in the formation of 'acid rain'.

Two kinds of pollutant are concerned in the production of acid rain. One is nitrogen oxides, which in damp air are oxidised to nitric acid. The other is sulphur dioxide, which is released into the atmosphere when sulphur-containing fuels are burnt. Sulphur dioxide dissolves easily in droplets of water in clouds, fog and rain to form sulphurous acid (H_2SO_3). This is oxidised by dissolved molecular oxygen to form sulphuric acid (H_2SO_4). The reaction is slow in the absence of light or specific catalysts. Transition metal ions such as those of iron(III), manganese(II) and copper(II) can also be present in low concentrations in water droplets, and are effective catalysts for the process. The reaction proceeds by many steps, but it is the step in which the catalyst is involved that determines the overall rate of the reaction.

❝ STOP PRESS ❞

In Europe the use of bromomethane to sterilise soil will be phased out by 2010.

Key ideas

- Radical substitution reactions can be initiated by ultraviolet radiation.

- Catalysts provide a lower-energy pathway for a reaction.

Answers to Questions

Chapter 1

1 Very short range, less than the diameter of the nucleus.
2 In the nucleus.
3 **a** Atomic number, $Z = 11$, mass number, $A = 23$
   b Atomic number, $Z = 13$, mass number, $A = 27$
   c Atomic number, $Z = 26$, mass number, $A = 56$
4 It is the electrons that determine an element's chemical properties, and all isotopes of carbon have six electrons.
5 The ratio carbon-14:carbon-12 started to decrease.
6 Chlorine
7 **a** M_r for ethanol is 46.
   b M_r for calcium hydroxide is 74.
   c M_r for ammonium sulphate is 132.
8 Peak at $1 = H^+$, $2 = H_2^+$, $12 = C^+$, $13 = CH^+$, $14 = CH_2^+$, $15 = CH_3^+$

Chapter 2

1 **a** Empirical formula = CH_2O
   b Molecular formula = $C_2H_4O_2$
2 **a** 2 mol
   b 0.25 mol
   c 1.5 mol
3 **a** 394 g
   b 8 g
   c 84 g
4 2.8 tonnes of sulphur dioxide
5 3.5 tonnes of sulphur trioxide
6 **a** $2SO_2 + O_2 \longrightarrow 2SO_3$
      So 67.2 dm³ SO_2 will produce 67.2 dm³ of SO_3.
   b $SO_2 + H_2SO_4 \longrightarrow H_2S_2O_7$
      22.4 dm³ SO_2 reacts with 98 g H_2SO_4
      So 224 dm³ SO_2 reacts with 980 g of H_2SO_4.
7 **a** Molar mass NaOH = 40 g mol⁻¹
      25 cm³ 1M solution contains 0.1 g NaOH.
   b Molar mass H_2SO_4 = 98 g mol⁻¹
      The concentration of the solution is 0.2M.
8 **a** $FeTiO_3 + 2H_2SO_4 \longrightarrow FeSO_4 + TiOSO_4 + 2H_2O$

152 g	gives	160 g
152 tonnes	gives	160 tonnes
760 tonnes	gives	$\frac{160}{152} \times 760$ tonnes
		= 800 tonnes $TiOSO_4$

b $Fe_2(TiO_3)_3 + 6H_2SO_4 \longrightarrow Fe_2(SO_4)_3 + 3TiOSO_4 + 6H_2O$

400 g	gives	3×160 g
		= 480 g
400 tonnes	gives	480 tonnes
760 tonnes	gives	$\frac{480}{400} \times 760$ tonnes
		= 912 tonnes
		$TiOSO_4$

9 **a** $Fe^{2+} + TiO_3^{2-} + 4H^+ + 2SO_4^{2-} \longrightarrow$
      $Fe^{2+} + SO_4^{2-} + TiO^{2+} + SO_4^{2-} + 4H^+ + 2O^{2-}$
      or, $TiO_3^{2-} \longrightarrow TiO^{2+} + 2O^{2-}$
   b $2Fe^{3+} + 3TiO_3^{2-} + 12H^+ + 6SO_4^{2-} \longrightarrow$
      $3TiO^{2+} + 3SO_4^{2-} + 2Fe^{3+} + 3SO_4^{2-} + 12H^+ + 6O^{2-}$
      or, $3TiO_3^{2-} \longrightarrow 3TiO^{2+} + 6O^{2-}$
      or, $TiO_3^{2-} \longrightarrow TiO^{2+} + 2O^{2-}$
10 **a** Chemical equations:
      $Fe(s) + H_2SO_4(aq) \longrightarrow FeSO_4(aq) + H_2(g)$
      $H_2(g) + Fe_2(SO_4)_3(aq) \longrightarrow 2FeSO_4(aq) + H_2SO_4(aq)$
   b Ionic equation:
      $H_2 + 2Fe^{3+} + 3SO_4^{2-} \longrightarrow 2Fe^{2+} + 2SO_4^{2-} + 2H^+ + SO_4^{2-}$
      or, $H_2 + 2Fe^{3+} \longrightarrow 2Fe^{2+} + 2H^+$
11 Recycling sulphuric acid consumes energy and is therefore expensive. Sulphuric acid converted to calcium sulphate can be sold to plasterboard manufacturers and is profitable.
12 By converting waste products to saleable commodities; the adoption of environmental strategies has been carried out in conjunction with improving the efficiency of the plant.
13 From the equation,
      $1 \text{ mol } CaCO_3 \longrightarrow 22.4 \text{ dm}^3 \text{ } CO_2$
      $100 \text{ g } CaCO_3 \longrightarrow 22.4 \text{ dm}^3 \text{ } CO_2$
      $1000 \text{ g } CaCO_3 \longrightarrow \frac{22.4}{100} \times 1000 \text{ dm}^3 \text{ } CO_2$
      $= 224 \text{ dm}^3$ carbon dioxide
14 $HCl(aq) + NaOH(aq) \longrightarrow NaCl(aq) + H_2O(l)$

Amount NaOH (mol)	$= 10 \times 10^{-3} \times 0.120$
	$= 1.2 \times 10^{-3}$ mol
Amount HCl	$= 1.2 \times 10^{-3}$ mol
Amount HCl (mol)	$=$ volume (dm³) $\times$ concentration (mol dm⁻³)
0.012 mol HCl	$= 9.5 \times 10^{-3} \times$ concentration

$$\text{Concentration (mol dm}^{-3}) = \frac{1.2 \times 10^{-3}}{9.5 \times 10^{-3}}$$
$$= 0.126 \text{ mol dm}^{-3}$$

Chapter 3

1 $2Na(s) + 2H_2O(l) \longrightarrow 2NaOH(aq) + H_2(g)$
$2K(s) + 2H_2O(l) \longrightarrow 2KOH(aq) + H_2(g)$

2 Rubidium and caesium are so reactive, that electrolysis of their molten compounds is needed to isolate the elements.

3 The inert gases are missing, as they had not yet been discovered.

4 Germanium

5 Transition elements, both first and second row.

6 The outer electron in potassium is 'shielded' from the nucleus by three full energy levels of electrons. Sodium's outer electron is shielded by only two full energy levels. This makes the electron in potassium easier to remove (its first ionisation energy is lower), which means that it reacts more readily.

7 The second ionisation energy is greater than the first for Group II elements, but there is a much bigger jump between the second and third ionisation energies. This is because they have two electrons in their outer shell.

8 A similar pattern in first ionisation energies as with Period 2 elements. Aluminium's is less than magnesium's because of the stability of the full s sub-shell.

9 Na: $1s^2\,2s^2\,2p^6\,3s^1$ ($1s^2\,2s^2\,2p^6$ is sometimes written as [Ne])

Mg:	[Ne]	$3s^2$
Al:	[Ne]	$3s^2\,3p^1$
Si:	[Ne]	$3s^2\,3p^2$
P:	[Ne]	$3s^2\,3p^3$
S:	[Ne]	$3s^2\,3p^4$ Ne = Neon
Cl:	[Ne]	$3s^2\,3p^5$
Ar:	[Ne]	$3s^2\,3p^6$

10

V:	[Ar]	$3d^3\,4s^2$
Cr:	[Ar]	$3d^5\,4s^1$
Mn:	[Ar]	$3d^5\,4s^2$
Fe:	[Ar]	$3d^6\,4s^2$ Ar = Argon
Co:	[Ar]	$3d^7\,4s^2$
Ni:	[Ar]	$3d^8\,4s^2$
Cu:	[Ar]	$3d^{10}\,4s^1$
Zn:	[Ar]	$3d^{10}\,4s^2$

11 They both have full electron levels. A full energy level of electrons provides relatively good shielding for all electrons in that level.

12 The high melting point of silicon oxide and silicates makes them able to withstand high temperatures, both in processing and in use.

Chapter 4

1 The positive cations are attracted to the negative 'sea' of delocalised electrons which surrounds them.

2
```
  ..           ..
H:N:H        H:O:
  x            x
  H            H
ammonia      water
```

3
```
H  .    . H
  +C:C+
H +    + H
   ethene
```

4
```
     x   x
H:C:::C:H
     x   x
    ethyne
```

5 **a**
```
        ..   2-
       xO:
  K+    ..
       K+
  potassium oxide
```

b
```
Na+
          ..
Na+   xN:
          x
Na+
sodium nitride
```

c
```
             ..   2-
            xO:
 Fe3+        ..
             ..   2-
            xO:
 Fe3+        ..
             ..   2-
            xO:
             ..
```

6 The noble gases are very unreactive. They form very few compounds.

7
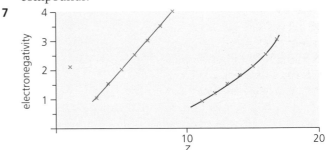

8 Electronegativity decreases down a group because of the increasing numbers of inner electrons which shield the attracting power of the nucleus for the outermost electrons.

9 **a** Ionic
b Ionic, though less so than in lithium fluoride
c Covalent and slightly polar
d Covalent and non-polar
e Covalent and slightly polar

10 Current can flow from an n-type semiconductor to a p-type semiconductor because free electrons in the n-type material can move into 'holes' in the p-type material. Current cannot flow from a p-type semiconductor to an n-type semiconductor because there are no free 'holes' in the n-type material for the electrons to move into. Current can therefore pass in only one direction: the junction acts as a 'one-way valve'.

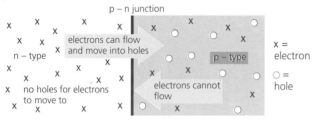

Chapter 5

1 The outer planets are all gaseous. They have no solid core.

2 **a** 0.015%

b 0.033%

3 $p \propto 1/V$ at constant temperature

$p \propto T$ at constant volume

Combining these two gives $pV/T = $ constant

$V \propto n$

So $pV/T = $ constant $\times n$

4 p is measured in Pa. 1 Pa is 1 N m^{-2}. Putting SI units into the gas equation:

N m^{-2} × m^3/K = [R] × mol

N m K^{-1} mol^{-1} = [R]

1 N m = 1 J

So units of R are J K^{-1} mol^{-1}.

5 8.79×10^{19} particles cm^{-3}

6 V_2 = $p_1 V_1 T_2 / T_1 p_2$

$= \dfrac{1.01 \times 10^5 \times 16 \times 250}{298 \times 0.007 \times 1.01 \times 10^5}$

= 1920

Volume = 1920 dm^3

7 Particle interactions are infrequent at low pressure because the particle density is low. At high temperature the kinetic energy is high, and the particle interactions are less significant.

8 Carbon dioxide is a linear molecule because there are double bonds between each carbon atom and oxygen atom, and no free rotation about the carbon atom. This leads to symmetry in electron distribution across the whole molecule.

9 Hydrogen bonding will occur in hydrogen fluoride (linear molecule), ammonia (trigonal pyramidal), hydrazine and ethanol.

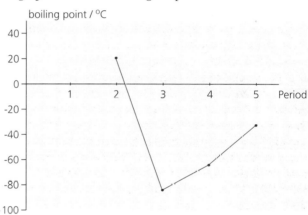

Hydrogen bonding will not occur in methane (tetrahedral) or hydrogen cyanide (linear), as in these molecules the hydrogen is not bonded to a highly electronegative element.

10 The graph has the following shape.

Hydrogen fluoride has a high boiling point because of hydrogen bonding. With other halogen hydrides, boiling point increases with increasing molecular mass.

11 Water has a higher latent heat of vaporisation than heptane. More energy is released when steam condenses than when heptane vapour condenses. The hydrogen bonds formed when steam condenses to water are a stronger intermolecular interaction than the van der Waals forces between the molecules in liquid heptane.

12 Water could be found in solid and vapour phases on Mars.

13 No. The phase diagram shows that carbon dioxide would be a gas under those conditions. The clouds are thought to be mainly a concentrated solution of sulphuric acid.

14 **a** Low melting point and boiling point, non-conduction of electricity.

b

stacked to form needle crystals

15 There are a lot of —OH groups in the glucose molecule. This leads to extensive hydrogen bonding between glucose and water molecules.

Chapter 6

1 **a** There is a large error caused by loss of heat to the surroundings during the experiment.

   b Heat energy transferred $= 200 \times 4.18 \times 16$
   $$= 13\,376 \text{ J or } 13.376 \text{ kJ}$$

   M_r methanol (CH_3OH) $= 32$

   Moles methanol burnt $= \dfrac{0.67}{32}$
   $$= 0.021 \text{ mol}$$

   Enthalpy of combustion $\dfrac{13.376}{0.021}$
   $$= 636.95 \text{ kJ mol}^{-1}$$

   $\Delta H_c = -636.95 \text{ kJ mol}^{-1}$

   In terms of enthalpy content, methanol is not a better fuel than ethanol.

2 $C_8H_{18}(l) + 12\frac{1}{2}O_2(g) \longrightarrow 8CO_2(g) + 9H_2O(l)$

     -250.0 0 8×-393.5 9×-285.8

     -250.0 $+$ $\Delta H_{reaction}$ $= -3148.0 \; + \; -2572.2$
   $$= -5720.2 \text{ kJ mol}^{-1}$$

   So $\Delta H_{reaction} = -5470.2 \text{ kJ mol}^{-1}$

   So standard enthalpy of combustion of octane
   $$= -5470.2 \text{ kJ mol}^{-1}$$

3 Production of fertilisers, pesticides, fuel – for irrigation (to pump water), for maintaining a constant fermentation temperature and for distillation – require crude oil products. A change in the price of crude oil will therefore alter the costs of ethanol production, as well as altering the cost of the competing fuel, petrol.

4 $C_6H_{12}O_6 \rightarrow 2C_2H_5OH + 2CO_2$

   One mole of glucose produces two moles of ethanol (and two moles of carbon dioxide) during fermentation.

5

   $\Delta H_1 = \Delta H_3 - \Delta H_2$

   $\Delta H_3 = 8[\Delta H_{f\ carbon\ dioxide(g)}] + 9[\Delta H_{f\ water(l)}]$
   $$= 8[-393.5] + 9[-285.8]$$
   $$= -3148 + -2572.2 \text{ kJ mol}^{-1}$$
   $$= -5720.2 \text{ kJ mol}^{-1}$$

   $\Delta H_2 = \Delta H_{f\ (octane(l))}$

   $\Delta H_1 = -5720.2 - -250.0$
   $$= -5470.2 \text{ kJ mol}^{-1}$$

   Standard enthalpy of combustion of octane
   $$= -5470.2 \text{ kJ mol}^{-1}$$

6 **a**

   Energy used to break bonds/kJ mol^{-1}:

   $18\ E(C—H) = 18 \times 413 = 7434$

   $7\ E(C—C) = 7 \times 347 = 2429$

   $12\frac{1}{2}\ E(O—O) = 12 \times 498 = 6225$

   Total enthalpy change $= 16\,088$ kJ mol^{-1}

   Energy released when bonds made/kJ mol^{-1}:

   $18\ E(O—H) = 18 \times 464 = 8352$

   $16\ E(C\!\!=\!\!O) = 16 \times 805 = 12\,880$

   Total enthalpy change $= 21\,232$ kJ mol^{-1}

   Standard enthalpy of combustion of octane
   $$= -5144 \text{ kJ mol}^{-1}$$

   b Remember, enthalpy changes of reaction calculated from bond enthalpies are only approximate.

Chapter 7

1 **a** In a sealed lemonade bottle, there is equilibrium between carbon dioxide gas and carbon dioxide dissolved in water.

   b There is equilibrium between bromine vapour and bromine liquid in a sealed gas jar.

2 **a** $K_c = \dfrac{[NO_2(g)]^2}{[N_2O_4(g)]}$

   b The units are mol dm^{-3}.

3 **a** $K_c = \dfrac{[N_2O_4(g)]}{[NO_2(g)]^2}$

   b The units for this equilibrium constant are mol^{-1} dm^3.

4 **a** Light brown: the nitrogen dioxide concentration is low.

   b Deep brown: the nitrogen dioxide concentration is high.

5 The dimerisation of nitrogen dioxide is exothermic; K_c for the dissociation of N_2O_4 increases with increasing temperature.

6 The reduction in pressure leads to production of more nitrogen dioxide, and the mixture appears more brown.

7 **a** More sulphur trioxide is produced.

   b There is no change – there are equal numbers of molecules on both sides of the equation.

8 **a** The forward reactions of methane with steam are endothermic. Increasing the temperature speeds up the achievement of equilibrium and increases the equilibrium constant. There are higher equilibrium yields of hydrogen at higher temperatures.

b Low pressure will encourage a high yield of hydrogen, as there are more molecules on the right-hand side of equation than on the left. The pressure cannot be less than atmospheric, as otherwise the gases cannot be pumped through the reactor.

9 More of the chemicals on the right-hand side of the equation are formed. The blue colour of the solution will deepen.

10 a More ethyl ethanoate will be produced, and the concentration of ethanoic acid decreases.

  b More ethanol and ethanoic acid will be produced.

  c More ethyl ethanoate will be produced, in order to maintain the equilibrium.

11 Food production depends on climate and on elimination of pests and crop diseases, as well as on having sufficient nitrogen in the soil. The fair distribution of food depends on a stable government that is willing to ensure fair shares of food for everyone.

Chapter 8

1 a $HCl(aq) + KOH(aq) \longrightarrow KCl(aq) + H_2O(l)$

  b $H_2SO_4(aq) + NaOH(aq) \longrightarrow Na_2SO_4(aq) + H_2O(l)$
  Both these can be represented by:
  $H^+(aq) + OH^-(aq) \longrightarrow H_2O(l)$

2 In methanol and methanoic acid, the O—H bond is polar. It can be broken to release H^+. The C—H bond in methane is not polar as the electronegativities of carbon and hydrogen are similar.

3 $HCOOH(l) + H_2O(l) \rightleftharpoons HCOO^-(aq) + H_3O^+(aq)$

4 a $CH_3(CH_2)_{16}COOH(l) + NaOH(aq) \longrightarrow$
$CH_3(CH_2)_{16}COO^-Na^+(s) + H_2O(l)$

  b $NH_4^+(aq) + OH^- \rightleftharpoons NH_3(aq) \ H_2O(l)$
  acid   base   base   acid

  c $CH_3COO^-(aq) + H_3O^+(aq) \rightleftharpoons CH_3COOH(aq) + H_2O(l)$
  base   acid   acid   base

5 $CH_3(CH_2)_{16}COOH(l) + NaOH(aq) \longrightarrow$
$CH_3(CH_2)_{16}COO^-Na^+(s) + H_2O(l)$

6 $[H^+] = 0.01$
$\log_{10} 0.01 = -2$
So pH = 2

7 a pH 1
  b pH 0.7
  c pH –0.7; very concentrated acids can have negative pH.

8 a $0.001 \ mol \ dm^{-3}$
  b $3.2 \times 10^{-6} \ mol \ dm^{-3}$

9 $1 \times 10^{-7} \ mol \ dm^{-3}$

10 a Endothermic, because ionisation increases with increasing temperature.

b The pH of water at 60 °C is less than 7, as the hydrogen ion concentration is greater than at 25 °C.

11 a pH 12
  b pH 13.5

12 $K_a = \dfrac{[CH_3(CH_2)_3COO^-(aq)] \ [H^+(aq)]}{[CH_3(CH_2)_3COOH(aq)]}$

13 Sodium nitrate is neutral because it is made from a strong acid (nitric acid) and a strong alkali (sodium hydroxide).

14 Both potassium hydroxide and sodium hydroxide are strong alkalis. Potassium ions and sodium ions have no effect on the ionisation of water.

15 Sodium citrate is more weakly alkaline than sodium ethanoate. The stronger the acid, the closer the pH of a salt from the acid and a strong base will be to pH 7. This means that citric acid is stronger than ethanoic acid.

16 The greasier the hair, the higher the proportion of detergent needed in the shampoo.

Chapter 9

1 A half-full sub-shell, i.e. $3d^5$, is comparatively stable. The arrangement $3d^5 \ 4s^1$ is more stable than $3d^4 \ 4s^2$.

2 Density, malleability, enthalpy of fusion, electronegativity.

3 a $3d^{10}$
  b $3d^9$
  c $3d^5$
  d $3d^3$

4 Oxidation half-equation:
$Fe^{2+} \rightarrow Fe^{3+} + e^-$
Reduction half-equation:
$Cl_2 + 2e^- \rightarrow 2Cl^-$
Full redox equation:
$2Fe^{2+} + Cl_2 \longrightarrow 2Fe^{3+} + 2Cl^-$

5 Hydrogen is +1, oxygen is –2. Two hydrogens (+2) plus four oxygens (–8) give –6. Overall the oxidation states of the elements must balance out as there is no charge on the compound. The charge on a sulphate ion is –2. Four oxygens give –8, leaving –6 to be cancelled out by sulphur. So the oxidation state of sulphur is +6.

6 MnO_4^-: each oxygen has an oxidation state of –2. This gives –8. The single negative charge on the ion gives –7 to be cancelled by the +7 oxidation state of manganese.

7 MnO_2: oxidation state of manganese is +4 (manganese(IV) oxide). $MnCl_2$: oxidation state of manganese is +2 (manganese(II) chloride).

8 $CuO + CO \rightarrow Cu + CO_2$
Copper changes oxidation state from +2 to 0. Carbon changes oxidation state from +2 to +4.

9 Four

10 a Manganate (VII) ions.

   b $MnO_2 + 2O_2^- = MnO_4^- + 3e^-$

11 $3d^7$ (cobalt(II) ions)

Chapter 10

1 About $5000\ cm^3$ (this is quite a large laboratory).

2 In high concentrations of hydrogen ions, at low pH, the equilibrium in Equation 2 moves to the left.

3 Low pH. Higher concentrations of HOCl are present at low pH.

4 3 ppm

5 $8.45 \times 10^{-5}\ mol\ dm^{-3}$

6 From −1 to 0

7 $Br_2\ (aq) + 2I^-\ (aq) \longrightarrow 2Br^-\ (aq) + I_2\ (aq)$

8 One atom of chlorine is oxidised from 0 to +1. One atom of chlorine is reduced from 0 to −1.

$$\begin{array}{c} \overset{0}{} \qquad\qquad \overset{-1}{} \\ Cl_2(g)\ +\ H_2O(l) \longrightarrow HOCl(aq)\ +\ H^+(aq)\ +\ Cl^-(aq) \\ \underset{0}{} \qquad\qquad \underset{+1}{} \end{array}$$

9 a Bromine is the most effective at pH 8.

   b Bromine is the most effective across the pH range 6–8.

10 a $Br_2(l) + H_2O(l) \rightleftharpoons HOBr\ (aq) + H^+\ (aq) + Br^-(aq)$

   b At low pH, there is a high concentration of free bromine.

11 $Ag^+(aq) + I^-(aq) \rightleftharpoons AgI(s)$

12 The grey colour is due to the silver formed during photochemical decomposition.

13 Iodine is less electronegative than chlorine. The iodide ion is larger than the chloride ion. The outer electrons on the chloride ion are more strongly attracted to the nucleus than the outer electrons on the iodide ion.

14 a From +6 to 0

   b $8H^+(aq) + SO_4^{2-}(aq) + 6I^-(s) \longrightarrow 3I_2(g) + S(s) + 4H_2O(l)$

15 a $NaBr(s) + H_2SO_4(l) \longrightarrow NaHSO_4(s) + HBr(g)$

   b $2Br^- \longrightarrow Br_2 + 2e^-$

Chapter 11

1 Carbohydrates such as sugars and starches. Some energy is supplied by protein and, for some people, by alcohol.

2 Saturated fatty acids 10%; unsaturated fatty acids 20%, i.e. a ratio of 10:20 or 1:2.

3 Octane

4 Molecular formula C_8H_{18}
Structural formula $CH_3CH_2CH_2CH_2CH_2CH_2CH_2CH_3$
Empirical formula C_4H_9

5 Myristic acid:
Molecular formula $C_{13}H_{27}COOH$
Structural formula

$$CH_3CH_2CH_2CH_2CH_2CH_2CH_2CH_2CH_2CH_2CH_2CH_2CH_2C \overset{\displaystyle O}{\underset{\displaystyle OH}{\big\langle}}$$

Stearic acid:
Molecular formula $C_{17}H_{35}COOH$
Structural formula

$$CH_3CH_2CH_2CH_2CH_2CH_2CH_2CH_2CH_2CH_2CH_2CH_2CH_2CH_2CH_2CH_2C \overset{\displaystyle O}{\underset{\displaystyle OH}{\big\langle}}$$

6 $CH_3CH{=}CHCH{=}CHCH_3$

7 The electrons are not only located in their normal orbits but also in the π bond created by the overlap of adjacent orbitals. They are no longer local to their atoms.

8 The area of high electron density in the double bond repels the remaining electrons and the H—C—H bond angle is lower.

9 Margarine contains more saturated and *trans*-unsaturated fatty acids as a result of hydrogenation. The carbon chains can lie side-by-side more easily and the margarine can solidify.

10 By titrating each oil in turn with a solution of bromine water. The yellow bromine water turns to colourless 1,2-dibromoethane. When all the unsaturated oil has been saturated, the bromine water no longer changes colour. The volumes of bromine water used give a comparison of the degrees of unsaturation.

11 Hydrogen bromide polarises. The H^+ is attracted to the high electron density area of the double bond and a carbonium ion is formed. This reacts with the Br^- ion to form bromoethane.

Chapter 12

1 a Pentane

$$\begin{array}{c}
\text{H} \ \ \text{H} \ \ \text{H} \ \ \text{H} \ \ \text{H} \\
| \ \ \ | \ \ \ | \ \ \ | \ \ \ | \\
\text{H}-\text{C}-\text{C}-\text{C}-\text{C}-\text{C}-\text{H} \\
| \ \ \ | \ \ \ | \ \ \ | \ \ \ | \\
\text{H} \ \ \text{H} \ \ \text{H} \ \ \text{H} \ \ \text{H}
\end{array}$$

b 2-methylbutane

$$\begin{array}{c}
\text{H} \ \ \ \text{H} \ \ \ \text{H} \ \ \text{H} \\
| \ \ \ \ | \ \ \ \ | \ \ \ | \\
\text{H}-\text{C}-\text{C}-\text{C}-\text{C}-\text{H} \\
| \ \ \ | \ \ \ | \ \ \ | \\
\text{H} \ \ \text{H}-\text{C}-\text{H} \ \ \text{H} \ \ \text{H} \\
\ \ \ \ \ \ | \\
\ \ \ \ \ \ \text{H}
\end{array}$$

c 2,2-dimethylpropane

$$\begin{array}{c}
\ \ \ \ \ \ \ \text{H} \\
\ \ \ \ \ \ \ | \\
\ \ \ \ \ \text{H}-\text{C}-\text{H} \\
\text{H} \ \ \ | \ \ \ \text{H} \\
| \ \ \ \ | \ \ \ \ | \\
\text{H}-\text{C}-\text{C}-\text{C}-\text{H} \\
| \ \ \ \ | \ \ \ \ | \\
\text{H} \ \ \text{H}-\text{C}-\text{H} \ \ \text{H} \\
\ \ \ \ \ \ | \\
\ \ \ \ \ \ \text{H}
\end{array}$$

2 Butan-2-ol and alanine are both chiral. Chlorofluoromethane (CH_2ClF) is not chiral.

3

4 Producing single isomers is more expensive than producing a racemate. The enantiomers have to be separated and isolated, which is a time-consuming and often costly process.

5 The optical isomers in our bodies have the L-form. It is possible that our bodies are better adapted for processing L-lactic acid than the D-isomer.

Chapter 13

1

$$\begin{array}{c}
\text{H} \ \ \text{CH}_3 \ \text{H} \ \ \text{CH}_3 \ \text{H} \\
| \ \ \ \ | \ \ \ \ | \ \ \ \ | \ \ \ \ | \\
\text{H}-\text{C}-\text{C}-\text{C}-\text{C}-\text{C}-\text{H} \\
| \ \ \ \ | \ \ \ \ | \ \ \ | \ \ \ | \\
\text{H} \ \ \text{CH}_3 \ \text{H} \ \ \text{H} \ \ \ \text{H}
\end{array}$$

2 There are not enough hydrogen atoms to produce only saturated hydrocarbons. At least one product must be an alkene.

3

$$\begin{array}{c}
\text{H} \ \ \ \ \ \ \ \ \text{H} \\
\ \ \ \diagdown \ \ \ \diagup \\
\ \ \ \ \ \text{C}=\text{C} \ \ \ \longrightarrow \ \ -(\text{CH}-\text{CH}_2)_n- \\
\ \ \diagup \ \ \ \ \ \ \diagdown \ \ \ \ \ \ \ \ \ \ \ \ \ \ \ | \\
\text{CH}_3 \ \ \ \ \ \ \ \text{H} \ \ \ \ \ \ \ \ \ \ \ \ \ \ \ \text{CH}_3
\end{array}$$

4 Octanoic acid.

5 The ester is methyl propanoate. The reaction is

$C_2H_5COOH(l) + CH_3OH(l) \longrightarrow C_2H_5COOCH_3(l) + H_2O(l)$
propanoic acid   methanol   methylpropanoate   water

6 a $\underset{\text{2-ethylhexan-1-ol}}{\text{CH}_3\text{CH}_2\text{CH}_2\text{CH}_2\overset{\displaystyle |}{\underset{\displaystyle C_2H_5}{\text{CH}}}\text{CH}_2\text{OH}}$

b $\underset{\text{hexanedioic acid}}{\begin{array}{c}\text{CH}_2\text{CH}_2\text{COOH} \\ | \\ \text{CH}_2\text{CH}_2\text{COOH}\end{array}}$

c 2CH₃(CH₂)₃CHCH₂OH + CH₂CH₂COOH $\longrightarrow$ 2H₂O + CH₂CH₂COOCH₂CH(CH₂)₃CH₃

$\underset{\text{2-ethylhexan-1-ol}}{\ \ \ \ \ \ \ | \ \ \ \ \ \ \ \ \ \ \ \ \ \ \ \ }$ $\underset{\text{hexanedioic acid}}{\ \ \ \ | \ \ \ \ \ \ \ \ }$ $\underset{\text{water}}{}$ $\underset{\text{2-ethylhexyladipate}}{\begin{array}{c}| \\ C_2H_5 \\ CH_2CH_2COOCH_2CH(CH_2)_3CH_3 \\ | \\ C_2H_5\end{array}}$

7 Generally, plasticisers move more freely into cheeses with a higher fat content. The exception is full-fat soft cheese.

8 The fat content of the food.

9 Microwave cooking increases the migration of plasticiser from ATBC-plasticised film.

Chapter 14

1 No. Carbon has four electrons available for bonding and this structure only uses three.

2 C_{60} would be very reactive.

3 The single bond involves only one electron from each carbon atom; the double bond involves two electrons from each carbon atom. This increased negative charge draws the positively charged nuclei closer together in the double bond.

4 Smallest radiowave = 10^7 nm. 1 nm = 10^{-9} m = 10^{-7} cm. Smallest radiowave is therefore $10^7 \times 10^{-7}$ cm = 1 cm.

5 It suggests that C_{70} is not spherically symmetrical, as C_{60} is.

6 C—C stretch: 800–1500 nm. C=C stretch: 5900–6200 nm.

7 C—C stretch at about 900 nm.

Chapter 15

1 Pentan-1-ol, primary alcohol

$$\begin{array}{c}
\text{H} \ \ \text{H} \ \ \text{H} \ \ \text{H} \ \ \text{H} \\
| \ \ \ | \ \ \ | \ \ \ | \ \ \ | \\
\text{H}-\text{C}-\text{C}-\text{C}-\text{C}-\text{C}-\text{OH} \\
| \ \ \ | \ \ \ | \ \ \ | \ \ \ | \\
\text{H} \ \ \text{H} \ \ \text{H} \ \ \text{H} \ \ \text{H}
\end{array}$$

Pentan-2-ol, secondary alcohol

$$\begin{array}{c}
\text{H} \ \ \text{H} \ \ \text{H} \ \ \text{H} \ \ \text{H} \\
| \ \ \ | \ \ \ | \ \ \ | \ \ \ | \\
\text{H}-\text{C}-\text{C}-\text{C}-\text{C}-\text{C}-\text{H} \\
| \ \ \ | \ \ \ | \ \ \ | \ \ \ | \\
\text{H} \ \ \text{H} \ \ \text{H} \ \ \text{OH} \ \text{H}
\end{array}$$

Pentan-3-ol, secondary alcohol

$$\begin{array}{c}
\text{H} \ \ \text{H} \ \ \text{H} \ \ \text{H} \ \ \text{H} \\
| \ \ \ | \ \ \ | \ \ \ | \ \ \ | \\
\text{H}-\text{C}-\text{C}-\text{C}-\text{C}-\text{C}-\text{H} \\
| \ \ \ | \ \ \ | \ \ \ | \ \ \ | \\
\text{H} \ \ \text{H} \ \ \text{OH} \ \text{H} \ \ \text{H}
\end{array}$$

2-methylbutan-1-ol, primary alcohol

```
      H   H   H   H
      |   |   |   |
  H—C—C—C—C—OH
      |   |   |   |
      H   H H—C—H H
              |
              H
```

3-methylbutan-2-ol, secondary alcohol

```
      H     H   OH  H
      |     |   |   |
  H—C—C—C—C—H
      |   |   |   |
      H   H H—C—H H   H
              |
              H
```

3-methylbutan-1-ol, primary alcohol

```
      H     H   H   H
      |     |   |   |
  H—C—C—C—C—OH
      |   |   |   |
      H   H H—C—H H   H
              |
              H
```

2-methylbutan-2-ol, tertiary alcohol

```
      H   H   OH  H
      |   |   |   |
  H—C—C—C—C—H
      |   |   |   |
      H   H H—C—H H   H
              |
              H
```

2,2-dimethylpropan-1-ol, Primary alcohol

```
              H
              |
      H H—C—H H
      |   |   |
  H—C—C—C—OH
      |   |   |
      H H—C—H H
              |
              H
```

2 butanal

```
      H   H   H       O
      |   |   |      ⫽
  H—C—C—C—C
      |   |   |      \
      H   H   H       H
```

pentanal

```
      H   H   H   H       O
      |   |   |   |      ⫽
  H—C—C—C—C—C
      |   |   |   |      \
      H   H   H   H       H
```

hexanal

```
      H   H   H   H   H       O
      |   |   |   |   |      ⫽
  H—C—C—C—C—C—C
      |   |   |   |   |      \
      H   H   H   H   H       H
```

3 −3

4 $CH_3CH_2CH_2OH(l) \xrightarrow{(-2H)} CH_3CH_2CHO(l) \xrightarrow{(+O)} CH_3CH_2COOH(l)$

5 a

```
      H     H   H
      |     |   |
  H—C—C—C—C—H
      ‖     |   |
      H  O  H   H
```

b Butan-2-one

6 a

```
      H   H   H   H
      |   |   |   |
  H—C—C—C—C—H
      |   |   |   |
      H   OH  H   H
```

b Butan-2-ol

Chapter 16

1 a

```
      H   H
      |   |
  H—C—C—Br
      |   |
      H   H
```

```
      H   H   H
      |   |   |
  H—C—C—C—Br
      |   |   |
      H   H   H
```

```
      H   H   H   H
      |   |   |   |
  H—C—C—C—C—Br
      |   |   |   |
      H   H   H   H
```

```
      H   H   H   H   H
      |   |   |   |   |
  H—C—C—C—C—C—Br
      |   |   |   |   |
      H   H   H   H   H
```

```
      H   H   H   H   H   H
      |   |   |   |   |   |
  H—C—C—C—C—C—C—Br
      |   |   |   |   |   |
      H   H   H   H   H   H
```

b About 178 °C

2 a

```
      H   H   H   ˙˙
      |   |   |   :OH                    OH₂                      H
      |   |   |                          |                        |
  H—C—C—C—Br      ⟶   C₂H₅—C····Br   ⟶   C₂H₅—C—OH
      |   |   |                          H₂                       |
      H   H   H                                                   H
```

b $C_3H_7Br + OH^- \longrightarrow C_3H_7OH + Br^-$

3 $C_3H_7Br + CN^- \longrightarrow C_3H_7CN + Br^-$

4 The reaction between $CH_3Br + CN^-$ will be fastest, as it has the lowest activation energy.

5

```
      H   H   H   H
      |   |   |   |
  H—C—C—C—C—H
      |   |   |   |
      H   H   Br  H
```

6 The second step in the S_N1 reaction will be the fastest step, where the carbonium ion intermediately reacts with hydroxide ions.

7

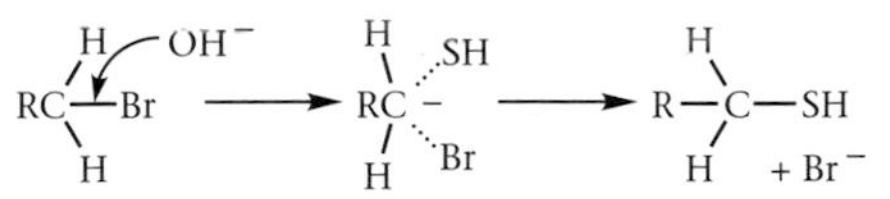

primary bromoalkane

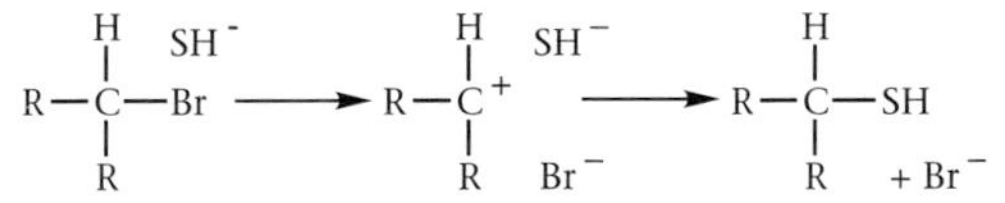

tertiary bromoalkane

8 Rate = $k[C_4H_9Br][HS^-]$

2.22×10^{-5} mol dm^{-3} s^{-1} = $k \times 0.2$ mol dm$^{-3} \times 0.1$ mol dm^{-3}

$k = 1.11 \times 10^{-3}$ mol^{-1} dm^3 s^{-1}

9 The rate equations are different: one is second order and the other is first order.

10

$$OH\cdot + O_3 \longrightarrow HOO\cdot + O_2$$
$$HOO\cdot + O\cdot \longrightarrow OH\cdot + O_2$$

Net effect $\qquad O\cdot + O_3 \longrightarrow O_2 + O_2$

12 a

$CH_2Cl_2 + Cl\cdot \longrightarrow CHCl_2\cdot + HCl$	propagation
$CHCl_2\cdot + Cl\cdot \longrightarrow CHCl_3$	termination
$CHCl_3 + Cl\cdot \longrightarrow CCl_3\cdot + HCl$	propagation
$CCl_3\cdot + Cl\cdot \longrightarrow CCl_4$	termination

b The reaction is propagated by the range of radicals produced, and several different chlorinated hydrocarbons are formed. It is difficult to control the reaction conditions so that only chloromethane is produced.

13 During the short time the reacting gases are in the converter they have the best chance of reaching the active part of the catalyst if it is spread out as widely as possible.

References

Chapter 1

Everett, K (1994). Death on the Rocks. *The Observer*, 30 January 1994, 27.

Chapter 3

Davy, H (1840). Collected Works, Volume IV. *Elements of Chemical Philosophy*. Smith, Elder and Co., Cornhill, London.

Mendeléev, D I (1889) The Periodic Law of the Chemical Elements. *Transactions of the Chemical Society*, **55** 634–56.

Segrè, E (1939). Element 43. *Nature*, **143** (18 March 1939) 460–61.

Chapter 10

Anderson, C (1991). Cholera Epidemic Traced to Risk Miscalculation. *Nature*, **354** (28 November 1991) 255.

Chapter 11

Coghlan, A (1991). Britain's Deadly Diet. *New Scientist*, 11 May 1991.

COMA Report (1991). United Kingdom Report of the Panel on Dietary Reference Values of the Committee on Medical Aspects of Food Policy. *Reports of Health and Social Subjects*, **41**. HMSO, London.

Family Guide to Alternative Medicine (1991). Readers' Digest Association, London.

Federation of Bakers. *Build 'em on Bread*. London (n.d.).

Laurance, J (1994). Fatty Diet Doubles Heart Risk. *The Times*, 4 February 1994.

Chapter 13

Hornsby, M (1990). Clingfilm May Endanger Health. *The Times*, 13 November 1990, 1.

Horsnell, M (1990). Makers Told to Carry Clingfilm Warning. *The Times*, 14 November 1990, 1.

McKee, V (1990). Debate on Packaging Heats Up. *The Times*, 15 November 1990, 22.

Ministry of Agriculture, Food and Fisheries (1987). Survey of Plasticisers in Food Contact Materials and in Foods. *Food Surveillance Paper*, **21**. HMSO, London.

Ministry of Agriculture, Food and Fisheries (1990). Plasticisers: Continuing Surveillance.The 30th Report of the Steering Group on Food Surveillance, the Working party on Chemical Contaminants from Food Contact Materials, Sub Group on Plasticisers. *Food surveillance Paper*, **30**. HMSO, London.

Selinger, B (1989). *Chemistry in the Market Place (4th Edition)*. Harcourt Brace Jovanovich, London.

Chapter 14

Baggott, J (1990). A New Field of Chemistry is Born. *New Scientist*, 13 October 1990, 18.

Kroto, H W, Heath, J R, O'Brien, S C, Curl, R F, and Smalley, R E (1985). C_{60}: Buckminsterfullerene. *Nature*, **318** (14 November 1985) 162–3.

Talbot, C (1993) The Third Allotropic Form of Carbon: The Fullerenes. *School Science Review*, **75** (270) 55–64.

Chapter 16

Moelwyn Hughes, E A (1971). *The Chemical Statistics and Kinetics of Solutions*. Academic Press, London.

Schwarzenbach, RP, Giger, W, Schaffner, C and Wanner, O (1985) Ground water contamination by volatile halogenated alkanes: abiotic formation of volatile sulfur compounds under anaerobic conditions. *Environmental Science and Technology*, **19**, 322 – 7.

Data section

Units

Chemists usually use the International System of Units (Système Internationale, or SI). The base SI units that are most often used in chemistry are shown in Table 1.

Table 1 Base SI units		
Quantity	Unit name	Symbol
length	metre	m
mass	kilogram	kg
time	second	s
electric current	ampere	A
temperature	kelvin	K
amount of substance	mole	mol

For convenience, any of the prefixes in Table 2 may be used with any unit: for example, the kilometre (1 km = 10^3m) and the milliampere (1 mA = 10^{-3}A) are often useful.

Table 2 Prefixes for units		
Prefix	Symbol	Meaning
tera	T	10^{12}
giga	G	10^9
mega	M	10^6
kilo	k	10^3
deci	d	10^{-1}
centi	c	10^{-2}
milli	m	10^{-3}
micro	µ	10^{-6}
nano	n	10^{-9}
pico	p	10^{-12}

Other units can be derived from the base units. For example, energy is normally measured in joules (symbol J), or multiples of joules (kJ, MJ), defined in terms of base units as kg m^2 s^{-2}. Some non-SI units can be converted to SI units as shown in Table 3.

Table 3 Unit conversions		
Unit	Symbol	SI equivalent
length	metre	m
atomic mass unit	u	1.661×10^{-27} kg
atmosphere	atm	101 325 Pa
degree Celsius	°C	1 K
litre	dm^3	10^{-3} m^3
tonne	t	10^3 kg

Formulae

Ideal gas equation

$pV = nRT$

Amount of substance

$$\text{number of moles} = \frac{\text{mass}}{\text{r.m.m}}$$

Equilibrium law

For the reaction

$mA + nB \rightleftharpoons pC + qD$

the equilibrium constant K_c is given by

$$K_c = \frac{[C]^p\,[D]^q}{[A]^m\,[B]^n}$$

where values in square brackets are equilibrium concentrations.

pH

$pH = -\log_{10}[H^+]$

Ionic product of water

$K_w = [H^+]\,[OH^-]$
$\quad = 1 \times 10^{-14}$ mol^2 dm^{-6} at s.t.p.

Order of reaction

For a zero-order reaction:

$$\frac{-d[A]}{dt} = k_o$$

$$\frac{-d[A]}{dt} = k_1[A]$$

For a first-order reaction:

$$\frac{-d[A]}{dt} = k_2\,[A]^2$$

For a second-order reaction:

Important values, constants and standards

Constant	Symbol	Value
molar gas constant	R	$8.31 \text{ J K}^{-1}\text{ mol}^{-1}$
Faraday constant	F	$9.65 \times 10^4 \text{ C mol}^{-1}$
Avogadro constant	L	$6.02 \times 10^{23}\text{ mol}^{-1}$
Planck constant	h	$6.63 \times 10^{-34}\text{ J Hz}^{-1}$
speed of light in a vacuum	c	$3.00 \times 10^{-8}\text{ m s}^{-1}$
mass of proton	m_p	$1.67 \times 10^{-27}\text{ kg}$
mass of neutron	m_n	$1.67 \times 10^{-27}\text{ kg}$
mass of electron	m_e	$9.11 \times 10^{-31}\text{ kg}$
electronic charge	e	$1.60 \times 10^{-19}\text{ C}$
molar volume of gas	V_m	$22.4 \text{ dm}^3\text{ mol}^{-1}$ (at s.t.p.)
specific heat capacity of water		$4.18 \text{ kJ kg}^{-1}\text{ K}^{-1}$

s.t.p. is approximately 101 kPa and 273 K (0 °C)

Infrared spectroscopy: characteristic absorption bands

Compound	Wavelength/nm
C—H stretching vibrations	
alkane	3376–3505
alkene	3231–3322
arene	3300
aldehyde	3448–3546
	3603–3703
C—H bending vibrations	
alkane	6734–7326
arene	11 364–14 300
O—H stretching vibrations	
alcohols	
(not hydrogen-bonded)	2740–2786
(hydrogen-bonded	2667–3125
carboxylic acids	
(hydrogen-bonded)	3030–4000
Carbon–halogen stretching vibrations	
C—F	7142–10 000
C—Cl	12 500–16 667
C—Br	16 667–20 000
C—I	about 20 000
C=C stretching vibrations	
alkene	5991–6079
arene	6250–6897
C=O stretching vibrations	
aldehydes, saturated alkyl group	5747–5814
ketones	5882–5952
carboxylic acids	
saturated alkyl	5797–5882
aryl (from arene)	5882–5952
esters (saturated)	5714–5763

Bond angles

Compound	Sequence	Angle	Bond	Bond length/nm
CCl_4	Cl—C—Cl	109.5	Cl—C	0.177
CH_4	H—C—H	109.5	H—C	0.109
C_2H_4	H—C—H	117.3	H—C	0.109
C_6H_6 (benzene)	C—C—C	120.0	C—C	0.1397
H_2O	H—O—H	104.5	H—O	0.096
NH_3	H—N—H	107.0	H—N	0.101
PCl_5	Cl—P—Cl	120.0	Cl—P	0.204
SF_6	F—S—F	90.0	F—S	0.156

Periodic table

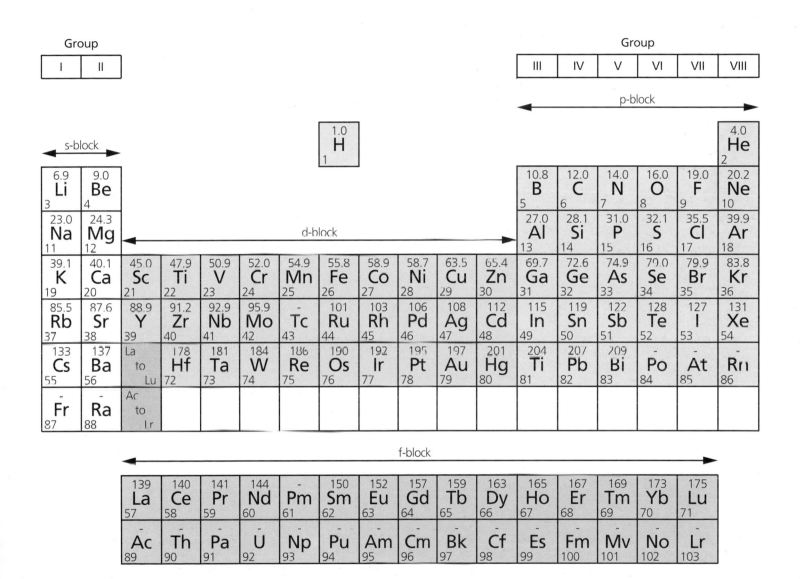

Group I, II

Group III, IV, V, VI, VII, VIII

p-block

s-block

d-block

f-block

1.0	
H	
1	

4.0
He
2

6.9	9.0
Li	**Be**
3	4

10.8	12.0	14.0	16.0	19.0	20.2
B	**C**	**N**	**O**	**F**	**Ne**
5	6	7	8	9	10

23.0	24.3
Na	**Mg**
11	12

27.0	28.1	31.0	32.1	35.5	39.9
Al	**Si**	**P**	**S**	**Cl**	**Ar**
13	14	15	16	17	18

39.1	40.1	45.0	47.9	50.9	52.0	54.9	55.8	58.9	58.7	63.5	65.4	69.7	72.6	74.9	79.0	79.9	83.8
K	**Ca**	**Sc**	**Ti**	**V**	**Cr**	**Mn**	**Fe**	**Co**	**Ni**	**Cu**	**Zn**	**Ga**	**Ge**	**As**	**Se**	**Br**	**Kr**
19	20	21	22	23	24	25	26	27	28	29	30	31	32	33	34	35	36

85.5	87.6	88.9	91.2	92.9	95.9	-	101	103	106	108	112	115	119	122	128	127	131
Rb	**Sr**	**Y**	**Zr**	**Nb**	**Mo**	**Tc**	**Ru**	**Rh**	**Pd**	**Ag**	**Cd**	**In**	**Sn**	**Sb**	**Te**	**I**	**Xe**
37	38	39	40	41	42	43	44	45	46	47	48	49	50	51	52	53	54

133	137	La to Lu	178	181	184	186	190	192	195	197	201	204	207	209	-	-	-
Cs	**Ba**		**Hf**	**Ta**	**W**	**Re**	**Os**	**Ir**	**Pt**	**Au**	**Hg**	**Ti**	**Pb**	**Bi**	**Po**	**At**	**Rn**
55	56		72	73	74	75	76	77	78	79	80	81	82	83	84	85	86

-	-	Ac to Lr
Fr	**Ra**	
87	88	

139	140	141	144	-	150	152	157	159	163	165	167	169	173	175
La	**Ce**	**Pr**	**Nd**	**Pm**	**Sm**	**Eu**	**Gd**	**Tb**	**Dy**	**Ho**	**Er**	**Tm**	**Yb**	**Lu**
57	58	59	60	61	62	63	64	65	66	67	68	69	70	71

-	-	-	-	-	-	-	-	-	-	-	-	-	-	-
Ac	**Th**	**Pa**	**U**	**Np**	**Pu**	**Am**	**Cm**	**Bk**	**Cf**	**Es**	**Fm**	**Mv**	**No**	**Lr**
89	90	91	92	93	94	95	96	97	98	99	100	101	102	103

Key

a
X
b

a = relative atomic mass
x = atomic symbol
b = atomic (proton) number

Selected data for some elements

Element	Symbol	Atomic number	Stable mass number (% abundance)	Molar mass/ g mol^{-1}	Melting point/ °C	Boiling point/ °C
Aluminium	Al	13	27(100)	26.9	660	2467
Argon	Ar	18	40(99.6), 36(0.34), 38(0.063)	39.9	−189	−186
Barium	Ba	56	138(71.7), 137(11.32), 136(7.81), 135(6.59)	137.3	725	1640
Beryllium	Be	4	9(100)	9.01	1278	2970
Boron	B	5	11(80.3), 10(19.7)	10.8	2300	2550
Bromine	Br	35	79(50.5), 81(49.5)	79.9	−7	59
Caesium	Cs	55	133(100)	132.9	29	669
Calcium	Ca	20	40(96.97), 44(2.06), 42(0.64)	40.1	839	1484
Carbon	C	6	12(98.9), 13(1.1)	12.0	3652	4827
Chlorine	Cl	17	35(75.5), 37(24.5)	35.5	−101	−35
Chromium	Cr	24	52(83.8), 53(9.55), 50(4.31)	52.0	1857	2670
Cobalt	Co	27	59(100)	58.9	1495	2870
Copper	Cu	29	63(69.1), 65(30.9)	63.5	1083	2567
Fluorine	F	9	19(100)	19.0	−220	−188
Helium	He	2	4(100)	4.0	−263	−269
Hydrogen	H	1	1(99.98), 2(0.015)	1.0	−259	−253
Iodine	I	53	127(100)	126.9	114	184
Iron	Fe	26	56(91.7), 54(5.8), 57(2.2)	55.8	1535	2750
Krypton	Kr	36	84(56.9), 86(17.4), 82(11.5), 83(11.5)	83.8	−157	−152
Lithium	Li	3	7(92.6), 6(7.4)	6.9	171	1342
Magnesium	Mg	12	24(78.6), 25(10.1), 26(11.3)	24.3	649	1107
Manganese	Mn	25	55(100)	54.9	1244	1962
Neon	Ne	10	20(90.9), 22(8.8)	20.2	−248	−246
Nickel	Ni	28	58(67.8), 60(26.2), 62(3.7)	58.7	1455	2730
Nitrogen	N	7	14(99.6), 15(0.4)	14.0	−210	−196
Oxygen	O	8	16(99.8), 18(0.2)	16.0	−218	−183
Phosphorus	P	15	31(100)	31.0	44(white)	280(white)
Potassium	K	19	39(93.2), 41(6.8)	39.1	63	760
Rubidium	Rb	37	85(72.15), 87(27.85)	85.5	39	686
Scandium	Sc	21	45(100)	45.0	1541	2831
Silicon	Si	14	28(92.2), 29(4.7), 30(3.1)	28.1	1410	2355
Sodium	Na	11	23(100)	23.0	98	883
Strontium	Sr	38	88(82.6), 86(9.9), 87(7.0)	87.6	769	1384
Sulphur	S	16	32(95), 34(4.2), 33(0.8)	32.1	119	445
Titanium	Ti	22	48(74), 46(8.0), 47(7.3), 49(5.5)	47.9	1660	3287
Vanadium	V	23	51(99.7), 50 (0.3)	50.9	1890	3380
Xenon	Xe	54	Many	131.3	−112	−107
Zinc	Zn	30	several	65.4	420	907

[1] Pauling electronegativity index
[2] m = metallic radius; v = van der Waals radius; c = covalent radius
[3] Superscript shows the charge on the ion

Electronegativity[1]	Atomic radius/[2] nm	Ionic radius/[3] nm	Ionisation energies/kJ mol^{-1}				
			1st	2nd	3rd	4th	
1.5	^{m}0.143	$^{+3}$ 0.053	578	1817	2745	11578	Al
–	^{v}0.190	–	1521	2666	3931	5771	Ar
0.9	^{m}0.224	$^{+2}$ 0.136	503	965			Ba
1.5	^{m}0.112	$^{+2}$0.027	900	1757	14849	21007	Be
2.0	^{m}0.098	$^{+3}$ 0.012	801	2427	3660	25026	B
2.8	^{c}0.114	$^{-1}$ 0.195	1140	2100	3500	4560	Br
0.7	^{m}0.272	$^{+1}$ 0.170	376	2420	3300		Cs
1.0	^{m}0.197	$^{+2}$ 0.100	590	1145	4912	6474	Ca
2.5	^{c}0.077	–	1086	2353	4621	6223	C
3.0	^{c}0.099	$^{-1}$ 0.180	1251	2297	3822	5158	Cl
1.6	^{m}0.129	$^{+3}$ 0.062	653	1592	2987	4740	Cr
1.8	^{m}0.125	$^{+2}$ 0.065	758	1646	3232	4950	Co
1.9	^{m}0.128	$^{+2}$ 0.073	746	1958	3554	5330	Cu
4.0	^{c}0.071	$^{-1}$ 0.133	1681	3374	6051	8408	F
–	^{v}0.180	–	2372	5251	–	–	He
2.1	^{c}0.037	$^{-1}$ 0.208	1312	–	–	–	H
2.5	^{c}0.133	$^{-1}$ 0.215	1008	1846	3200	–	I
1.8	^{m}0.126	$^{+3}$ 0.055	759	1561	2958	5290	Fe
–	^{v}0.200	–	1351	2368	3565	5070	Kr
1.0	^{m}0.157	$^{+1}$ 0.074	520	7298	11815	–	Li
1.2	^{m}0.160	$^{+2}$ 0.072	738	1451	7733	10541	Mg
1.5	^{m}0.137	$^{+2}$ 0.067	717	1509	3249	4940	Mn
–	^{v}0.160	–	2081	3952	6122	9370	Ne
1.8	^{m}0.125	$^{+2}$ 0.070	737	1753	3394	5300	Ni
3.0	^{c}0.075	$^{-3}$ 0.171	1402	2856	4578	7475	N
3.5	^{c}0.073	$^{-2}$ 0.140	1314	3388	5301	7469	O
2.1	^{c}0.110	$^{-3}$ 0.190	1012	1903	2912	4957	P
0.8	^{m}0.235	$^{+1}$ 0.138	419	3051	4412	5877	K
0.8	^{m}0.250	$^{+1}$ 0.149	403	2632	3900	5080	Rb
1.3	^{m}0.164	$^{+3}$ 0.075	631	1235	2389	7089	Sc
1.8	^{c}0.118	$^{+4}$ 0.040	789	1577	3232	4356	Si
0.9	^{m}0.191	$^{+1}$ 0.102	496	4563	6913	9544	Na
1.0	^{m}0.215	$^{+2}$ 0.113	550	1064	4210	5500	Sr
2.5	^{c}0.102	$^{-2}$ 0.185	1000	2251	3361	4564	S
1.5	^{m}0.147	$^{+4}$ 0.061	658	1310	2653	4175	Ti
1.6	^{m}0.135	$^{+3}$ 0.064	650	1414	2828	4507	V
–	^{v}0.220	–	1170	2047	3100		Xe
1.6	^{m}0.137	$^{+2}$ 0.075	906	1733	3833	5730	Zn

Selected data for some inorganic compounds

Compound	Formula	State	Molar mass/g mol^{-1}	T_m/K	T_bK	ΔH/kJ mol^{-1}
Aluminium fluoride	AlF$_3$	s	84.0	1564 (sub)	–	−1504
Aluminium chloride	AlCl$_3$	s	133.3	463	451 (sub)	−704
Aluminium oxide	Al$_2$O$_3$	s	102.0	2345	3253	−1676
Caesium fluoride	CsF	s	151.9	955	1524	−553
Caesium chloride	CsCl	s	168.4	918	1563	−443
Caesium oxide	Cs$_2$O	s	281.8	763 (in N$_2$)	673 (dec)	−346
Carbon monoxide	CO	g	28.0	74	82	−110
Carbon dioxide	CO$_2$	g	44.0	217 (at 5.2atm)	195	−393
Hydrogen fluoride	HF	g	20.0	190	293	−271
Hydrogen chloride	HCl	g	36.5	158	188	−92.3
Hydrogen bromide	HBr	g	80.9	185	206	−36.4
Hydrogen iodide	HI	g	127.9	222	238	26.5
Water	H$_2$O	l	18.0	273	373	−286
Hydrogen sulphide	H$_2$S	g	34.1	188	212	−20.6
Lithium fluoride	LiF	s	25.9	1118	1949	−616
Lithium chloride	LiCl	s	42.4	878	1613	−408.6
Lithium oxide	Li$_2$O	s	29.9	>1973	—	−598
Magnesium chloride	MgCl$_2$	s	95.2	987	1685	−641
Magnesium oxide	MgO	s	40.3	3125	3873	−602
Hydrazine	N$_2$H$_4$	l	32.0	275	387	50.6
Ammonia	NH$_3$	g	17.0	195	240	−46.1
Nitrogen chloride	NCl$_3$	l	120.4	<233	<344	230.1
Phosphorus(III) choride	PCl$_3$	l	137.3	161	349	−320
Phosphorus(V) choride	PCl$_5$	s	208.2	435 (sub.)	440 (dec.)	−443
Silicon(IV) chloride	SiCl$_4$	l	169.9	203	331	−687
Silicon dioxide	SiO$_2$	s	60.1	1883	2503	−911
Sodium fluoride	NaF	s	42.0	1266	1968	−574
Sodium chloride	NaCl	s	58.4	1074	1686	−411
Sodium bromide	NaBr	s	102.9	1020	1663	−361
Sodium oxide	Na$_2$O	s	62.0	1548 (sub.)	–	−414
Sulphur(II) chloride	SCl$_2$	g	103.0	195	332 (dec.)	−20
Sulphur(IV) chloride	SCl$_4$	l	173.9	243	258 (dec.)	−56
Sulphur(IV) oxide	SO$_2$	g	64.1	200	263	−297
Sulphur(VI) oxide	SO$_3$	l	80.1	290	318	−441

s=solid, l=liquid, g=gas

T_m = melting point; sub=sublimes; dec=decomposes

T_b = boiling point at 1 atm

ΔH_f = Standard molar enthalpy change of formation at 298 K and 1 atmosphere

Selected data for some organic compounds

Compound	Formula	State	Molar mass/g mol^{-1}	T_m/K	T_b/K	ΔH_c/kJ mol^{-1}	ΔH_f/kJ mol^{-1}
Alkanes							
Methane	CH_4	g	16.0	91.1	109.1	−890	−75
Ethane	CH_3CH_3	g	30.1	89.8	184.5	−1560	−85
Propane	$CH_3CH_2CH_3$	g	44.1	83.4	231.0	−2219	−104
Butane	$CH_3(CH_2)_2CH_3$	g	58.1	134.7	272.6	−2876	−126
Pentane	$CH_3(CH_2)_3CH_3$	l	72.2	143.1	309.2	−3509	−173
Hexane	$CH_3(CH_2)_4CH_3$	l	86.2	178.1	342.1	−4163	−199
Alkenes							
Ethene	$CH_2{=}CH_2$	g	28.1	104.1	169.4	−1411	+52
Propene	$CH_2{=}CHCH_3$	g	42.1	87.9	225.7	−2058	+20
But-1-ene	$CH_2{=}CHCH_2CH_3$	g	56.1	87.8	266.8	−2717	−0.4
trans-But-2-ene	$CH_3CH{=}CHCH_3$	g	56.1	167.6	274.0	−2705	−12
cis-But-2-ene	$CH_3CH{=}CHCH_3$	g	56.1	134.2	276.8	−2709	−8
Arenes							
Benzene	C_6H_6	l	78.1	278.6	353.2	−3267	+49
Halogenoalkanes							
Fluoromethane	CH_3F	g	34.0	131.3	194.7	−	−247
Chloromethane	CH_3Cl	g	50.5	176.0	248.9	−764.0	82
Bromomethane	CH_3Br	g	94.9	179.5	276.7	770	−37
Iodomethane	CH_3I	l	141.9	206.7	315.5	−815	−15
Dichloromethane	CH_2Cl_2	l	84.9	178.0	313.1	−606	−124
Trichloromethane	$CHCl_3$	l	119.4	209.6	334.8	−474	−135
Tetrachloromethane	CCl_4	l	153.8	250.1	349.6	−360	−130
Alcohols							
Methanol	CH_3OH	l	32.0	179.2	338.1	−726	−239
Ethanol	CH_3CH_2OH	l	46.1	155.8	351.6	−1367	−277
Propan-1-ol	$CH_3CH_2CH_2OH$	l	60.1	146.6	370.5	−2021	−303
Propan-2-ol	$CH_3CHOHCH_3$	l	60.1	183.6	355.5	−2006	−318
Butan-1-ol	$CH_3(CH_2)CH_2OH$	l	74.1	183.6	390.3	2676	327
Pentan-1-ol	$CH_3(CH_2)_3CH_2OH$	l	88.2	194.1	411.1	−3329	−354
Hexan-1-ol	$CH_3(CH_2)_4CH_2OH$	l	102.2	226.4	431.1	−3984	−379
Aldehydes							
Methanal	HCHO	g	30.0	181.1	252.1	−571	−109
Ethanal	CH_3CHO	g	44.1	152.1	293.9	−1167	−191
Propanal	CH_3CH_2CHO	l	58.1	192.1	321.9	−1821	−217
Ketones							
Propanone	CH_3COCH_3	l	58.1	177.8	329.3	−1816	−248
Butanone	$CH_3CH_2COCH_3$	l	72.1	186.8	352.7	−2441	−276
Carboxylic acids							
Methanoic	HCOOH	l	46.0	281.5	373.7	−254	−425
Ethanoic	CH_3COOH	l	60.1	289.7	391.0	−874	−484
Propanoic	CH_3CH_2COOH	l	74.1	252.3	414.1	−1527	−511
Butanoic	$CH_3CH_2CH_2CO_2H$	l	88.1	268.6	438.6	−2183	−534

ΔH_c = standard molar enthalpy change of combustion; other abbreviations as in previous table

Bond lengths and bond energies

Bond	in	Bond length/ nm	Bond energy/ kJ mol^{-1}	Bond	in	Bond Length/ nm	Bond energy/ kJ mol^{-1}
Br—Br	Br$_2$	0.228	193	O—Si	SiO$_2$(s)	0.161	466
Br—H	HBr	0.141	366	O=Si	SiO$_2$(g)	–	638
Cl—Cl	Cl	0.199	243	O=Si	SiO	–	805
Cl—H	HCl	0.127	432	P—P	P$_4$	0.221	198
F—F	F$_2$	0.142	158	P=P	P$_2$	0.189	485
F—H	HF	0.092	568	C—C	average	0.154	347
I—I	I$_2$	0.267	151	C=C	average	0.134	612
H—I	HI	0.161	298	C≡C	average	0.120	838
H—H	H$_2$	0.074	435	C—H	average	0.108	413
H—Si	SiH$_4$	0.148	318	C—H	CH$_4$	0.109	435
H—Ge	GeH$_4$	0.153	285	C—F	average	0.138	467
H—N	NH$_3$	0.101	391	C—F	CH$_3$F	0.139	452
H—P	PH$_3$	0.144	321	C—F	CF$_4$	0.132	485
H—As	AsH$_3$	0.152	297	C—Cl	average	0.177	346
H—O	H$_2$O	0.096	464	C—Cl	CCl$_4$	0.177	327
H—S	H$_2$S	0.134	364	C—Cl	C$_6$H$_5$Cl	0.170	–
H—Se	H$_2$Se	0.146	313	C—Br	average	0.194	290
Na—Na	Na$_2$	0.308	72	C—Br	CBr$_4$	0.194	285
K—K	K$_2$	0.392	49	C—I	average	0.214	228
N—N	N$_2$H$_4$	0.145	158	C—I	CH$_3$I	0.214	234
N=N	C$_6$H$_{14}$N$_2$	0.120	410	C—N	average	0.147	286
N≡N	N$_2$	0.110	945	C=N	average	0.130	615
N—O	HNO$_2$	0.120	214	C≡N	average	0.116	887
N=O	NOF, NOCl	0.114	587	C—N	phenylamine	0.135	–
N=P	PN	0.149	582	C—O	average	0.143	358
O—O	H$_2$O$_2$	0.148	144	C—O	CH$_3$OH	0.143	336
O—O	O$_3$	0.128	302	C=O	CO$_2$	0.116	805
O=O	O$_2$	0.121	498	C=O	HCHO	0.121	695
S—S	S$_8$	0.205	266	C=O	aldehydes	0.122	736
S=S	S$_2$	0.189	429	C=O	ketones	0.122	749
O—S	SO$_3$	0.143	469	C=O	CO	0.113	1077
Si—Si	Si(s), SiH$_4$	0.235	226	C—Si	(CH$_3$)$_4$Si, SiC(s)	0.187	307

Glossary

Absorption spectrum   The amounts of radiation absorbed by a substance at different wavelengths, usually displayed on a print-out produced by a **spectrometer**.

Acid   A substance which has a tendency to release **protons** (hydrogen ions). A strong acid, such as nitric acid, releases hydrogen ions readily. Weak acids, such as ethanoic and other organic acids, release hydrogen ions far less readily.

Acid dissociation constant   A measure of the extent to which an **acid** releases hydrogen ions. For the dissociation of any weak acid, HA, the dissociation constant K_a is given by:

$$K_a = \frac{[A^-]\,[H^+]}{[HA]}$$

where the square brackets ([ ]) indicate **equilibrium** concentrations in aqueous solution.

Activation energy   The minimum energy required by particles in collision to bring about a chemical reaction.

Addition polymerisation   The **addition reaction** of many molecules of monomer to form one large molecule of **polymer**. No other substances are formed. Ethene forms polythene by addition polymerisation.

Addition reaction   A reaction in which two molecules react together to form one molecule.

Alcohols   Alcohols have the general formula R—OH, where R is an **alkyl group**. Their names end in –ol. Ethanol, C_2H_5OH, is an alcohol. A primary alcohol has the general formula

$$R-\overset{\displaystyle H}{\underset{\displaystyle H}{\overset{|}{\underset{|}{C}}}}-OH$$

A secondary alcohol has the general formula

$$R-\overset{\displaystyle H}{\underset{\displaystyle R^1}{\overset{|}{\underset{|}{C}}}}-OH$$

A tertiary alcohol has the general formula

$$R-\overset{\displaystyle R^2}{\underset{\displaystyle R^1}{\overset{|}{\underset{|}{C}}}}-OH$$

Aldehyde   A carbonyl compound with the general formula

The names of aldehydes end in –al. Ethanal, CH_3CHO, is an aldehyde.

Alkali   A **base** which dissolves in water, releasing hydroxide ions (OH^-).

Alkane   A hydrocarbon with the general formula C_nH_{2n+2}. The first three alkanes are CH_4, C_2H_6 and C_3H_8.

Alkene   A hydrocarbon with the general formula C_nH_{2n}. Alkene molecules contain double bonds. The first two alkenes are C_2H_4 and C_3H_6.

Alkyl group   A group of atoms with the general formula CnH_{2n+1}—, forming part of a molecule.

Allotropes   Different forms of the same element, having different structures. Carbon has several allotropes: diamond, graphite and the fullerenes.

Amphoteric   Having both **acidic** and **basic** properties. For example, aluminium oxide is an amphoteric oxide. It forms salts both with acids and with alkalis.

Arene   An aromatic compound which is a hydrocarbon. All arenes contain one or more benzene rings. Benzene and naphthalene are arenes.

benzene   naphthalene

Aromatic compounds   Organic compounds which contain one or more benzene rings. All **arenes** are aromatic compounds, as are phenol and phenylamine.

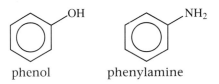

phenol   phenylamine

Atom   A single unit of an element.

Atomic mass   *See* **relative atomic mass**

Atomic number (symbol Z)   The number of protons (and therefore electrons) present in an **atom**.

Atomic radius   The distance from the centre of the **nucleus** to the outermost **electrons** in an **atom**.

Avogadro constant   The number of particles contained in one **mole** of a substance: 6.022×10^{23} mol^{-1}.

Bactericide   A chemical that will kill bacteria. The halogens can all act as bactericides.

Base   A substance which has a tendency to gain **protons**. Bases which dissolve in water are called **alkalis**. Strong bases gain protons readily.

Biomass   Biological material; often refers just to plant material.

Bond energy (symbol E)   The bond enthalpy: the amount of energy released when the bond is formed, which equals the amount of energy absorbed when the bond is broken.

Buffer   A mixture whose **pH** does not change appreciably when acids or alkalis are added to it. Most buffers are mixtures of a weak **acid** or weak **base** with a corresponding **salt**.

Carbonium ion   A positively charged group containing carbon and hydrogen atoms. Examples are

$$\begin{array}{ccc} & H & H \\ & | & | \\ H - & C - & C^+ \\ & | & | \\ & H & H \end{array} \qquad \begin{array}{c} H \\ | \\ H - C^+ \\ | \\ H \end{array}$$

Carbonyl compounds   Compounds containing the group >C==O. They include **aldehydes** and **ketones**.

Carbonyl group   The functional group >C==O.

Carboxylic acids   Organic **acids** having the general formula

$$R - C \overset{OH}{\underset{O}{<}}$$

Their names end in –oic acid. Ethanoic acid has the formula CH_3COOH.

Catalyst   A substance that alters the rate of a chemical reaction by changing the **activation energy**. A catalyst remains chemically unchanged at the end of the reaction. A catalyst that lowers the rate of a reaction is often called an inhibitor.

Chiral compounds   Compounds whose molecules are asymmetrical, and thus are different from their mirror images. They are **optically active**.

Chirality   The absence of symmetry in a molecule.

Chloramines   Compounds containing both chlorine and nitrogen derived from an amine group (NH_2). Chloramines are used as disinfectants. The simplest chloramines are monochloramine, NH_2Cl, and dichloramine, $NHCl_2$.

Closed system   A **system** from which reactants and products cannot escape, and to which they cannot be added. Chemical **equilibrium** is only possible in a closed system.

Combined chlorine   The term given to chlorine that is bonded in a molecule in such a way that it is unavailable to act as a **bactericide**.

Complex ion   An **ion** that contains a central atom to which other atoms or ions are bonded. In a **transition metal** complex, the transition metal is the central atom. The atoms or ions bonded to the central atom are called **ligands**. Examples include $Cu(NH_3)_4^{2+}$, the tetraamminecopper(II) ion.

Coordinate bond   A **covalent bond** in which the shared **electron pair** originates from the same atom. It can be written as $X \rightarrow Y$, showing that the shared electron pair originated from X.

Coordination number   The number of **ligands** to which a central metal atom is bonded in a **complex ion**. For example, in the tetraamminecopper(II) ion, $Cu(NH_3)_4^{2+}$, the coordination number of copper is four.

Covalent bond   A bond in which two atoms share one or more pairs of electrons. A hydrogen molecule, H—H, has a single covalent bond. In a double covalent bond there are two shared pairs of electrons. The oxygen molecule, O==O, has a double covalent bond.

Cracking   The process of breaking up the long-chain hydrocarbons in crude oil into shorter-chain hydrocarbons that can be used in the chemical industry and for petrol.

Crude oil   A mixture of hydrocarbons formed naturally by the decomposition of marine animals over millions of years.

Dative covalent bond   Another name for a **coordinate bond**.

Dehydration reaction   A reaction in which water is eliminated.

Delocalised electrons   Electrons that are not located on one particular atom, but are free to move between all atoms in the structure. There are delocalised electrons in both benzene and graphite.

Dextrorotatory   An **optical isomer** that rotates the plane of **plane-polarised light** to the right (clockwise) is dextrorotatory; written as D- or (+)-.

Dipole   Consists of a positive charge and an equal negative charge separated by a short distance. Temporary dipoles form in non-polar molecules, such as nitrogen, because at any instant electron distribution around the molecule may not be quite even. Some molecules, such as hydrogen chloride, are **polar**. They have permanent dipoles because the electron distribution is always uneven. Bonding between atoms of different **electronegativity** causes this unevenness.

Dissociated   Refers to a compound that is broken up into its constituent **atoms** or **ions**.

Dot-and-cross diagram A means of representing the electrons in a molecule. Electrons are drawn as either dots or crosses, to indicate their original atom.

Electron A negatively charged particle. Electrons orbit the atomic **nucleus** in **energy levels**. Atoms of different elements have different numbers of electrons. The number of electrons is always equal to the **atomic number** of the element.

Electron density map A diagram of a molecule in which lines connect areas of equal electron density. It shows the position of the atoms (or ions) and gives information about the bonding.

Electron pairs Bonding electron pairs occur in a **covalent bond** between two atoms, and normally include one electron from each atom except in the case of a **coordinate bond**. Non-bonding electron pairs, or lone pairs, take no part in bonding. For example, a hydrogen chloride molecule has one bonding electron pair, together with three non-bonding electron pairs on the chlorine atom.

Electronegativity The tendency of the atoms of an **element** to gain **electrons**. Elements whose atoms gain electrons easily are the most electronegative. Elements whose atoms lose outer electrons easily are described as being electropositive. Caesium is the most electropositive element. Fluorine is the most electronegative element.

Electrophile An electron-seeking group. Electrophiles are positively charged. Examples include the nitryl group, $-NO_2^+$.

Electrophilic addition A reaction in which an **electrophile** is attracted to an area of high electron density. The electrophile adds on to the atom or group – an **addition reaction**.

Electrophilic substitution A reaction in which an **electrophile** is attracted to an area of high electron density. The electrophile replaces an atom or group – a **substitution reaction**.

Element A substance which cannot be broken down into any simpler substance by chemical means. All **atoms** of an element have the same **atomic number**.

Elimination reaction A reaction in which the products include a small molecule, often water. The small product molecule is said to be eliminated from the reacting molecule(s).

Empirical formula The simplest formula of a compound, showing the ratios of the numbers of atoms in the molecule. For example, CH_3 is the empirical formula of ethane, C_2H_6.

Emulsify To make a suspension of very small droplets of one liquid in another. Detergents help to form an emulsion of oil in water.

Enantiomer One of the **optical isomers** of a **chiral compound**.

Endothermic reaction A chemical reaction in which energy is absorbed.

Energy level One of the fixed range of energies to which electron energies in atoms are limited; sometimes described as **shells** and **sub-shells**. An electron in an atom requires a particular amount or quantum of energy to move from one energy level to the next.

Enthalpy Energy content.

Enthalpy change An amount of energy that is transferred (absorbed or released).

Enthalpy change of combustion. The amount of energy transferred when one **mole** of a substance burns completely in oxygen under **standard conditions**.

Enthalpy change of hydrogenation The amount of energy transferred when one **mole** of a substance reacts completely with hydrogen under **standard conditions**.

Enthalpy change of vaporisation The amount of energy required to convert one **mole** of a liquid to a gas at its boiling point.

Equilibrium The state reached in a **reversible reaction** at which the rates of the two opposing reactions are equal, so that the system has no further tendency to change. This is a dynamic equilibrium, as reactants and products are both still being formed, but at equal rates.

Equilibrium constant The ratio of products to reactants in an **equilibrium** mixture. K_c relates to concentrations of reactants and products at equilibrium. For the reaction

$$nA(l) + mB(l) \rightleftharpoons pC(l) + qD$$

$$K_c = \frac{[C(l)]^p \, [D(l)]^q}{[A(l)]^n \, [B(l)]^m}$$

where the square brackets ([ ]) are **equilibrium** concentrations.

Ester A compound with the general formula

Esters are formed by the reaction of an alcohol with a carboxylic acid in the presence of a strong acid catalyst.

Exothermic reaction A chemical reaction in which energy is released.

Fermentation The process by which, for example, the micro-organism yeast converts glucose into ethanol and carbon dioxide in order to release energy.

Fossil fuels Fuels that have been formed by the slow decomposition of plant and animal material. They include coal, oil, natural gas and peat.

Fraction   A product of **fractional distillation**, collected over a specific temperature range; a part of crude oil containing hydrocarbons of similar chain length.

Fractional distillation   Process used to separate the components of crude oil into groups of hydrocarbons of similar chain length. The process involves heating the crude oil until it vaporises and collecting the products within a set boiling point range.

Free chlorine   The chlorine available for a reaction, particularly as a **bactericide**, normally in the form of chlorate(I) ions.

Giant atomic structure   A structure that contains many millions of atoms all bonded together. Diamond and graphite have giant atomic structures.

Geometric isomer   A geometric isomer is an example of a **stereoisomer**. Geometric isomers have *cis* and *trans* forms.

Half-equation   Part of the equation for a **redox reaction**, showing the oxidation or reduction of one particular element. Two half-equations, showing the simultaneous oxidation and reduction steps, make up the full equation for the redox reaction. For example, the reaction
$$Zn(s) + Cu^{2+}(aq) \longrightarrow Zn_{2+}(aq) + Cu(s)$$
is made up from two half-equations
$$Zn(s) \longrightarrow Zn^{2+} + 2e^- \quad \text{oxidation}$$
$$Cu^{2+}(aq) + 2e^- \longrightarrow Cu(s) \quad \text{reduction}$$

Half-life   The time taken for half the atoms in a sample of a radioactive material to decay. Polonium–214 has a half-life of 1.5×10^{-4} seconds. Uranium–238 has a half-life of 4.5×10^9 years.

Heterogeneous catalysis   A reaction for which the **catalyst** and the reactants are in different phases. Examples include the use of a solid iron catalyst in the reaction of nitrogen gas and hydrogen gas to form ammonia (Haber process).

Heterogeneous equilibrium   An **equilibrium** in which the reactants are in different phases. An example is the equilibrium mixture obtained by heating ammonium chloride in a sealed tube:
$$NH_4Cl(s) \rightleftharpoons NH_3(g) + HCl(g)$$

Heterolytic bond breaking   The breaking of a single covalent bond (a bonding pair of electrons) so that the two electrons remain on one atom. **Ions** are formed. The atom taking the two electrons is negatively charged. The atom with no electrons from the bond is positively charged. Examples include the dissociation in solution of hydrogen bromide:
$$H{:}Br(g) \longrightarrow H^+(aq) + Br{:}^-(aq)$$

Homogeneous catalysis   A reaction for which the **catalyst** and the reactants are in the same phase. Examples include the catalysis of the oxidation of sulphuric(IV) acid by transition metal ions in solution.

Homogeneous equilibrium   An **equilibrium** in which all the reactants are in the same phase. An example is the equilibrium mixture obtained by heating hydrogen and iodine in a sealed tube:
$$H_2(g) + I_2(g) \rightleftharpoons 2HI(g)$$

Homologous series   A series of organic compounds with the same general formula, each member of the series having one more carbon atom in its molecule than the last. For example, the **alkanes** form a homologous series.

Homolytic bond breaking   The breaking of a single covalent bond (a bonding pair of electrons) so that one electron remains with each atom. The species formed are called **radicals** and each has an unpaired electron. The gas-phase dissociation of chlorine is an example:
$$Cl{:}Cl \longrightarrow Cl\cdot + Cl\cdot$$

Hydration energy   The energy released when an ionic lattice dissolves in water, and water molecules surround the positive and negative ions.

Hydrogen bonding   The **intermolecular bonding** between **dipoles** in adjacent molecules in which hydrogen is bonded to a very electronegative element. For example, intermolecular hydrogen bonding exists in water (H_2O), ammonia (NH_3) and hydrogen fluoride (HF):
$$H{-}F\cdots H{-}F$$
$$\Uparrow$$
hydrogen bond

Hydrogenation   The **addition reaction** of a compound with hydrogen.

Ideal gas   A gas made up of particles of negligible size, with no forces acting between them. Ideal gases exist only in theory, not in practice, but nitrogen, oxygen, hydrogen and the inert gases behave like ideal gases at high temperature and low pressure. Under these conditions they obey the ideal gas equation.

Ideal gas equation   A mathematical description of the relationship between volume, temperature and pressure for an **ideal gas**:
$$pV = nRT$$
where n is the number of moles of gas. R is the same for every gas, and is called the **molar gas constant**. It has the value of 8.314 J K^{-1} mol^{-1}, when pressure (p) is measured in N m^{-2} (Pa), volume (V) is measured in m^3 and temperature (T) is measured in K.

Intermolecular bonding   Bonding between molecules; the phrase does not refer to bonding within molecules. There are several types of intermolecular bonding, including **van der Waals forces** and **hydrogen bonds**.

Ion A particle, consisting of an **atom** or group of atoms, that carries a positive or negative electric charge. An atom forms an ion when it loses or gains one or more electrons.

Ionic equations A concise method of writing down the important changes that affect the ions directly involved in a chemical reaction.

Ionic product of water The product of the concentrations of hydrogen ions and hydroxide ions in pure water:
$$K_w = [H^+][OH^-]$$
At 25 °C, K_w is 10^{-14} mol^2 dm^{-6}. Pure water has a neutral **pH**.

Ionisation energy The energy required to remove one **mole** of **electrons** from one mole of atoms of an **element** so that the electrons are no longer under the influence of the positive charge of a **nucleus**. The energy required to remove one mole of the outermost electrons from one mole of atoms of the element is called the first ionisation energy of the element. The atom becomes a positively charged ion:
$$X(g) \longrightarrow X^+(g) + e^-$$
Removing a further mole of electrons represents the second ionisation energy:
$$X^+(g) \longrightarrow X^{2+}(g) + e^-$$

Isomers Compounds that have the same **molecular formula** but different **structural formulae**.

Isotopes **Atoms** that have the same **atomic number** but different **mass numbers**. They are atoms of the same element, with the same numbers of protons and electrons but different numbers of neutrons. The isotopes of chlorine, for example, are written as chlorine-35 and chlorine-37 (or ^{35}Cl and ^{37}Cl), where 35 and 37 are mass numbers.

Ketone A **carbonyl compound** with the general formula

$$\overset{R}{\underset{R^1}{\diagup}} C{=}O$$

Propanone, CH_3COCH_3, is a ketone.

Kinetics of reaction or **rate of reaction** The study of factors that affect the way in which the concentration of the reactants and products changes with time during a chemical reaction.

Laevorotatory An **optical isomer** that rotates the plane of plane-polarised light to the left, or anticlockwise, is laevorotatory; written as L- or (–)-.

Lattice A geometrical arrangement of points. Crystal structures are based on lattices, with the particles positioned at the points.

Lattice energy The energy transferred when one **mole** of an ionic crystal, say AB, is formed from one mole of its gaseous **ions**:
$$A^+(g) + B^-(g) \longrightarrow AB(s)$$
For example, the lattice energy of sodium chloride is –775 kJ mol^{-1}.

Le Châtelier's principle When an equilibrium reaction mixture is subjected to a change in conditions, the composition of the mixture adjusts to counteract the change. For example, if the concentration of one of the reactants in an equilibrium mixture is suddenly increased, the equilibrium will adjust so as to reduce the increase in concentration.

Ligand An **atom** or **ion** which is able to bond to a central metal atom in a **complex ion**. A ligand can do this because it has a non-bonding electron pair which can form a **coordinate bond** with the central atom. For example, the non-bonding pair on nitrogen in ammonia form the N-Cu bond in $Cu(NH_3)_4^{2+}$, the tetraamminecopper(II) ion.

Limiting reactant In most chemical reactions in practice one reactant is present in excess of another. The smaller amount of the latter reactant limits the amount of product that will be formed: this reactant is the limiting reactant.

Mass number (symbol A) The number of protons plus the number of neutrons present in an atom.

Mass spectroscopy A technique used to find the **relative atomic mass** (symbol A_r) of an element or the **relative molecular mass** (symbol M_r) of a compound. It identifies the types and amounts of any isotopes present.

Maxwell-Boltzmann distribution A mathematical description of the energy distribution among the molecules in a gas. The fraction of molecules having an energy higher than a particular value E is given by a mathematical expression ($e^{-E/RT}$).

Molar gas constant (symbol R) The proportionality constant in the **ideal gas equation**.

Molar mass The mass of one **mole** of a substance. For example, the molar mass of magnesium is 24 g mol^{-1}.

Molar volume (symbol V_m) The volume occupied by one **mole** of any gas. It is 22.4 dm^3 at standard temperature and pressure.

Molarity The concentration of a solution expressed in mol dm^{-3}.

Mole An amount of substance that contains 6.022×10^{23} particles. These may be atoms, ions, molecules or electrons.

Molecular formula A formula showing the number and types of atoms present in a molecule. For example, the molecular formula for calcium carbonate is $CaCO_3$.

Monomer   A molecule that can react with many other similar molecules to build up a large molecule, or most **polymer** plastic materials are polymers; for example, polythene is a polymer of the monomer ethene.

Neutralisation   The reaction of an **acid** and a **base** to form a **salt** and water. Hydrogen ions react with hydroxide ions to form water:
$$H^+(aq) + OH^-(aq) \longrightarrow H_2O(l)$$
Not all salts have a neutral **pH**.

Neutron   A neutral (uncharged) mass particle found in the atomic **nucleus**. Its mass is approximately 1 atomic unit.

Nucleophile   An atom or group of atoms that is attracted to a positive charge. NH_3, OH^- and H_2O can act as nucleophiles.

Nucleophilic addition reaction   A reaction in which a **nucleophile** is attracted to a positive charge. An **addition reaction** then takes place between the nucleophile and the positively charged molecule or group. Examples include the reaction of the cyanide ion with **carbonyl compounds**.

Nucleophilic substitution reaction   A chemical reaction in which one **nucleophile** replaces another in a molecule. For example, in the reaction of bromoethane with alkali, the hydroxide ion (nucleophile) replaces the bromide ion in the bromoethane molecule:
$$C_2H_5Br + OH^- \longrightarrow C_2H_5OH + Br^-$$

Nucleus   The central part of an **atom**, around which the **electrons** orbit. It consists of positively charged **protons** and neutral **neutrons**, tightly packed together.

Optical activity   The ability of a substance to rotate the plane of **plane-polarised light**.

Optical isomers   Compounds whose molecules, though alike in every other way, are mirror images of each other. Optical isomers are **chiral**, and can rotate the plane of **plane-polarised light**.

Order of reaction   The relationship between the concentration of a reactant or product and the rate of the reaction as expressed in the **rate equation**. For example, if the rate is proportional to $[X]^y$, the order of reaction is y with respect to X. The overall order of the reaction is the sum of the powers in the rate equation. Orders of reaction are usually zero, one or two. For example, for the reaction of bromoethane with alkali, the rate equation is
$$\text{rate} = k[C_2H_5Br][OH^-]$$
The reaction is first order with respect to bromoethane, first order with respect to hydroxide ions and second order overall. The order of reaction can only be found experimentally.

Organic chemistry   The chemistry of carbon compounds. Several million different carbon compounds are known.

Oxidation   A process in which a species loses electrons. It can also be defined as an increase in **oxidation state** for an element. Oxidation and **reduction** occur together in a **redox reaction**.

Oxidation state   The charge that an element would have if it were totally ionically bonded. For example, the oxidation state of hydrogen in water is +1, and that of oxygen in water is –2, even though water is covalently bonded. Oxidation state can change in a **redox reaction**.

Oxidising agent   An element or compound that gains electrons from a **reducing agent**, which itself loses electrons in the process. The oxidising agent is reduced, and the reducing agent is oxidised.

Parts per million (ppm)   A unit often used to express low concentrations. It is not always easy to visualise such low concentrations. Analogies can help: one part per million is one second in 12 days of your life, or one penny out of £10 000. 1 ppm is the same as 1 mg per 1000 g (1 mg per 1kg).

Periodic Table   A classification of the **elements** in order of their **atomic numbers**. Elements with similar properties appear in columns, known as groups. Metals lie on the left of the Table and non-metals on the right, with a gradual change of properties across the rows, or periods.

pH   A measure of hydrogen ion concentration (acidity). The pH of a solution is the negative log to the base 10 of the hydrogen ion concentration in the solution:
$$pH = -\log_{10}[H^+]$$

Plane-polarised light   Light in which all vibrations take place in the same plane or direction.

Plasticiser   A substance added to a plastic in order to increase its flexibility.

Polar molecule   A covalent molecule which contains atoms with different **electronegativities**. The **electron density** of the bonding electrons lies towards the more electronegative atom.

Polarimeter   An instrument for measuring the amount of rotation of **plane-polarised light** by an **optical isomer**.

Polymer   A large molecule formed from many smaller **monomer** molecules reacting together. Examples of polymers include plastics like polythene, and synthetic fibres like nylon and Terylene.

Polymerisation   The reaction of **monomers** to form **polymers**.

Precipitate   An insoluble (solid) product formed when two solutions are mixed.

Proton   A positively charged particle found in the atomic **nucleus**. It has a mass of approximately 1 atomic unit.

Protonation   The addition of a proton, written as H^+, to another molecule or particle.

Racemate   A 50:50 (moles) mixture of the optical isomers of a compound. A racemate is not itself optically active, because the optical activities of the isomers (one **dextrorotatory**, one **laevorotatory**) cancel each other out.

Radical   A species which has an unpaired electron available for bonding. A radical is formed by **homolytic bond breaking**.

Radical substitution reaction   A reaction in which one **radical** is substituted for another in a reaction. For example, in the reaction between chlorine and methane, chlorine radicals (atoms) replace hydrogen atoms.

Radioactive decay   The process by which the atoms of certain elements break up into smaller atoms, emitting energy as they do so. Protons, neutrons or electrons may also be emitted during this process.

Rate of reaction   The change over time of the concentration of a reactant or a product of a reaction. Its units are $mol\ dm^{-3}\ s^{-1}$.

Rate constant (symbol K)   The proportionality constant in a rate equation.

Rate equation   A mathematical description of the way in which the **rate of a reaction** depends on the concentrations of reactants. The rate equation for a reaction

A + B ⟶ products can be written:

rate = $k[A]^m[B]^n$

where m and n are the **orders of reaction** with respect to A and B. The rate equation has to be determined by experiments and cannot be deduced from the chemical equation.

Rate-determining step   The slowest step in a reaction. The rate of this step determines the overall rate of reaction. Many reactions have more than one step between reactants and products. For example, the reaction between nucleophiles and primary halogenoalkanes takes place in two steps.

Redox reaction   A reaction in which **oxidation** and **reduction** both occur. One species is oxidised, while another is reduced. The two processes are sometimes shown as **half-equations**.

Redox titration   A procedure in which amounts of **reducing agent** or **oxidising agent** can be determined accurately in a **redox reaction**. An indicator is need to show the point at which all of the **limiting reactant** has reacted. Potassium manganate(VII) is an **oxidising agent** commonly used in such titrations, and since it is intensely coloured (purple) acts as its own indicator.

Reducing agent   An element or compound that loses electrons to an **oxidising agent**, which itself gains electrons in the process. The reducing agent is oxidised, and the oxidising agent is reduced.

Reduction   A process in which a species gains electrons. It can also be defined as a decrease in **oxidation state** for an element. Reduction and **oxidation** occur together in a **redox reaction**.

Refluxing   Boiling a liquid in a flask with a condenser attached, so that the vapour condenses and flows back into the flask. This keeps the liquid at its boiling point without any loss by evaporation.

Relative atomic mass (symbol A_r)   The mass of one atom of an element compared with one-twelfth of the mass of one atom of carbon-12.

Relative molecular mass (symbol M_r)   The mass of one molecule of an element or compound compared with one-twelfth of the mass of one atom of carbon-12.

Reversible reaction   A chemical reaction which can take place in both directions and so is incomplete. A mixture of reactants and products is obtained when the reaction reaches **equilibrium**. The composition of the equilibrium mixture is the same whether the reaction starts from the substances on the left-hand or the right-hand side of the reaction equation.

Salt   A compound formed when an **acid** reacts with a **base**. The pH of a solution of a salt depends on the relative strengths of the acid and base from which it is formed. A strong acid reacting with a strong base gives a salt that will dissolve to give a solution of pH 7. A strong acid reacting with a weak base gives a salt that forms a solution of pH less than 7.

Saturated organic compound   An organic compound that contains only single bonds between the carbon atoms in its molecule.

Semiconductor   A material that is midway between an insulator and a conductor. Semiconductors are insulators at standard temperature, but their conductivity increases as the temperature rises.
n-type semiconductors have a negative charge. Silicon is doped with Group 5 atoms, which provide extra electrons to move throughout the semiconductor.
p-type semiconductors have a positive charge. Silicon is doped with Group 3 atoms, which leaves 'holes' into which other electrons can move.

Shell   A term that is sometimes used to describe the principal electron energy levels in an atom. The numbers 1, 2, 3... denote the shells, and are the same as the periods in the **Periodic Table**.

Spectrometer An instrument used to study the absorption of electromagnetic radiation by substances. There are different types of spectrometer (infrared, ultraviolet, NMR and so on) according to the type of radiation that is being studied.

Standard conditions A temperature of 298 K (or 25 °C) and a pressure of 1 atmosphere.

Standard enthalpy change of combustion (symbol ΔH_c) The energy transferred when one **mole** of a substance burns completely in oxygen under standard conditions.

Standard enthalpy change of formation (symbol ΔH_f) The energy absorbed when one **mole** of a substance is formed from its elements in their standard states.

Stereoisomers Isomers having the same **molecular formula** and **structural formula** but with different arrangements of their atoms in space. **Optical** and **geometrical isomers** are stereoisomers.

Strong nuclear force The attractive force within the **nucleus**.

Structural formula A formula that shows how the atoms are bonded together in a compound. It can either be written out in full, with each bond shown, or by writing groups of atoms in sequence.

Structural isomers Isomers having the same **molecular formula**, but different **structural formulae**. Butane and 2-methylpropane are structural isomers of C_4H_{10}.

Sub-shell A term used to describe the detail of orbitals or energy levels in an atom. Each sub-shell contains pairs of electrons. Sub-shells are given letters: s holds up to one electron pair, p holds up to 3 electron pairs, d holds up to 5 electron pairs.

Substitution reaction A reaction in which an atom or group forming part of a molecule is replaced by a different atom or group.

Surroundings The environment in which a chemical reaction takes place. The immediate surroundings include the vessel and any other associated apparatus, nearby objects and the atmosphere around them. Strictly speaking, the term applies to *every* object that is not a component of the reaction mixture (the **system**).

System In chemistry, the term is used to mean the reaction mixture.

Threshold limit value (TLV) The highest level of a toxic gas in air to which it is believed that workers can be exposed without harm; usually given in **parts per million** in air.

Transition metals Elements that have incomplete electron **sub-shells** in their **atoms** or **ions**. First-row transition metals (scandium to copper) have incomplete d sub-shells.

Triple point The conditions of temperature and pressure at which all three phases of a substance (solid, liquid and gas) can exist together. For water the triple point is at 273.16 K and 610 N m^{-2}.

Unsaturated organic compound A compound that contains one or more double bonds between the carbon atoms in its molecule.

van der Waals forces A form of **intermolecular bonding**. They are forces between **temporary dipoles** in adjacent molecules. Van der Waals forces are between one-hundredth and one-tenth as strong as typical covalent bonds.

Index

Key ideas are highlighted in the index by **bold text** and by **bold page numbers** for key/glossary definitions

Photo Acknowledgements

The publishers would like to thank the following for permission to reproduce photographs:

p 1 Science Photo Library, p 6 (top left and right) Science Photo Library, (bottom) Sygma, p 9 Popperfoto, p 10 Ardea, p 13 Jerry Mason, p14 (top) Jerry Mason, (bottom) Barnaby's Picture Library, p 16 Jerry Mason, p 20 Jerry Mason, p 22 Jerry Mason, p 23 (top) Jerry Mason, (bottom) National Trust Photo Library, p 26 (left and right) Science Photo Library, p 28 Andrew Lambert, p 34 The Royal Society, p 37 Andrew Lambert, p 38 (top) Science & Society Photo Library, (bottom) Eye Ubiquitous, p 39 (top) Paul Brierley, (bottom left) Intel, (bottom right) Tony Stone Worldwide, p 42 Tony Stone Worldwide, p43 Science Photo Library, p 46 The Image Bank, p 48 Science Photo Library, p 49 (left and right) NASA, p 51 Mary Evans Picture Library, p 53 Chris Bonnington Library, p 57 Heather Angel, p 58 Science Photo Library, p 59 Shout, p 62 NASA, p 63 (top left) Colorific, (top right) Still Pictures, (bottom) South American Pictures, p 64 Colorific, p 65 Colorific, p 66 Anthony Blake Photo Library, p 68 Allsport, p 69 Telegraph Colour Library, p 70 (left) The Image Bank, (right) The Image Bank, p 73 Tony Stone Worldwide p 74 Tony Stone Worldwide, p 75 Holt Studios, (inset) Ardea, p 76 (left) Tony Waltham, (right) BASF, p 77 Andrew Lambert, p 82 Andrew Lambert, p 83 Nobel Foundation, P 87 Janine Wiedel, p 88 (top) Bridgeman Art Library, (bottom) The Image Bank, p 89 The Image Bank, p 90 Tony Stone Worldwide, p 91 Andrew Lambert, p 92 Janine Wiedel, p 94 Bubbles, p 95 Eye Ubiquitous, p 99 Johnson & Johnson, p 101 (left and right) Janine Wiedel, p 102 (all photographs) Janine Wiedel, p 105 J Malone, E Lewenstein, P Lane: The Crafts Council Photo Library, p 107 Trustees of the British Museum, p 108 Geoscience Features, p 111 Science Photo Library, p 112 Tony Stone Worldwide, (right) J Allan Cash, p 113 (left) Imperial War Museum, London, (right) Environmental Picture Library, p 115 (left) Philip Sapwell, (right) Janine Wiedel, p 118 (top) Science Photo Library, (bottom left) Janine Wiedel, (bottom right) Panos Pictures, p 120 Kodak Research Laboratory, p 121 Heather Angel, p 123 Zefa, p 124 (left and right) Zefa, p 125 (left and right) Science Photo Library, p 127 Hutchison Library, p 130 Zefa, p 132 Janine Wiedel, p 135 (left) Tito Simbali, (right) Rex Features, p 136 Janine Wiedel, p 140 Andrew Lambert, p 142 (left) Janine Wiedel, (centre and right) Photos Horticultural, p 143 Telegraph Colour Library, p 144 (left and right) Janine Wiedel, p 145 The Complete Picture, p 147 Panos Pictures, p 152 Robert Harding Picture Library, p 155 (left) Science Photo Library, (right) Network, p 156 (top) Richard Smalley/ Professor Harry Kroto University of Sussex, (bottom) The Natural History Museum, London, p 157 (top) GRAPHIS, Michel Proulx (Professor Harry Kroto, University of Sussex), (bottom) Science Photo Library p 160 The Image Bank, p 162 Science Photo Library, p 164 Jerry Mason, P 165 (left and right) Shout, p 168 Topham Picture Source, p 169 (top) John Feltwell, (bottom) Robert Harding Picture Library, p170 ICI, p 171 (left and right) Andrew Lambert, p 173 (top) J Allan Cash Photo Library, (bottom) Shout, p 175 (top) Network, (bottom) Impact, p 176 Central Science Laboratory, p 179 Holt Studios, p 180 Tony Stone Worldwide, p 185 Science Photo Library, p 187 Impact, p 188 Ecoscene.